5000 copies printed on the occasion of the exhibition,
CALIFORNIA SCULPTURE SHOW

California/International Arts Foundation
Exhibition coordinators: Lyn Kienholz and Marc Pally,
Los Angeles, California

Fisher Gallery, University of Southern California
Director: Selma Holo, Ph.D.
Staff: Kay Allen, Marie de Alcuaz
Exhibition design: Trevor Norris

Exhibition selection: Henry T. Hopkins, Director,
San Francisco Museum of Modern Art

Catalogue design: Nancy Zaslavsky, Ultragraphics,
Venice, California
Cover lettering: Morris Zaslavsky
Production artist: Lupe Marmolejo

Translators
French: Jeanne Hart
German: Barbara Algin and Martin Ashoff
Spanish: Antonio Forés and Fernando Martinez-Gil

Catalogue editing and typography: Barbara McAlpine,
La Habra, California
Typography is Univers light and extra bold

Text paper is 80-pound Condat Dull. Cover paper is Grandee
Cover, 80-pound, Barcelona Gray.

Lithography: Lithographix, Inc., Los Angeles, California

Cover printing: Crown Sojourn, Pico Rivera, California

Color separations: Heinz Weber, Inc., Los Angeles, California

International Standard Book Number: 0-917571-00-2

Library of Congress Catalog Card Number: 84-70848

© 1984 California/International Arts Foundation,
Los Angeles, California

california
sculpture
S · H · O · W

FISHER GALLERY
UNIVERSITY OF SOUTHERN CALIFORNIA
LOS ANGELES, CALIFORNIA, U.S.A.
JUNE 2 AUGUST 12, 1984

C.A.P.C.
MUSÉE D'ART CONTEMPORAIN DE BORDEAUX
BORDEAUX, FRANCE
OCTOBER 1984

STÄDTICHE KUNSTHALLE
MANNHEIM, W. GERMANY
FEBRUARY 1985

YORKSHIRE SCULPTURE PARK
WEST BRETTON, ENGLAND
MAY 1985

SONJA HENIES OG NIELS ONSTADS STIFTELSER
HØVIKODDEN, NORWAY
SEPTEMBER 1985

This catalogue is published in conjunction with the exhibition, CALIFORNIA SCULPTURE SHOW. The California/International Arts Foundation is grateful for financial support from the Los Angeles Olympic Organizing Committee.

The Olympic Arts Festival is produced by the Los Angeles Organizing Committee with support from the Times Mirror Company, the official festival sponsor.

The project is also supported by grants from Target Stores; the University of Southern California; The James Irvine Foundation; National Endowment for the Arts, Washington, D.C., a federal agency; and the L.J. and Mary C. Skaggs Foundation.

Olympic Arts Festival Los Angeles 1984

June 1 – August 12, 1984

Contents

6 **Introduction**
Robert J. Fitzpatrick
Director, Los Angeles Olympic Arts Festival

7 **Exhibition Catalogue**

8 **Acknowledgment**
Lyn Kienholz

10 **Acknowledgment**
Selma Holo, Ph.D.

12 **Foreword**
Henry T. Hopkins
Director, San Francisco Museum of Modern Art

16 **Sculpture is Realer than Painting**
Jan Butterfield

28 **Sensuous Constructivism in California Sculpture**
Melinda Wortz

41 **The Artists**

139 **Biographies**

153 **Bibliographies**

167 **Photography Credits**

Introduction

The *California Sculpture Show* is a uniquely important component of the 1984 Olympic Arts Festival. This exhibition by the California/International Arts Foundation is an opportunity to share some extraordinary work by a group of major artists whom we are fortunate to have living in California. The work is all very different—what it has in common is an intensely personal vocabulary and viewpoint that could not be mistaken for that of any other group of artists in the world. This major exhibit, organized especially for this occasion, travels directly from the Olympic Arts Festival to Bordeaux, France, where it begins its European tour.

The Olympic Arts Festival is pleased to have helped make possible the *California Sculpture Show*. The Los Angeles Olympic Organizing Committee expresses its appreciation to the Times Mirror Company for its official sponsorship of the Festival, as well as to Lyn Kienholz of the California/International Arts Foundation, Henry Hopkins of the San Francisco Museum of Modern Art, and Dr. Selma Holo of the University of Southern California's Fisher Gallery.

Robert J. Fitzpatrick, Director
Olympic Arts Festival

La *Exhibición de Escultura de California* es un componente particularmente importante de los Festivales Artísticos de los Olímpicos de 1984. Esta exposición patrocinada por la Fundación de Arte Internacional y de California constituye una oportunidad de compartir parte de la obra extraordinaria de un grupo de destacados artistas que para fortuna nuestra residen en California. El conjunto de la obra rezuma variedad—lo unificador radica en una perspectiva y vocabulario intensamente personales que no puede ser confundido con ningún otro grupo de artistas en el mundo. Esta gran exposición, organizada especialmente para esta ocasión, se trasladará directamente desde los Festivales de Arte de los Olímpicos a Burdeos, Francia, donde iniciará su gira europea.

El comité de los Festivales de Arte de los Olímpicos se complace en haber hecho posible la *Exhibición de Escultura de California*. El Comité Organizador de los Juegos Olímpicos de Los Angeles expresa su agradecimiento a la Compañía Times Mirror por su patrocinio oficial de los Festivales, asi como a Lyn Kienholz de la Fundación de Arte International y de California, a Henry Hopkins del Museo de Arte Moderno de San Francisco, y a la Dra. Selma Holo de la Galería Fisher de la Universidad del Sur de California.

Robert J. Fitzpatrick, Director
Festivales de Arte de los Olímpicos

L'*Exposition de Sculpture californienne* apporte une contribution rès importante au Festival Olympique des Arts. Cette exposition présentée par la California/International Arts Foundation est l'occasion de faire apprécier d'un vaste public les oeuvres extraordinaires produites par un groupe d'artistes que nous avons la chance d'avoir, vivant parmi nous, en Californie. Ces oeuvres sont toutes très différentes—ce qui en fait l'unité est l'intensité de leur vocabulaire personnel ainsi qu'une certaine façon de voir qui ne pourraient être celles d'aucun autre artiste au monde. Cette exposition majeure, qui a été organisée spécialement à l'occasion du Festival Olympique d'Art, voyagera ensuite directement à Bordeaux, en France, où elle commencera son tour d'Europe.

Le Festival Olympique des Arts est heureux d'avoir pu rendre possible l'*Exposition de Sculpture californienne*. Le Comité d'Organisation Olympique de Los Angeles remercie la Times Mirror Compagnie d'avoir officiellement accepté de parrainer le Festival, ainsi que Lyn Kienholz de la California/International Arts Foundation, Henry Hopkins, Directeur du Musée d'Art Moderne de San Francisco et Dr. Selma Holo de la Fisher Gallery de l'Université de Californie du Sud.

Robert J. Fitzpatrick, Directeur
Festival Olympique des Arts

Die *California Sculpture Show* ist ein in einzigartiger Weise wichtiger Beitrag zu dem olympischen Festival der Künste 1984. Diese Ausstellung der California/International Arts Foundation bietet die Gelegenheit, an einigen außerordentlichen Arbeiten einer Gruppe von bedeutenden Künstlern, die glücklicherweise bei uns in Kalifornien leben, teilzuhaben. Die Werke sind sehr unterschiedlich—was sie gemeinsam haben, ist ein eindringlich persönliches Vokabular und Gesichtspunkte, die nicht mit denen irgendeiner anderen Gruppe von Künstlern in der Welt verwechselt werden können. Diese bedeutende Ausstellung, die besonders für diesen Anlaß ins Leben gerufen wurde, geht auf direktem Wege von dem olympischen Festival der Künste nach Bordeaux, Frankreich, wo sie den Anfang ihrer Europa-Tour nimmt.

Das olympische Festival der Künste ist erfreut, zu der Realisierung der *California Sculpture Show* beigetragen zu haben. Das olympische Organisationskomitee in Los Angeles ist folgenden zu Dank verpflichtet: der Times Mirror Gesellschaft als offizieller Sponsor des Festivals, ebenso Lyn Kienholz von der California/International Arts Foundation, Henry Hopkins vom San Francisco Museum of Modern Art und Dr. Selma Holo von der Fisher Gallery der University of Southern California.

Robert J. Fitzpatrick, Direktor
Olympischen Festivals der Künste

Exhibition Catalogue

Robert Arneson

Ground Zero, 1984
Bronze
26 × 80 × 80"
66 × 203 × 203 cm
Lent by the artist

Charles Arnoldi

Not Marble nor Gilded Monument, 1982
Cast and welded bronze
102 × 78 × 86"
259 × 198 × 218 cm
Lent by James Corcoran Casting, Inc.

Bruce Beasley

Artemon, 1984
Stainless steel
192 × 384 × 120"
488 × 975 × 305 cm
Lent by the artist

Fletcher Benton

Balanced/Unbalanced Wheels, 1982
Painted steel
360 × 336 × 84"
914 × 853 × 213 cm
Lent by the artist

Guy Dill

Siduri, 1983
Cast reinforced pigmented concrete
132 × 114 × 48"
335 × 290 × 122 cm
Lent by the artist and Flow Ace Gallery

Jud Fine

Horizontal Pillar #5, 1983
Steel, wood, galvanized steel,
copper, rubber, wire, string
36 × 960 × 9"
91 × 2438 × 23 cm
Lent by Margo Leavin Gallery

Tom Holland

Norton, 1983
Acrylic urethane on aluminum
144 × 60 × 60"
366 × 152 × 152 cm
Lent by James Corcoran Gallery

Robert Hudson

Figure of Speech, 1984
Steel
170 × 104 × 62"
432 × 264 × 157 cm
Lent by the artist

Manuel Neri

Carriona Figure No. 2, 1981
Marble with oil-based pigment
58 × 16 × 12"
147 × 41 × 30 cm
From a private collection

Sam Richardson

Split and Tied, 1984
Steel, bronze, acrylic urethane enamel
132 × 60 × 72"
335 × 152 × 183 cm
Lent by the artist

Michael Todd

Nataraja I, 1982
Steel
216 × 192 × 96"
549 × 488 × 244 cm
Lent by the artist

DeWain Valentine

Sky Gate III, 1984 (maquette)
Laminated glass, bronze
114 × 96 × 24"
290 × 244 × 61 cm
Lent by the artist

Acknowledgment

The idea for this exhibition originated with Peter Murray, director of the Yorkshire Sculpture Park in England, who had talked with Bruce Beasley about presenting an exhibit of West Coast sculpture. The fact that so little art in general, and sculpture in particular, from this state has received recognition overseas was a condition to be corrected. With Peter committed to accepting such a show, the planning began.

I was fortunate from the beginning to have had the support of Henry Hopkins, director of the San Francisco Museum of Modern Art. Henry carefully thought out the needs of the exhibition and the state of sculpture in California today. His selections represent the vitality, diversity, and sense of adventure that characterize California artists at their best.

While in the last few years a generation of women sculptors has emerged in California, the preceding generations, including those represented in this exhibition, produced very few. Among those working, some are in such categories as site-specific or conceptual and/or performance, categories not included in this exhibit. Hopefully the prejudices that have kept so many women from sculpture are disappearing.

Robert Fitzpatrick, director of the Olympic Arts Festival, through his consistent and early support and inspiring energy, encouraged me in the belief that anything and everything is possible. During the Olympics the *California Sculpture Show* is particularly fortunate to be housed at Fisher Gallery on the University of Southern California campus, which has given me the enormous privilege of working with its director, Selma Holo. Selma's constant stream of brilliant ideas and her sense of humor are a source of wonder and inspiration. To Jean-Louis Froment, director of the Centre d'Art Plastique Contemporain in Bordeaux, France, countless thanks are offered for agreeing to host the exhibit at its first stop of the international tour.

The California/International Arts Foundation is grateful to the Times Mirror Company for supporting the Olympic Arts Festival. Important support for this exhibition also has been provided by Target Stores, The James Irvine Foundation, the National Endowment for the Arts, the L.J. and Mary C. Skaggs Foundation, and the University of Southern California. We are indeed grateful to these supporters, not only for the very necessary funds provided, but for their encouraging moral support.

Finally, it is to the artists we must all be grateful—for their dedication and for producing wonderful work to be shared with the world.

Lyn Kienholz, Founder/President
California/International Arts Foundation

La idea para esta exposición se originó en Peter Murray, director del Parque de Escultura de Yorkshire en Inglaterra, después de un diálogo con Bruce Beasley sobre la posibilidad de presentar una exposición de escultura de la costa Oeste. Ambos coincidieron en que la falta de reconocimiento en el extranjero del arte de este estado en general, y de su escultura en particular, debería ser corregida. La planificación comenzó cuando Peter se comprometió a aceptar la mencionada exhibición.

Yo tuve la fortuna desde el principio de recibir el apoyo de Henry Hopkins, director del Museo de Arte Moderno de San Francisco. Henry consideró cuidadosamente las necesidades de la exposición y el estado de la escultura en la California actual. Su selección es representativa de la vitalidad, diversidad y el sentido de aventura que mejor caracterizan a los artistas de California.

Mientras que en los últimos años ha surgido una generación de mujeres escultoras en California, las generaciones precedentes, incluídas las representadas en esta exposición, produjeron muy pocas. Entre las activas algunas caen dentro de categorías tales como aquéllas específicas de lugar o conceptuales y/o de ejecución, categorías no incluídas en esta exposición. Esperamos que desaparezcan los prejuicios que han impedido el acceso de tantas mujeres a la escultura.

Robert Fitzpatrick, director de los Festivales de Arte de las Olimpiadas, por medio de su rápido y consistente apoyo y de su energía inspiradora, me animó a creer fervientemente que no hay imposibles. Durante los Juegos Olímpicos la *Exhibición de Escultura de California* ha tenido la particular fortuna de estar localizada en la Galería Fisher en el campus de la Universidad del Sur de California lo cual me ha otorgado el enorme privilegio de trabajar con su directora Selma Holo. El efluvio de brillantes ideas de Selma y su sentido del humor constituyen una fuente de maravilla y de inspiración. Quisiera enviar mis más expresivas gracias a Jean-Louis Froment, director del Centre d'Art Plastique Contemporain de Burdeos, Francia, por aceptar la exposición en la primera etapa de su gira internacional.

La Fundación de Arte Internacional y de California desea expresar su agradecimiento a la Compañía Times Mirror por su apoyo de los Festivales de Arte Olímpicos. También mencionar a la Target Stores, La Fundación James Irvine, la Fundación Nacional para las Artes, la Fundación L.J. y Mary C. Skaggs, y la Universidad del Sur de California por su importante apoyo. Estamos muy agradecidos a estos patrocinadores, no sólo por los fondos tan necesarios que han otorgado, sino también por su alentador apoyo moral.

Finalmente, deseamos mostrar nuestro agradecimiento a los artistas por su dedicacion y por producir obras maravillosas que todo el mundo puede compartir.

Lyn Kienholz, Fundadora/Presidenta
Fundación de Arte International y de California

Ce fut Peter Murray, Directeur du Yorkshire Sculpture Park, en Angleterre, qui eut l'idée de cette exposition. Il avait parlé avec Bruce Beasley de la possibilité de monter une exposition pour présenter la sculpture de la Côte Ouest des Etats-Unis. Le fait que l'art de la Californie, en général, et sa sculpture en particulier, soient si mal connus outre-mer demandait qu'on y remédie. Une fois que Peter eut accepté l'exposition, le planning put commencer.

J'eus la chance, dès le début, de recevoir l'aide d'Henry Hopkins, Directeur du San Francisco Museum of Modern Art. Henry réfléchit avec soin aux besoins de l'exposition ainsi qu'à la condition de la sculpture californienne contemporaine. Ses choix représentent la vitalité, la diversité, et l'esprit aventureux qui caractérisent les meilleures oeuvres des artistes de Californie.

Tandis qu'au cours des quelques dernières années, une génération de femmes-sculpteurs est apparue en Californie, les femmes étaient très peu nombreuses dans les générations précédentes, y compris celles représentées dans cette exposition. Il est à espérer que les préjugées qui avaient tenu les femmes à l'écart de la sculpture sont en train de disparaître.

Robert Fitzpatrick, Directeur du Festival Olympique des Arts, grâce à l'aide constante qu'il m'accorda très tôt et grâce à son énergie, m'a portée à croire que tout est possible. Pendant les Jeux Olympiques, l'*Exposition de Sculpture Californienne* est particulièrement fortunée d'être l'hôte de la Fisher Gallery, sur le campus de l'Université de Californie du Sud, ce qui m'a donné l'énorme privilège de travailler avec sa directrice, Selma Holo. Il émane de Selma un flot ininterrompu d'idées brillantes qui, joint à son sens de l'humour, font d'elle une source d'émerveillement et d'inspiration. Je tiens à remercier aussi Jean-Louis Froment, directeur du Centre d'Art Plastique Contemporain de Bordaux, en France, pour avoir accepté de recevoir l'exposition pendant la première étape de sa tournée internationale.

La California/International Arts Foundation est reconnaissante à la Times Mirror Company du soutien qu'elle apporte au Festival Olympique des Arts. L'exposition a également reçu une aide importante des Target Stores, de la James Irvine Foundation, du National Endowment for the Arts, de la L.J. and Mary C. Skaggs Foundation et de l'Université de Californie du Sud. A tous, nous disons: «Merci!», non seulement pour les fonds très nécessaires qu'ils nous ont donnés, mais aussi pour leur encouragement et leur sontien moral.

Finalement, c'est envers les artistes que nous devons tous être très reconnaissants—pour leur dévouement à leur art et pour avoir créé des oeuvres merveilleuses qu'il nous est donné, maintenant, de partager avec le monde entier.

Lyn Kienholz, Fondatrice/Présidente
California/International Arts Foundation

Die Idee zu dieser Ausstellung stammt von Peter Murray, dem Direktor des Yorkshire Sculpture Parks in England, der mit Bruce Beasley über eine Kunstausstellung der Bildhauerei der Westküste gesprochen hatte. Die Tatsche, daß so wenig Kunst von diesem Staat im allgemeinen und der Bildhauerei im besonderen in Übersee Anerkennung gefunden hat, war ein Zustand, der verbessert werden sollte. Nachdem Peter sich verpflichtet hatte, solch eine Ausstellung ins Leben zu rufen, begann die Planung.

Glücklicherweise hatte ich von Anfang an die Unterstützung von Henry Hopkins, dem Direktor des San Francisco Museum of Modern Art. Henry überlegte sich genau die Bedürfnisse der Ausstellung und des heutigen Standes der Bildhauerei in Kalifornien. Seine Auswahl repräsentiert die Vitalität, Mannigfaltigkeit und Abenteuerlust, die kalifornische Künstler im besten Sinne charakterisieren.

Während in den letzten paar Jahren eine Generation weiblicher Bildhauer in Kalifornien aufgekommen ist, brachten die vorhergehenden Generationen, einschließlich jener auf der Ausstellung vertretenen, sehr wenige hervor. Unter den Schaffenden befinden sich einige in solchen Kategorien wie ort- oder konzeptuell und/oder darstellungsgebunden, Kategorien, die nicht auf dieser Ausstellung zu finden sind. Es ist zu hoffen, daß die Vorurteile, die soviele Frauen von der Bildhauerei ferngehalten haben, verschwinden werden.

Robert Fitzpatrick, der Direktor des olympischen Festivals der Künste, bestärkte mich durch seine beständige und frühzeitige Unterstützung und inspirierende Tatkraft in dem Glauben, daß alles und jedes möglich ist. Die *California Sculpture Show* kann sich besonders glücklich schätzen, während der olympischen Spiele in der Fisher Gallery auf dem Campus der University of Southern California untergebracht zu sein, was mir das Privileg zuteil werden ließ, mit deren Direktorin, Selma Holo, zusammenarbeiten zu dürfen. Selmas ständige Flut an außergewöhnlichen Ideen und ihr Sinn für Humor sind eine Quelle des Wunders und der Inspiration. Jean-Louis Froment, der Direktor des Centre d'Art Plastique Contemporain in Bordeaux (Frankreich), soll mit Nachdruck dafür gedankt werden, daß er sich bereit erklärt hat, Gastgeber der Ausstellung auf der ersten Station ihrer internationalen Tour zu sein.

Die California/International Arts Foundation dankt der Times Mirror Company für die Unterstützung des olympischen Festivals der Künste. Wichtige Unterstützung für diese Ausstellung kam von Seiten der Target Stores, der James Irvine Foundation, des National Endowment for the Arts, der L.J. and Mary C. Skaggs Foundation und der University of Southern California. Wir sind in der Tat diesen Trägerschaften dankbar, nicht nur für den sehr notwendigen Fonds, sondern auch für deren ermutigende moralische Unterstützung.

Letztlich müssen wir allen Künstlern unseren Dank aussprechen—für ihre Hingabe und für das Schaffen wundervoller Werke, an denen die Welt teilhaben soll.

Lyn Kienholz, Bergründerin/Präsidentin
California/International Arts Foundation

Acknowledgment

The year 1984 is full of implication for humankind, much of it Orwellian in nature. For Los Angeles, though, the summer of the year carries with it meaning of another kind—a significance derived from the quest for and the appreciation of excellence, as symbolized by the Olympic Games.

For the past three years, Fisher Gallery at the University of Southern California has been the focus of a long stream of artists and arts organizations from all over the globe, requesting the privilege of using the museum space during this summer's Olympic Arts Festival. Fisher's location (across from the Los Angeles Coliseum) guaranteed enormous exposure for the chosen exhibition. Furthermore, Fisher's ongoing commitment to showcasing works of the highest quality would no doubt bestow further validation upon the art. It was a large responsibility, therefore, to decide just which exhibition to present at USC for the summer of 1984.

John Gordon, Dean of the School of Fine Arts, and I spent many hours debating what the best possible material for Fisher's exhibition might be. We culled suggestions that included an international design show, any number of nationalistic presentations, art historical surveys of all kinds, and art emanating from California itself. We finally decided that the most challenging and exciting offering we could make to our visitors from near and far alike would be to choose and display a unique aspect of our own California art.

It was at this time that Lyn Kienholz, founder and president of the California/International Arts Foundation, suggested that the University of Southern California be the host institution to a large-scale exhibition, which would be organized by Henry Hopkins, director of the San Francisco Museum of Modern Art. Our response was unanimous and immediate. We were reinforced in our decision when Lyn informed us that the *California Sculpture Show* would travel to the Centre d'Art Plastique Contemporain at Bordeaux, France. Following Bordeaux, it would then carry these remarkable California artists' visions to a number of other European cities as well.

I am grateful to Dean Gordon for his involvement in the decision-making process and for his continuing support of Fisher Gallery's efforts. Working with Lyn Kienholz and the California/International Arts Foundation has been an ongoing delight. The University of Southern California demonstrated its special commitment to the project by making a large financial donation for the production of this catalogue; without USC's support it would not have been possible to offer a publication of this quality and scope. In sum, I am especially pleased that the search for excellence, epitomized by the 1984 summer Olympic season, has been made to dovetail with USC's exhibition representing some of the finest creative efforts in contemporary California sculpture.

Selma Holo, Ph.D., Director
Fisher Gallery
University of Southern California

Este año de 1984 está lleno de implicaciones para la humanidad, muchas de ellas de naturaleza orweliana. Para Los Angeles, sin embargo, el verano de este año contiene un significado de otra índole—un significado derivado de la búsqueda y la apreciación de la excelencia, como lo simbolizan los Juegos Olímpicos.

Durante los últimos tres años, la Galería Fisher de la Universidad del Sur de California ha sido el punto de encuentro de un desfile interminable de artistas y organizaciones artísticas procedentes de todo el mundo, que han solicitado el privilegio de usar los locales del museo durante los Festivales de Arte de las Olimpiadas de este verano. La ubicación de la Galería Fisher (enfrente del Coliseo de Los Angeles) garantizaba un enorme potencial para la mencionada exposición, y además su continuo compromiso de exhibir obras de la más alta calidad no requiere, sin duda alguna, mayor ratificación artística. Por lo tanto, constituyó una enorme responsabilidad el decidir el tipo de exposición a presentar en el verano de 1984 en USC.

John Gordon, Decano de la Facultad de Bellas Artes, y una servidora, pasamos muchas horas discutiendo cual sería el mejor material posible para la exposición de la Galería Fisher. Recogimos sugerencias entre las que se incluía una exhibición de diseño internacional, un número indeterminado de representaciones nacionales de cada país, estudios histórico-artísticos de todo tipo, y el arte que emana de la propia California. Finalmente decidimos que la oferta más fascinante e interesante que podríamos hacer a nuestros visitantes propios y extraños, sería la de seleccionar y exhibir un aspecto singular de nuestro propio arte de California.

Fué precisamente por este tiempo cuando Lyn Kienholz, fundadora y presidenta de la Fundación de Arte Internacional y de California, sugirió que la Universidad del Sur de California fuera la institución anfitriona de una exposición en gran escala a ser organizada por Henry Hopkins, director del Museo de Arte Moderno de San Francisco. Nuestra respuesta fue unánime e inmediata. Nuestra decisión se vio consolidada cuando Lyn nos informó que la *Exhibición de Escultura de California* viajaría al Centre d'Art Plastique Contemporain, de Burdeos, Francia. Después de Burdeos, las visiones de estos notables artistas californianos serían llevadas también a diversas otras ciudades europeas.

Quisiera expresar mi agradecimiento al Decano Gordon por su participación en el proceso de tomas de decisión y por su incondicional apoyo a los esfuerzos de la Galería Fisher. Trabajar con Lyn Kienholz y la Fundación de Arte Internacional de California ha sido un continuo placer. La Universidad del Sur de California demostró su especial afán de colaboración en el proyecto al otorgar una sustancial donación para la producción de este catálogo. Sin esta ayuda de USC no hubiera sido posible ofrecer una publicación de esta calidad y alcance. En suma, me complace especialmente manifestar que en la búsqueda de la excelencia, que tiene su exponente en la temporada olímpica del verano de 1984, no se han eludido esfuerzos creativos más sobresalientes de la escultura contemporánea de California.

Selma Holo, Ph.D., Directora
Galería Fisher
Universidad del Sur de California

L'année 1984 est lourde de sous-entendus pour l'humanité, la plupart orwelliens de nature. Pour Los Angeles, toutefois, l'été de cette année prend un sens spécial—il signifie la quête et l'appréciation de l'excellence, symbolisées par les Jeux Olympiques.

Depuis trois ans, la Fisher Gallery de l'Université de Californie du Sud a été le focus d'une longue théorie d'artistes et d'organisations artistiques du monde entier qui sollicitaient le privilège d'utiliser l'espace offert par le musée pendant le Festival Olympique des Arts, cet été. La situation de la Fisher Gallery (en face du Coliseum de Los Angeles) garantissait à l'exposition qui serait choisie une énorme visibilité. De plus, la tradition de la Fisher Gallery, qui n'expose que des oeuvres de la plus haute qualité, serait une sorte de reconnaissance supplémentaire de la valeur des oeuvres d'art exposées. Décider du choix d'une exposition pour USC, pour l'été de 1984, représentait donc une énorme responsabilité.

John Gordon, Doyen de l'Ecole des Beaux Arts, et moi, nous avons passé de nombreuses heures à débattre ce qui pourrait convenir le mieux. Nous recueillîmes des suggestions allant d'une exposition Internationale de «design», à des revues historiques de toutes sortes, en passant par une infinité d'expositions nationales, pour en arriver à l'art émanant de la Californie elle-même. Et nous en arrivâmes à la conclusion que la présentation la plus intéressante que nous pourrions offrir à nos visiteurs venus de près et de loin serait celle qui leur proposerait un unique aspect de l'art de la Californie.

Ce fut à ce moment-là que Lyn Kienholz, fondatrice et présidente de la California/International Arts Foundation, suggéra que l'Université de Californie du Sud soit l'hôte d'une exposition de larges proportions qu'organiserait Henry Hopkins, directeur du San Francisco Museum of Modern Art. Notre réponse fut unanime et immédiate. Notre enthousiasme grandit encore lorsque Lyn nous informa que la *California Sculpture Show* irait ensuite au Centre d'Art Plastique Contemporain, à Bordeaux, en France, et qu'après avoir quitté Bordeaux, elle emporterait les visions de ces remarquables artistes californiens vers un certain nombre de villes européennes.

Je suis reconnaissante au Doyen Gordon d'avoir pris part aux débats qui précédèrent la décision et de continuer à soutenir les efforts de la Fisher Gallery. Travailler avec Lyn Kienholz et la California/International Arts Foundation a été et continue à être un plaisir. L'Université de Californie du Sud a manifesté son intérêt pour le projet en faisant un don financier important destiné à faciliter la réalisation de ce catalogue; sans le soutien de USC, il n'aurait pas été possible d'offrir une publication de cette qualité et de cette compétence. En bref, je suis particulièrement heureuse que la quête de l'excellence, que symbolise la saison Olympique de l'été de 1984, coïncide avec l'exposition de USC qui représente quelques uns des efforts créatifs les plus remarquables réalisés dans le domaine de la sculpture californienne contemporaine.

Selma Holo, Ph.D., Directrice
Fisher Gallery
Université de Californie du Sud

Das Jahr 1984 ist voller Ungewißheiten für die Menschheit, viele von ihnen im Orwellschen Sinn. Für Los Angeles jedoch trägt der Sommer des Jahres eine andere Bedeutung—eine Bedeutung, die von der Suche nach und der Anerkennung von hervorragenden Leistungen abgeleitet ist, so wie sie durch die olympischen Spiele zum Ausdruck kommen.

Während der letzten drei Jahre war die Fisher Gallery an der University of Southern California der Kulminationspunkt eines Stromes von Künstlern und Kunstorganisationen aus aller Welt, die sich um das Privileg bemühten, die Museums Räume während des diesjährigen Festivals der Künste benutzen zu können. Die Örtlichkeiten der Fisher Gallery (gegenüber vom Los Angeles Coliseum) würden der gewählten Ausstellung eine Garantie für eine außergewöhnlich günstige Lage bieten. Darüber hinaus würde die andauernde Verpflichtung der Fisher Gallery, Werke höchster Qualität auszustellen, ohne Zweifel den Werken ein weiteres Werturteil verleihen. Gerade deshalb bedurfte es einer besonderen Anforderung zu entscheiden, welche Ausstellung für den Sommer 1984 an der USC vorzusehen.

John Gordon, der Dekan des Instituts der Schönen Künste und ich verbrachten Stunden damit zu beratschlagen, welches die bestmöglichen Gegenstände für die Fisher Ausstellung sein würden. Wir sammelten Anregungen und Vorschläge, u.a. eine internationale Kunstdesign-Ausstellung, eine Anzahl nationaler Darstellungen, kunsthistorischer Abrisse aller Art und Kunst, die von Kalifornien selbst kamen. Wir kamen zu dem Entschluß, daß es die herausforderndste und anregendste Darbietung für unsere Besucher von nah und fern sein würde, einen einzigartigen Aspekt unserer kalifornischen Kunst auszuwählen und darzustellen.

Zu diesem Zeitpunkt schlug die Begründerin und Präsidentin der California/International Arts Foundation vor, daß die University of Southern California Gastgeberin für eine großangelegte Ausstellung sei, die von Henry Hopkins, dem Direktor des San Francisco Museum of Modern Art organisiert würde. Unsere Antwort war einmütig und prompt. Wir wurden in unserer Entscheidung bestärkt, als Lyn uns darüber informierte, daß die *California Sculpture Show* zum Centre d'Art Plastique Contemporain in Bordeaux (Frankreich) reisen würde. Im Anschluß an Bordeaux würde sie diese bemerkenswerten Phantasien kalifornischer Künstler auch zu einer Reihe anderer europäischer Städte führen.

Ich danke Dekan Gordon für seine Mithilfe im Entscheidungsprozeß und für seine fortwährende Unterstützung der Bemühungen der Fisher Gallery. Die Zusammenarbeit mit Lyn Kienholz und der California/International Arts Foundation war eine stete Freude. Die University of Southern California betonte ihr besonderes Interesse an diesem Projekt durch einen großen finanziellen Beitrag zur Herstellung dieses Katalogs. Ohne USCs Unterstützung wäre es nicht möglich gewesen, eine Publikation dieser Qualität und diesen Umfangs anzubieten. Zusammenfassend gesagt bin ich überaus erfreut, daß die Suche nach Vortrefflichkeit, gekrönt durch die Olympischen Sommerspiele 1984, eng verbunden wurde mit der Ausstellung der USC, welche einige der besten kreativen Leistungen in zeitgenössischer kalifornischer Bildhauerei darstellt.

Selma Holo, Ph.D., Direktorin
Fisher Gallery
University of Southern California

Foreword

Robert Arneson, Charles Arnoldi, Bruce Beasley, Fletcher Benton, Guy Dill, Jud Fine, Tom Holland, Robert Hudson, Manuel Neri, Sam Richardson, Michael Todd, and DeWain Valentine represent a solid cross-section of two generations of sculptors who have chosen to live and work in California. Each has an established reputation within the western region, and several are reaching out toward national and international recognition.

These twelve artists were selected for this particular exhibition for a variety of reasons. Primary among these was the consistently high quality of work of each artist over an extended period of time, as well as the fact that each has developed a distinctive, quickly identifiable personal style in medium, method, and content. As such, these artists symbolize the diversity and imagination inherent in the work of California sculptors today.

Another factor that was considered in the selection process was the stated desire to have the exhibition travel to Europe. With this in mind, the work chosen is of large scale, and it is sculpture that does not demand unusual space, site, and installation requirements. Highly regarded conceptual, performance, and site-specific work being created by California artists will have to wait for another go-around.

Five of the artists are from Southern California, and seven are from the San Francisco Bay Area; other than that rather loose geographical designation, there are few clearly identifiable features of the art attaching it to one locale or the other. It might be observed that Robert Arneson, the only artist working in clay included in the exhibition, in his irreverent and iconoclastic statements, can be related to the "Funk" movement associated with San Francisco in the 1960s, and that DeWain Valentine's crisp work in glass or plastic can be associated with the "fetish finish" attitude prevailing in Los Angeles in the 1960s and early 1970s. Apart from these two rather obvious observations, the other artists are partaking of an international vocabulary that is more difficult to define except in formal terms, and which seems to have no clear regional association.

The following extended essays by Jan Butterfield and Melinda Wortz delve more deeply into the work itself. Let it suffice here to say that among the twelve artists, almost every medium known to art has been explored and incorporated in traditional and nontraditional ways—clay, fiber, wood, plastic, glass, steel, bronze, marble, leather, stitchery, and paint combine in a series of visually stimulating manifestations that characterize the delightful inventory of American sculpture created in California.

Henry T. Hopkins, Director
San Francisco Museum of Modern Art

Robert Arneson, Charles Arnoldi, Bruce Beasley, Fletcher Benton, Guy Dill, Jud Fine, Tom Holland, Robert Hudson, Manuel Neri, Sam Richardson, Michael Todd y DeWain Valentine constituyen una sólida muestra representativa de dos generaciones de escultores que decidieron vivir y trabajar en California. Cada uno de ellos posee una reputación reconocida en el oeste de los Estados Unidos y algunos están comenzando a ser reconocidos nacional e internacionalmente.

Los doce artistas de esta exposición particular fueron seleccionados por una variedad de razones. La primera fue la consistente alta calidad de la obra de cada artista durante un largo período de tiempo, asi como el hecho de que cada uno de ellos ha desarrollado un estilo personal distintivo, fácilmente identificable en contenido, materiales y método. Como tales, estos artistas simbolizan la diversidad e imaginación inherentes a los escultores de California de nuestros días.

Otro factor que fue considerado en el proceso de selección consistió en el reiterado deseo de trasladar la exposición a Europa. Con ésto en mente, las obras seleccionadas son de gran escala y precisamente la escultura no requiere espacios, locales o instalación insólitos. Las obras que están siendo creadas por artistas californianos con una ejecución considerada altamente conceptual y para ser exhibida en lugares específicos tendrán que esperar otra ocasión.

Cinco de los artistas proceden de California del Sur, y siete de la Bahía de San Francisco; aparte de esta bastante vaga localizacion geográfica, existen pocos rasgos artísticos distintivos que puedan identificarlos con una localidad u otra. Puede observarse que Robert Arneson, el único artista incluido en esta exposición que trabaja la arcilla, en sus irreverentes e iconoclastas afirmaciones, puede ser relacionado con el movimiento «Funk» asociado con el San Francisco de los años 60 y que la intensa obra de DeWain Valentine en vidrio o plástico puede ser asociada con la actitud de «acabado de fetiche» prevalente en Los Angeles durante los años 60 y principios de los 70. Aparte de estas dos muy obvias observaciones, los demás artistas comparten un vocabulario internacional de más difícil definición a no ser que lo hagamos en términos formales, lo cual no permite asociarlos con una zona geográfica definida.

En los siguientes y extensivos ensayos Jan Butterfield y Melinda Wortz exploran con mayor profundidad en la obra misma. Basta decir aquí que entre los doce artistas, se ha explorado casi cualquier material artístico conocido y se han incorporado a formas tradicionales y no tradicionales—arcilla, fibra, madera, plástico, vidrio, acero, bronce, mármol, cuero, bordados y pintura—combinadas en una serie de manifesaciones de gran estímulo visual que caracterizan el delicioso inventario de la escultura americana creada en California.

Henry T. Hopkins, Director
Museo de Arte Moderno de San Francisco

Robert Arneson, Charles Arnoldi, Bruce Beasley, Fletcher Benton, Guy Dill, Jud Fine, Tom Holland, Robert Hudson, Manuel Neri, Sam Richardson, Michael Todd et DeWain Valentine représentent une excellente sélection de deux générations de sculpteurs qui ont choisi de vivre et de travailler en Californie. Chacun d'eux a établi sa réputation sur la Côte Ouest [des Etats-Unis] et plusieurs d'entre eux ont acquis une renommée nationale et internationale.

Ces douze artistes ont été choisis pour cette exposition pour diverses raisons, la première étant que leurs oeuvres se sont maintenues à un haut niveau de perfection depuis de nombreuses années et la seconde, que chacun d'eux s'est créé un style distinct, personnel, que l'on reconnaît rapidement, dans le choix du matériau, la méthode et le contenu. En tant que tels, ces artistes symbolisent la diversité et l'imagination qui président à l'oeuvre des sculpteurs californiens d'aujourd'hui.

Un autre facteur qui a influencé la sélection fut le désir, de faire faire le tour de l'Europe à cette exposition. Dans cette perspective, la sculpture choisie est à grande échelle, et c'est une sculpture qui ne demande pas un espace, un site ou une installation spéciaux. Certaines oeuvres conceptuelles nécessitant un site spécifique, créées par des artistes californiens, bien que jouissant d'une très haute estime, devront attendre une autre exposition.

Parmi les artistes, cinq sont de Californie du Sud et sept viennent de la Baie de San Francisco; au-delà de cette appartenance géographique assez vague, il est assez difficile de trouver des caractéristiques qui rattachent un artiste à un groupe plutôt qu'à l'autre. Notons que Robert Arneson, le seul artiste présenté dans cette exposition à travailler avec de l'argile, pourrait, par ses déclarations irrévérencieuses et iconoclastes, être rattaché au movement «Funk» des années soixante, à San Francisco, et que le travail nerveux de DeWain Valentine, sur verre ou plastique, peut être associé à l'attitude «fetish finish» qui domina, à Los Angeles, pendant les années soixante et au commencement des années soixante-dix. A ces exceptions près, qui sont assez évidentes, les autres artistes partagent un vocabulaire international qu'il est plus difficile de définir, sinon de façon formelle, et qui ne semble pas avoir d'association régionale définie.

Les essais suivants, de Jan Butterfield et de Melinda Wortz, s'adressent plus particulièrement à l'oeuvre elle-même. Disons simplement qu'à eux douze, les artistes dont les oeuvres sont présentées ici ont exploré et assimilé, de manière traditionnelle et non-traditionnelle, tous les media auxquels l'art a recours pour s'exprimer: argile, fibre, bois, plastique, verre, acier, bronze, marbre, cuir, travail à l'aiguille et peinture, qui se marient pour créer une série de manifestations visuelles stimulantes merveilleusement représentative des trésors de la sculpture américaine créée en California.

Henry T. Hopkins, Directeur
Musée d'Art Moderne de San Francisco

Robert Arneson, Charles Arnoldi, Bruce Beasley, Fletcher Benton, Guy Dill, Jud Fine, Tom Holland, Robert Hudson, Manuel Neri, Sam Richardson, Michael Todd und DeWain Valentine stellen einen soliden Querschnitt zweier Generationen von Bildhauern dar, die Kalifornien gewählt haben, um dort zu leben und zu arbeiten. An der Westküste hat jeder einen festen Ruf, und einige sind auf dem Wege zur nationalen und internationalen Anerkennung.

Diese zwölf Künstler wurden aus mehrfachen Gründen für diese besondere Ausstellung ausgesucht. Hauptgrund war die durchweg hohe Qualität der Arbeiten eines jeden Künstlers über einen ausgedehnten Zeitraum, wie auch die Tatsache, daß jeder einen charakteristischen, leicht erkennbaren persönlichen Stil in Medium, Methode und Gehalt entwickelt hat. Als solche symbolisieren diese Künstler die Vielfältigkeit und Vorstellungskraft, die der Arbeit kalifornischer Bildhauer heute zu eigen ist.

Ein anderer Aspekt, der bei der Auswahl berücksichtigt wurde, war der ausdrückliche Wunsch, die Ausstellung nach Europa zu schicken. In diesem Sinne sind die Ausstellungsgegestände großen Ausmaßes, und nicht zuletzt ist es die Skulptur, die keine ungewöhnlichen Forderungen an Raum, Platz und Entwicklung stellt. Hoch angesehene konzeptuelle vorführungs- und platzgebundene Werke, die von kalifornischen Künstlern geschaffen wurden, müssen auf eine andere Gelegenheit warten.

Fünf der obengenannten Künstler kommen aus Südkalifornien und sieben von dem San Francisco-Bay-Gebiet. Abgesehen von jenen ziemlich vagen geographischen Begriffsbestimmungen, gibt es wenig klar erkennbare Wesenzüge der Kunstwerke, die sich mit der einen oder anderen Örtlichkeit in Verbindung bringen lassen. Es ließe sich feststellen, daß Robert Arneson als einziger mit Ton arbeitender Künstler dieser Ausstellung wegen seiner freizügigen und ikonoklastischen Bemerkungen mit der «Funk» Bewegung von dem San Francisco der 60er Jahre und ebenso, daß DeWain Valentines klare Arbeit in Glas oder Plastik mit der «fetish finish» Haltung, die in Los Angeles in den 60er und frühen 70er Jahren vorherrschte, in Verbindung gebracht werden kann. Neben diesen zwei ziemlich offensichtlichen Beobachtungen nehmen die anderen Künstler an einem internationalen Vokabular teil, das schwieriger zu definieren ist, abgesehen von formalen Begriffen, und welches keinen eindeutig regionalen Bezug zu haben scheint.

Die folgenden umfangreicheren Essays von Jan Butterfield und Melinda Wortz gehen näher auf die Arbeiten selbst ein. Beschränken wir uns hier darauf zu sagen, daß unter diesen zwölf Künstlern fast jedes der Kunst bekannte Medium erforscht und in traditionellen und nicht-traditionellen Weisen vereinigt wurden—nämlich Ton, Faser, Holz, Plastik, Glas, Stahl, Bronze, Marmor, Leder, Stichart und Farbe verbinden sich in einer Serie von visuell stimulierenden Erscheinungen, die das reizende Inventar der in Kalifornien geschaffenen amerikanischen Skulptur charakterisieren.

Henry T. Hopkins, Direktor
San Francisco Museum of Modern Art

Essays

Sculpture is Realer than Painting

Sculpture produced in California is an anomaly. Much of it is more diverse in color and imagery than work produced almost anywhere else in the country. The fact that a great deal of California sculpture is expressionist and painterly seems, on the surface, to be a contradiction in terms, yet in reality it is an interesting extension of both qualities.

In the present exhibition Robert Arneson, Tom Holland, Robert Hudson, Manuel Neri, Sam Richardson, and Chuck Arnoldi represent the painterly aspect of California sculpture—an aspect concerned with highly colored and often gestural works, frequently narrative in an idiosyncratic fashion. The largest proportion of these painterly sculptors is based in Northern California rather than in the southern part of the state, for reasons we shall examine later. Of all the artists in this exhibition who work in an expressionist fashion and/or with color, only Chuck Arnoldi resides in Southern California.

Although this exhibition features major West Coast sculptors, three of those included in the gestural/figurative area *began* as painters (Holland, Neri, and Richardson), two others *became* painters (Hudson and Arnoldi), and the remaining sculptor (Arneson) has been active in recent years in printmaking and drawing. It follows that these factors would account substantially for their acute awareness of surface and color in relation to their present sculpture.[1]

The qualities of a statement articulated in a two-dimensional medium and one made in a three-dimensional medium are markedly different, yet all the artists examined in this essay seem to have made that leap intuitively. Theoretically, the developmental process of any major artist is unique. That is to say, the process through which he or she arrives at the statement materialized by the mature work is a circuitous one, which no one else would be likely to come upon or choose to follow. Why, then, do we find such curious parallels in the mature work of a number of artists? For one thing, it seems clear that in the 1980s we are witnessing a disintegration and dissolution of the (arbitrary) boundaries between painting and sculpture. This dissolution makes the concept of lineal sculptural development null and void. Secondly, it has become increasingly obvious that painting, while practiced as a two-dimensional activity, is conceptually a three-dimensional one. The painter working in the 1980s often deals with hypothetical space that is fully three-dimensional and/or with the illusion of three dimensions in the actual work. Clement Greenberg's critical canons of flatness of surface and utter separation of disciplines (the better to self-criticize as well as to maintain the implicit sculpturalness of sculpture and the painterliness of painting) were never given much credibility on the West Coast to begin with. It is almost as if Greenberg felt that infiltration of the genetic structure would somehow contaminate the breed. In fact, the once forbidden merger between painting and sculpture has been a fortuitous one for it has created a remarkable hybrid—a hybrid which is clearly sculpture rather than painting as we have known it. In its use of materials and imagery, the new hybrid combines the most notable aspects of both, and in so doing has contributed powerful, innovative qualities to the genre of sculpture, which, in turn, have greatly increased its capacity for communication.

Sculpture came late to full maturity and innovation, as Barbara Haskell has noted: "The creative atmosphere and international recognition achieved by Abstract Expressionist painting was not shared by American sculpture until the sixties. . . . By the early sixties American sculpture became as prominent and as vital as painting."[2]

If there was a vitality in the sculpture of the early 1960s, it was not until the last part of those years and the beginning of the 1970s that true innovation began to take place—innovation that took it beyond the boundaries of its implicit sculpturalness and demanded that it be examined in a new context. In 1967 Lucy Lippard noted: "Perhaps the most important aspect of sculpture today is its apparent potential as a vehicle of advance—both formal and evocative, or sensuous. This comprises its most crucial relationship to painting for it is only with the avant-garde's decreasing interest in painting that sculpture has come to the fore. This is a very literal period. *Sculpture, existing in real space and physically autonomous is realer than painting.*"[3]

Sculpture is "realer" than painting. At the end of the 1960s and in the beginning of the 1970s, artists such as Smithson, Heizer, and Christo radically altered our concepts of size and scale by creating site-specific "earth works" so grandiose in concept and implication that they challenged our imagination. At the same period of time Robert Irwin, Maria Nordman, Doug Wheeler, Michael Asher, Eric Orr, and others created room environment pieces of a "light and space" nature that resulted in a reinvestigation of our perceptual processes from a phenomenological and experiential point of view. Major contributions were also made in a category we shall term "colored sculpture" (which for our purposes shall be recognized as distinct from "painted sculpture," in that the latter utilizes color almost as an afterthought, and the former incorporates it as an integral part of the statement and the skin). Early on, that category included a diversity of artists such as John Chamberlain, Dan Flavin, Claes Oldenburg, and George Segal on the East Coast, and Kenneth Price, William Geis, Robert Hudson, and Robert Arneson in the West.

In her essay in the *American Sculpture of the Sixties* catalogue, Lucy Lippard discusses the formal role of color in sculpture: "It [color] is used illusionistically to disperse and minimize volume, to separate shapes in space, making heavy forms seem weightless, light ones heavy, near forms farther away and far ones closer. And it is used to unify, to make a form more "real," isolating it from the environment and asserting the piece as a self-contained whole."[4] Yet historically a conflict existed between this formal approach to color and the relative success of its actual application or function. In spite of the addition of color, sculpture (which through the ages had essentially been no-color—the "no-color" of its material, be it marble, wood, bronze, et cetera) still focused on *material* and *structure*. Lippard quotes Clement Greenberg on Anthony Caro in a story illustrating this dilemma: "Clement Greenberg's complaint about Anthony Caro's color could be applied to any number of other sculptors: 'I know of no piece of his, not even an unsuccessful one, that does not *transcend* its color, or whose specific color or combination of colors does not detract from the quality of the whole (especially when there is more than one color). In every case I have the impression that the color is aesthetically (as well as literally) provisional—that it can be changed at will without affecting quality.' "[5]

The qualities of three-dimensionality and of weight, density, and gravity, classically regarded as the hallmarks of sculpture, have never been associated with color. In fact, in the history of the western sculptural tradition, color has always been virtually a secondary consideration, if not an afterthought. Even polychromatic Greek sculpture was merely an attempt to make the work appear life-like without compromising an integral part of the statement. It was decorative rather than structural. By the same token, the gilded surfaces of much religious art of the fourteenth, fifteenth, and sixteenth centuries were intended primarily to convey religiorealism and spirituality, rather than to serve the purpose of modeling or definition. Not until the late 1950s and the beginning of the

1960s did color on sculpture come into its own. On the East Coast (as we have already noted) it remained for sculptors such as John Chamberlain, Dan Flavin, Claes Oldenburg, and George Segal to make color the paramount issue, linking it inextricably with form. To Flavin that meant "painting" with it —with brilliantly colored light, spilling it over walls and ceilings. To Oldenburg it was first a matter of *applying* color (as he did earlier with plasters), and then integrating it part and parcel with the skin of the work as well as using it as an integral element of his bright, ironical Pop statements.

It is perhaps germane to the following discussion to note that as an artist who created colored sculpture, Oldenburg came to this sensibility *via drawing*, a requisite he shares with the West Coast artists in this exhibition. In fact, his early, beautifully drawn "monuments" were never intended to be executed—they were simply fancies of the artist's eye and hand.

Working in an entirely different fashion, John Chamberlain created sculptures of highly colored crushed automobile parts, providing an extraordinary example of the infusion of color into the sculptural structure.

In George Segal's later works, color became the skin and bones of many of his figures.

Of the West Coast artists working in the arena of colored sculpture, the largest number came from the Bay Area. (Another group, composed of artists such as DeWain Valentine, Peter Alexander, and Larry Bell, all from Los Angeles, comprises still another category. Although their works might properly be interpreted to fit within the definition of colored sculpture as we have defined it here, in actuality these artists were working in glass and plastic at the edges of Los Angeles' "Light and Space Movement," and their concerns were more specifically with transparency, reflection, light, and space than with color per se.) Only Kenneth Price in Los Angeles used color structurally, as if it were a solid entity.

Why is it that many of the artists included in this exhibition are painterly? Fully half the artists in this exhibition use color as an integral part of their statement. The remaining artists are more purely sculptural and/or constructivist (as Wortz's essay indicates). How is it that in addition to the usual involvement with lineal sculptural concerns, the work of these artists slid almost unobtrusively into the arena of painting? Part of the answer lies in the context of place. San Francisco has always been a "painter's town." Early on one can tie that to the presence of such important "painter's painters" as Clyfford Still, Mark Rothko, and Ad Reinhardt, who taught at the San Francisco Art Institute in its "Golden Era" from 1945 to 1950, and to the later influx to the school of major artists, both as teachers and pupils—painters such as Elmer Bischoff, Hassel Smith, Richard Diebenkorn, Joan Brown, Manuel Neri, and many others.

There was another important center at the California College of Arts and Crafts in the early 1950s, when painters Richard Diebenkorn and Nathan Oliveira taught there (Oliveira later took up Stanford as his permanent base, and Diebenkorn began to teach at UCLA where he has a profound effect on the painting community in Southern California). Yet another hotbed of painting and sculpture, one with eccentric narrative qualities in addition to its propensity for high color, has been located at the University of California, Davis, since the beginning of the 1960s. U.C. Davis has been greatly affected by the presence of such important figures as Roy De Forest, Wayne Thiebaud, and Robert Arneson, and has produced a large number of significant painterly artists who work in ceramics.

Because the Bay Area is a painter's town, it is difficult if not impossible to come up with a lengthy list of pure "sculptors" who work in what sculptor Richard Shaw has termed the "YO HO BILL HELP ME TOTE THIS BIG HEAVY BEAM OVER HERE" school (the primary exceptions being Brian Wall, Pete Voulkos, and younger sculptors David Anderson and David Bottini). For the most part, Bay Area artists who attended any one of these influential schools intending to become sculptors became painters because there was so much painting excitement in the air. Nobody forced it, artists just veered in that direction. Their works were eccentric, funky, highly colored, and erratic. They painted over them in a way that had never been done before. They also worked with throwaway materials such as plaster—partly because it was so inexpensive, but also, and importantly, because it could be manipulated like paint. If one had to be a sculptor, the thing was to be so in the most painterly way possible. It seems clear that in Northern California from the mid 1940s on, painters and sculptors tended to occupy themselves with very similar problems— problems that were concerned directly with the power of an image rather than the technical properties of a specific material.

Whether Manuel Neri's plaster or marble polychromed figures stepped out of Joan Brown's Bay Area figurative paintings, or whether Joan Brown often incorporated Neri's figures in her paintings makes no difference—the crucial feature is their symbiosis. Similarly, Nathan Oliveira's paintings, with their haunted, ghostly figures, are a poetic ancestor of them both. Neri has far more in common with those artists than he does with other sculptors, since his concerns with the figure parallel theirs. By the same token, the brightly colored humorous/ironical ceramic works of Robert Arneson have much in common with the works of his teaching cronies Roy De Forest and Wayne Thiebaud. They share an interest in highly colored narrative depiction, based partially or wholly on fancy. Tom Holland and Robert Hudson are long-term teachers at the San Francisco Art Institute, where there is a grand historical legacy of Abstract Expressionism. They both create major sculptural works: Holland in vibrant, gestural, post-cubist fashion, and Hudson in a post-Kandinsky son-of-Dada kind of way. Interestingly, they are both as active (and strong) as painters as they are sculptors. This is also true of William Wiley. Wiley is not included in this presentation simply because he does not create large-scale works that can be exhibited outdoors (a factor which predetermined the intent of this exhibition). Yet he would otherwise qualify. Richard Shaw is another powerful sculptor who works primarily in small scale, with ceramics as his material, and who integrates trompe l'oeil painting into his works in much the same way that Robert Hudson does with his sculptures.

Sam Richardson, among all the artists we are examining, uses the most restraint and delicacy with color (though not of image). He is one of the few Bay region artists of note who does not appear to be influenced by Abstract Expressionism. He is, however, involved with painterly concerns. His delicate miniature landscapes and large-scale environmental pieces are derived from painting, solely from Richardson's own painting and not from any other source. As an artist he is conceptually a loner, although the complex, large-scale room pieces and outdoor works produced over the last decade are always completed with the assistance of a crew.

Chuck Arnoldi's uncannily realistic "thickets," now cast in bronze, derive from the brightly colored "twig" works he has produced for more than a decade. As a student at Chouinard Art Institute in Los Angeles in the late 1960s, Arnoldi came into his own as an artist during a time when the "process and materials" sensibility was in full swing. In Los Angeles during that period, painting was "dead," and the only recourse for a young artist appeared to be a sculptural one. It has only been in the last few years, since gaining national attention as a sculptor, that Arnoldi has turned to painting, creating gigantic sculptural paintings of wood with the use of a chain saw. His works, therefore, are as much a function of his locale as are those of the Bay Area artists, yet he arrived at them entirely differently, as we have seen.

All of the artists discussed have expanded their boundaries and have amplified both our *sense* of the sculptural object and its purpose or meaning. The "colored sculpture" included in this exhibition is not only highly representative of the sort of work currently being done on the West Coast, but it clearly suggests a way to an ever-widening role of figuration, narration, and humor within the tradition of twentieth-century sculpture.

Jan Butterfield
December 1983

1. As noted by Melinda Wortz in this catalogue, the other six sculptors participating in the exhibition began as painters as well, and of those, Fletcher Benton still is active as a painter.

2. Barbara Haskell, "Two Decades of American Sculpture," *Two Hundred Years of American Sculpture*, New York: Whitney Museum of American Art, 1976, p. 187.

3. Lucy Lippard, "As Painting is to Sculpture: A Changing Ratio," *American Sculpture of the Sixties*, Los Angeles: Los Angeles County Museum of Art, 1967, p. 31.

4. Lucy Lippard, p. 33.

5. Lucy Lippard, pp. 106–09.

La escultura es más real que la pintura

La escultura producida en California es anómala. Gran parte de ella supera en color e imagen a las obras producidas en casi cualquier otra parte del país. El que la mayoría de la escultura realizada en California sea expresionista y pictórica parece, superficialmente, una contradicción de términos, sin embargo en la realidad es una interesante extensión de ambas cualidades.

En la presente exposición Robert Arneson, Tom Holland, Robert Hudson, Manuel Neri, Sam Richardson y Chuck Arnoldi representan el aspecto picórico de la escultura californiana—un aspecto procupado por obras a menudo gestuales y de alto colorido, frecuentemente narrativas de una forma idiosincrática. La proporción más grande de estos escultores pictóricos proviene de California del Norte más que de la parte sur del estado, por razones que examinaremos más tarde. De todos los artistas de esta exposición cuyo trabajo encuadra en la moda expresionista y/o colorista, solamente Chuck Arnoldi reside en California del Sur.

Aunque esta exposición presenta importantes escultores de la costa Oeste, tres de ellos incluídos en la tendencia gestual/figurativa, *comenzaron* como pintores (Holland, Neri y Richardson), dos de ellos *se hicieron* pintores (Hudson y Arnoldi), y el escultor restante (Arneson) ha estado activo en los últimos años en la impresión y el dibujo. Estos factores dan cuenta sustancial de la aguda conciencia de la superficie y del color a su escultura actual.[1]

Las cualidades de una declaración artística articulada en un medio bidimensional y otra en un medio tridimensional son marcadamente diferentes, no obstante, todos los artistas examinados en este ensayo parecen haber dado este salto intuitivamente. Teóricamente, el proceso evolutivo de cualquier artista de primera fila es único. Esto es, el proceso a través del cual el o la artista llega a una declaración artística materializada por su trabajo maduro, es circular; un proceso al que nadie llegaría probablemente por sí mismo o eligiera seguir. Entonces, ¿en qué momento encontramos paralelos tan curiosos en la obra madura de muchos artistas? Una cosa sí parece clara, y es que en los años 80 se está evidenciando una desintegración y disolución de los límites (arbitrarios) entre la pintura y la escultura. Esta disolución convierte en futil y vacío el concepto del desarrollo lineal escultural. En segundo lugar, es cada vez más obvio que la pintura, mientras se ejecute como una actividad bidimensional, es conceptualmente una actividad tridimensional. El pintor activo en los años 80 a menudo se enfrenta al espacio hipotético que es completamente tridimensional y/o produce la ilusión de las tres dimensiones en la obra real. Los cánones críticos de la superficie lisa y la total separación de disciplinas de Clement Greenberg nunca recibieron mucha credibilidad, de hecho, en la Costa Oeste (siendo la mencionada separación lo más apropiado para la auto-crítica asi como para mantener la esculturalidad implícita de la escultura y lo pictórico de la pintura). Es como si Greenberg sintiera que la infiltración de la estructura genética pudiera contaminar de algún modo el cultivo. En efecto, la convergencia a veces olvidada entre la pintura y la escultura ha sido fortuita puesto que ha creado un notable híbrido—un híbrido que es claramente escultura más que pintura, tal y como nosotros la conocemos. En su empleo de los materiales y la imagen el nuevo híbrido combina los aspectos más notables de ambos y de esta manera ha proporcionado cualidades poderosas e innovadoras al género de la escultura, el cual, a su vez, ha incrementado enormemente su capacidad de comunicación.

Como Barbara Haskell ha hecho notar, la escultura alcanzó tarde la madurez e innovación plenas: «La atmósfera creativa y el reconocimiento internacional alcanzados por la pintura Expresionista Abstracta no fueron compartidos por la escultura americana hasta los años 60. . . . A principios de los sesenta la escultura americana se hizo tan prominente y vital como la pintura.»[2]

Aunque hubo vitalidad en la escultura de principios de los sesenta no fue hasta finales de esos años y comienzos de los setenta cuando se inició la verdadera innovación—innovación que la llevó màs allá de los límites de su esculturalidad con la exigencia que fuera examinada en un nuevo contexto. En 1967 Lucy Lippard propone: «Quizá el aspecto más importante de la escultura de hoy día es su evidente potencial como vehículo de avance—tanto formal como evocativo o sensual. Esto comprende una relación altamente crucial para la pintura, puesto que sólo debido al interés cada vez menor de la vanguardia hacia la pintura ha permitido a la escultura adquirir un papel preponderante. Este es un período muy literal. *La escultura, físicamente autónoma y existiendo en el espacio real, es más real que la pintura.*»[3]

La escultura *es* «más real» que la pintura. Hacia finales de los sesenta y a comienzos de los setenta, algunos artistas como Smithson, Heizer y Christo alteraron radicalmente nuestros conceptos de tamaño y escala por medio de la creación de «obras terrenales» específicas de lugar tan grandiosas en concepto y en implicación que desafiaban la imaginación. Por el mismo tiempo Robert Irwin, Maria Nordman, Doug Wheeler, Michael Asher, Eric Orr y otros creaban piezas ambientales de una naturaleza «luminosa y espacial» que redundó en una reinvestigación de nuestros procesos perceptuales desde un punto de vista fenomenológico y de experiencia. También se efectuaron importantes contribuciones dentro de una categoría que llamaremos «escultura cromática», que para nuestros propósitos reconoceremos como distinta de la «escultura pintada,» en cuanto la última utiliza el color casi como un sucedáneo, mientras que la primera lo incorpora como parte integral de la declaración artística y de la textura. Con anterioridad, en esa categoría se incluía una diversidad de artistas, tales como John Chamberlain, Dan Flavin, Claes Oldenburg y George Segal en la costa Este y Kenneth Price, William Geis, Robert Hudson y Robert Arneson en la Oeste.

En su ensayo que aparece en el catálogo de la *Escultura Americana de los sesenta*, Lucy Lippard analiza el papel formal del color en la escultura: «[El color] se usa de forma ilusionista para minimizar y dispersar el volumen, para separar formas en el espacio, haciendo que las formas pesadas parezcan ligeras, las ligeras pesadas, las formas cercanas parecen lejanas y las lejanas, cercanas. Además se usa para unificar, para darle más ‹realidad› a una forma, aislándola del entorno y reafirmando la pieza como un todo contenido en sí mismo.[4] No obstante existió un conflicto histórico entre esta aproximación formal al color y el éxito relativo de su aplicación o función reales. A pesar de la adición del color la escultura todavía seguía centrándose en el *material* y la *estructura* (escultura que a través de los tiempos esencialmente no había recurrido al color—nos referimos al «no-color» de su material, ya fuera el mármol, madera, bronce, et cetera). Lippard cita a Clement Greenberg refiriéndose a Anthony Caro en una anécdota que ilustra este dilema: «La queja de Clement Greenberg sobre el color de Anthony Caro podría ser aplicada a un número indeterminado de escultores: ‹No conozco ninguna de sus piezas, ni siquiera una de poco éxito, que no *transcienda* su color, o cuyo color específico o combinación de colores no se aparte de la cualidad del conjunto (especialmente cuando hay más de un color‹. En cualquier caso tengo la impresión de que el color es estéticamente (asi como literalmente) provisional—que puede ser cambiado a voluntad sin afectar la cualidad.›»[5]

Las cualidades de la tridimensionalidad y las del peso,

densidad y gravedad, contempladas clásicamente como los hitos de la escultura, nunca han estado asociados con el color. De hecho, en la historia de la tradición de la escultura occidental el color ha sido siempre una consideración virtual secundaria, cuando no una idea adicional. Incluso la escultura policromada griega fue meramente un intento de hacer que la obra artística se semejara a la vida real sin comprometerla como parte integral de la declaración artística. Era más decorativa que estructural. Por la misma razón, las superficies doradas de gran parte del arte religioso de los siglos catorce, quince y dieciséis estaban primariamente concebidos para expresar espiritualidad y realismo religioso, más que para servir al propósito de modelar o definir. No fue hasta finales de los años 50 y principios de los 60 que el color en la escultura cobró fuerza propia. En la costa Este (como ya hemos mencionado) fue tarea de escultores como John Chamberlain, Dan Flavin, Claes Oldenburg y George Segal hacer del color la cuestión primordial, enlazándolo inextricablemente con la forma. Para Flavin eso significaba «pintar» con él—con luminosidad brillantemente colorista y derramándolo sobre paredes y techos. Para Oldenburg fue sobre todo una cuestión de *aplicación* del color (como lo había hecho anteriormente con sus yesos), y luego integrándolo completamente a la corteza de la obra y usándolo como elemento integral de sus declaraciones artístico-irónicas de su arte Pop.

Es quizá pertinente a la siguiente discusión el hacer notar que como artista creador de escultura cromática, Oldenburg alcanzó esta sensibilidad *vía el dibujo*, un requisito que comparte con los artistas de la costa oeste de esta exposición. En efecto, sus «monumentos» primerizos, bellamente esbozados, nunca fueron concebidos para ser ejecutados—eran simples caprichos de ojos y manos del artista.

Trabajando de una forma completamente diferente, John Chamberlain creó esculturas con recambios de automóviles aplastadas y de alto colorido, aportando un extraordinario ejemplo de la infusión del color en la estructura escultural.

En las obras tardías de George Segal el color se convirtió en la parte integral de muchas de sus figuras.

De entre los artistas de la costa oeste que trabajaban en el campo de la escultura cromática, el número mayor procede de la zona de la Bahía de San Francisco. (Otro grupo, compuesto de artistas como DeWain Valentine, Peter Alexander y Larry Bell, todos naturales de Los Angeles, todavía consitue otra categoría. Aunque sus obras pueden ser interpretadas adecuadamente dentro de la definición de escultura cromática tal y como la hemos definido aquí, en realidad estos artistas estuvieron trabajando con vidrio y plástico en contacto con el «Movimiento de Luz y de Espacio» de Los Angeles, y estaban preocupados mas específicamente por la transparencia, los reflejos, la luz y el espacio que por el color per se.) Solamente Kenneth Price usó estructuralemente el color en Los Angeles, como si fuera una identidad sólida.

¿Cuál es la razón de que muchos de los artistas incluídos en esta exposición sean pictóricos? Justamente la mitad de los artistas de esta exposición utilizan el color como parte integral de su declaración artística. Los restantes artistas son más propiamente esculturales y/o constructivistas (tal y como indica Wortz en su ensayo). ¿Cómo puede ser que además de la normal preocupación por la escultura lineal la obra de estos artistas se puede haber deslizado claramente hacia el terreno de la pintura? Parte de la respuesta está en el contexto del lugar. San Francisco siempre ha sido una «ciudad de pintores.» Esto se relaciona con la anterior presencia de «pintores de pintores» tan eminentes como Clyfford Still, Mark Rothko y Ad Reinhardt quienes enseñaron en la Academia de Arte de San Francisco en la «Época Dorada,» desde 1945 a 1950, y al flujo posterior de artistas destacados tanto profesores como alumnos—pintores de la talla de Elmer Bischoff, Hassel Smith, Richard Diebenkorn, Joan Brown, Manuel Neri y muchos otros.

A principios de los años 50 hubo otro centro importante en la Escuela Superior de Artes y Oficios de California donde enseñaron los pintores Richard Diebenkorn y Nathan Oliveira (posteriormente Oliveira trasladó a Stanford su base permanente y Diebenkorn comenzó a enseñar en UCLA donde sigue teniendo un profundo efecto en la comunidad de pintores de California del Sur). Todavía puede localizarse otro foco de pintura y escultura, de excéntricas cualidades narrativas, además de su propensión al intenso cromatismo, en la Universidad de California, Davis, desde el comienzo de los años 60. La Universidad de California en Davis ha sido altamente influída por la presencia de figuras tan importantes como Roy De Forest, Wayne Thiebaud y Robert Arneson y ha generado un gran número de artistas pictóricos significativos que trabajan con la cerámica.

Debido a que la zona de la Bahía de San Francisco es una zona de pintores, es difícil si no imposible elaborar una lista larga de «escultores» puros que trabajen en lo que el escultor Richard Shaw ha calificado como la escuela del «OYE BILL, AYUDAME A CAMBIAR DE LUGAR ESTE MUNDO DE TABLON» (cuyas excepciones eran Brian Wall, Pete Voulkos y escultores más jóvenes como David Anderson y David Bottini). En su mayoría, los artistas de la Bahía de San Francisco que asistieron a alguna de estas influyentes escuelas y que intentaban hacerse escultores, se hicieron pintores debido a que había un ambiente de euforia hacia la pintura. Nadie se vio forzado, los artistas tomaron simplemente esa dirección. Sus obras eran excéntricas, esotéricas, de colores intensos, y erráticas. Fueron pintadas como nunca lo habían sido antes. También trabajaron con materiales de desecho como el yeso—en parte porque era tan barato, pero también, y esto es importante, porque podía manipularse como la pintura. Si la intención de uno era ser escultor, la cuestión era serlo de la forma más pictórica posible. Parece evidente que a partir de mediados de los años 40 en adelante, los pintores y escultores de California del Norte tendían a ocuparse de problemas muy similares—problemas directamente relacionados con el poder de la imagen más que con las propiedades técnicas de un material específico.

No importa que las figuras policromadas en yeso o mármol de Manuel Neri surgieran de las pinturas figurativas de Joan Brown de la Bahía de San Francisco, ni que Joan Brown incorporara a menudo figuras de Neri en sus pinturas—el rasgo crucial radica en su simbiosis. Similarmente, las pinturas de Nathan Oliveira con sus figuras perturbadas y fantasmagóricas, constituyen un precedente poético de ambos. Neri tiene mucho más en común con aquellos artistas que con otros escultores, puesto que su preocupación por la figura es paralela a la de ellos. Por la misma razón, los trabajos de cerámica de brillantes colores irónico-humoristas de Robert Arneson tienen mucho en común con las obras de sus maestros y colegas Roy De Forest y Wayne Thiebaud. Ellos comparten un interés por la representación narrativa altamente colorista, basada parcial o totalmente en la fantasía. Tom Holland y Robert Hudson son profesores establecidos en la Academia de Arte de San Francisco donde existe un grandioso legado histórico del Expresionismo Abstracto. Ambos se dedican a crear grandes obras esculturales: Holland de forma vibrante, gestual y post-cubista, y Hudson de una forma a lo hijo-de-Dada post-Kandinsky. Curiosamente, ambos son pintores tan activos (y poderosos) como escultores. Esto también es verdad de William Wiley. Wiley no está incluído en esta presentación simplemente porque no crea trabajos a gran escala que puedan ser exhibidos en el exterior (un factor que subyace a la intención de esta exposición). De lo contrario hubiera sido incluído. Richard Shaw es otro poderoso escultor que trabaja primordialmente a pequeña escala, con cerámica como material, y que integra pintura trompe l'oeil a sus obras de forma muy parecida a como Robert Hudson lo hace con sus esculturas.

Sam Richardson usa la mayor moderación y delicadeza con el color (aunque no con la imagen) de entre todos los artistas que estamos examinando. El es uno de los pocos artistas de la zona de la Bahía, de cierto renombre que parece no estar influído por el Expresionismo Abstracto. Sin embargo, está procupado por la cuestión pictórica. Sus delicados paisajes en miniatura y piezas ambientales a gran escala se derivan de la pintura, de la propia pintura de Richardson exclusivamente y no de cualquier otra fuente. Como artista es conceptualmente un solitario, aunque las piezas interiores y obras exteriores complejas y a gran escala, producidas durante la última década, siempre son terminadas con la ayuda de un equipo de personas.

Las «espesuras» misteriosamente realistas de Chuck Arnoldi, ahora forjadas en bronce, se derivan de las obras de «ramas» brillantemente coloristas que ha producido durante más de una década. A finales de los años 60 siendo estudiante en el Instituto Chouinard de Los Angeles, Arnoldi se encontró a si mismo como artista durante un período en el que la sensibilidad hacia los «procesos y materiales» estaba en pleno auge. En Los Angeles, durante aquel período, la pintura estaba «muerta» y el único recurso del artista joven parecía ser la escultura. El cambio de Arnoldi a la pintura ha ocurrido en los años, desde que ganó atención nacional como escultor, con la creación de pinturas esculturales gigantescas de madera usando una sierra automática. Sus obras, por lo tanto, son tanto una función de su procedencia geográfica como de los artistas del área de la Bahía, aunque por caminos enteramente diferentes, como ya hemos visto.

Todos los artistas aquí comentados han expandido sus límites y han amplificado tanto nuestro sentido del objeto escultural como su propósito o significado. La «escultura cromática» incluída en esta exposición no sólo es representativa del tipo de trabajo que se realiza actualmente en la costa oeste, sino que sugiere claramente un camino hacia un papel cada vez más amplio de la figuración, la narración y el humor dentro de la tradición escultórica del siglo veinte.

Jan Butterfield
Diciembre 1983

1. Como sugiere Melinda Wortz en este catálogo los otros seis escultores que participan en la exposición también comenzaron como pintores, y de ellos, Fletcher Benton es todavía un pintor activo.
2. Barbara Haskell, «Dos Décadas de Escultura Americana,» en *Doscientos años de Escultura Americana*, Nueva York: Museo Whitney de Arte Americano, 1976, pág. 187.
3. Lucy Lippard, «Lo que la Pintura es a la Escultura: una relación cambiante,» en *Escultura Americana de los sesenta*, Museo de Arte del Condado de Los Angeles, 1967, pág. 31.
4. Lucy Lippard, pág. 33.
5. Lucy Lippard, págs. 106–09.

La Sculpture est plus reelle que la peinture

La sculpture de Californie est une anomalie. Pour une large part, on y trouve des couleurs et une imagerie plus diverses que dans le travail exécuté n'importe où ailleurs dans le pays. Le fait qu'un bon nombre de sculptures californiennes soient expressionistes et picturales semble, en apparence, contradictoire, cependant, en réalité, elles y gagnent une richesse supplémentaire.

Dans cette exposition, Robert Arneson, Tom Holland, Robert Hudson, Manuel Neri, Sam Richardson et Chuck Arnoldi représentent la tendance picturale de la sculpture californienne—une tendance qui aime les oeuvres très colorées et souvent gestuelles, fréquemment narratives d'une façon idiosyncratique. Les peintres de ce groupe sont, en majorité, basés en Californie du Nord plutôt qu'au Sud de l'Etat, pour des raisons que nous examinerons plus tard. De tous les artistes représentés dans cette exposition et travaillant d'une manière expressionniste, avec ou sans couleur, seul Chuck Arnoldi réside en California du Sud.

Bien que cette exposition soit une exposition des principaux sculpteurs de la Côte Ouest, trois d'entre eux, qui font partie du groupe gestuel/figuratif, *commencèrent leur carrière* en tant que peintres (Holland, Neri et Richardson), deux autres *devinrent des peintres* (Hudson et Arnoldi), quant au dernier (Arneson), il s'intéresse, depuis ces dernières années, à la gravure et au dessin. Il s'ensuit que ces facteurs expliquent en grande partie la sensibilité extrême de ces artistes à la surface et à la couleur dans leurs sculptures présentes.[1]

Les qualités du message exprimé à travers un medium en deux dimensions et celles d'un message exprimé à travers un medium en trois dimensions sont très différentes, cependant, tous les artistes examinés dans cet essai semblent avoir franchi le pas intuitivement. En théorie, l'évolution d'un artiste est unique. C'est à dire que la façon dont il ou elle arrive à maturité et exprime cela dans son oeuvre n'est pas directe et lui appartient en propre. Pourquoi, alors, trouve-t-on de telles ressemblances curieuses entre les oeuvres d'un grand nombre d'artistes parvenus à maturité? Un fait est clair: il semble que dans les années quatre-vingts, nous assistions à la désintégration et à la dissolution des limites (arbitraires) entre sculpture et peinture. Cette dissolution rend nul et sans effet le concept de dévelopement sculptural linéaire. Deuxièmement, il devient du plus en plus évident que la peinture, tout en étant exécutée en deux dimensions, est, conceptuellement en trois dimensions. Le peintre travaillant dans les années quatre-vingts traite souvent un espace hypothétique qui est bel et bien en trois dimensions et/ou qui donne l'illusion des trois dimensions. Les canons critiques de Clement Greenberg relatifs à la platitude des surfaces et à la stricte séparation des disciplines (dont le but était l'auto-critique autant que le désir de sauvegarder la sculpturalité implicite de la sculpture et la picturalité de la peinture) n'ont jamais été très respectés sur la Côte Ouest. C'est presque comme si Greenberg avait pressenti que l'infiltration de la structure génétique allait, d'une manière ou d'une autre, contaminer l'espèce. En fait, la fusion, jadis interdite, de la peinture et de la sculpture a été accidentelle et elle a créé un hybride remarquable—qui appartient nettement à la sculpture au lieu de rester dans le domaine de la peinture telle que nous la connaissions. Par l'emploi des matériaux et de l'imagerie, le nouvel hybride combine les aspects les plus remarquables de chaque discipline et, ce faisant, a doué la sculpture de qualités innovatives puissantes qui, à leur tour, ont considérablement augmenté son pouvoir de communication.

Ainsi que l'a fait remarquer Barbara Haskell, la sculpture est venue tard à maturité, à être capable d'innover: «L'atmosphère créatrice et la renommée internationale dont jouissait la peinture expressionniste abstraite n'ont été partagées par la sculpture américaine que dans les années soixante. . . . C'est alors que la sculpture américaine devint aussi importante et vitale que la peinture.»[2]

Si la sculpture du début des années soixante ne manquait pas de vitalité, ce ne fut pas avant la fin de la décade et le début des années soixante-dix que de véritables innovations commencèrent à se produire—innovations qui l'entraînèrent au-delà des limites de sa sculpturalité implicite et qui nécessitèrent qu'on l'examine dans un contexte nouveau. Lucy Lippard faisait observer, en 1967: «Peut-être l'aspect le plus important de la sculpture d'aujourd'hui est-il son potentiel apparent comme véhicule de progrès—à la fois formel et suggestif ou sensuel. Cela inclut ses rapports, d'une importance cruciale avec la peinture car, ce fut seulement à cause de la perte d'intérêt manifestée par l'avant-garde à l'égard de la peinture que la sculpture est passée au premier plan. Nous vivons une période très littérale. *La sculpture, existant dans un espace réel et physiquement autonome, est plus réelle que la peinture.*»[3]

La sculpture est "plus réelle" que la peinture. A la fin des années soixate et au commencement des années soixante-dix, des artistes tels que Smithson, Heizer et Christo bouleversèrent radicalement nos concepts de dimensions et d'échelle en créant, dans un site spécifique, des «earth works» (travaux en argile) si grandioses par leur conception et par ce qu'ils impliquaient qu'ils défièrent notre imagination. Au même moment, Robert Irwin, Maria Nordman, Doug Wheeler, Michael Asher, Eric Orr et d'autres créèrent des oeuvres d'intérieur du type «lumière et espace» qui eurent pour résultat de nous faire ré-examiner nos procédés de perception d'un point de vue phénoménologique et empirique. Des contributions majeures furent aussi faites dans une catégorie que nous appellerons «sculpture colorée» (que nous distinguerons de la «sculpture peinte», en ce sens que cette dernière emploie la couleur presque comme après-coup alors que la première l'incorpore comme faisant partie intégrale de tout). Très tôt, cette catégorie comprit des artistes aussi divers que John Chamberlain, Dan Flavin, Claes Oldenburg et George Segal sur la Côte Est et Kenneth Price, William Geis, Robert Hudson et Robert Arneson à l'Ouest.

Dans son essai écrit pour le catalogue intitulé *American Sculpture of the Sixties*, Lucy Lippard parle du rôle formel de la couleur en sculpture: «Elle [la couleur] est employée de façon à créer illusion pour disperser et minimiser le volume, pour séparer les formes dans l'espace, pour donner l'impression que les formes lourdes ne pèsent pas, que celles qui sont légères sont lourdes, pour éloigner ce qui est proche et rapprocher ce qui est loin. Elle est aussi employée à unifier, à donner plus de «réalité» à une forme, en l'isolant de son environnement et en lui permettant de s'affirmer comme un tout autonome.»[4] Cependant, historiquement, il existait un conflit entre la théorie de la couleur et le succès relatif de son emploi ou de sa fonction réelle. En dépit de l'addition de la couleur, la sculpture (qui, au cours des âges, était traditionnellement restée privée de couleur—n'ayant, pour toute couleur que celle des matériaux qu'elle utilisait, que ce soit le marbre, le bois, le bronze, et caetera) continuait à mettre l'accent sur le *matériau* et la *structure*. Lippard cite Clement Greenberg parlant d'Anthony Caro dans une annecdote qui illustre ce dilemne: «Ce que reproche Clement Greenberg à Anthony Caro à propos de la couleur pourrait s'appliquer à de nombreux autres sculpteurs: «Je ne connais pas une seule de ses oeuvres, pas même une oeuvre ratée, qui ne *transcende* pas sa couleur, ou dont la couleur spécifique ou les combinaisons de couleurs ne diminuent pas la qualité de l'ensemble (surtout quand il y a plus d'une couleur). Dans tous les cas, j'ai toujours l'impression que la couleur est, esthétiquement (aussi bien que littéralement) provisoire—qu'on peut la transformer à volonté sans affecter la qualité [de l'oeuvre].»[5]

La tri-dimensionalité, le poids, la densité la pesanteur que l'on considère traditionnellement comme appartenant en propre à la sculpture, n'ont jamais été associées avec la couleur. En fait, dans l'histoire de la sculpture occidentale, la couleur a toujours été reléguée au second rang, comme ajoutée après-coup. La couleur polychrome des Grecs était elle-même un simple effort pour donner à l'oeuvre l'apparence de la vie sans en compromettre la structure. Elle était purement décorative. De même, les surfaces dorées des oeuvres de l'art religieux des XIVe, XVe et XVIe sicles avaient pour but d'en souligner le caractère sacré et la spiritualité, plutôt que le modelé. Ce ne fut qu'à la fin des années cinquante et au début des années soixante que la couleur commence à jouer un rôle en sculpture. Sur la Côte Est (ainsi que nous l'avons déjà fait remarquer), ce fut à des sculpteurs tels que John Chamberlain, Dan Flavin, Claes Oldenburg et George Segal qu'il revint de donner à la couleur une place de premier plan, en la liant indissolublement à la forme. Pour Flavin, cela signifiait «peindre»—avec une lumière brillamment colorée qu'il répandait sur les murs et sur les plafonds. Pour Oldenburg, il s'agissait d'abord d'*appliquer* la couleur, (comme avant il avait appliqué des plâtres), et puis de l'intégrer complètement à la surface de l'oeuvre autant que de l'employer comme un élément de ses oeuvres Pop, brillantes et ironiques.

Il est peut-être approprié de noter qu'en tant qu'artiste qui créa des sculptures colorées, Oldenburg acquit cette sensibilité *par le dessin*, caractéristique qu'il partage avec les artistes de la Côte Ouest dont les oeuvres sont ici exposées. En fait, ses premiers «monuments» si bien dessinés n'étaient pas destinés à être réalisés—ce n'étaient que des fantaisies nées de l'oeil et de la main de l'artiste.

Travaillant d'une toute autre manière, John Chamberlain créa des sculptures composées de morceaux d'automobiles compressées, fournissant ainsi un exemple extraordinaire de la fusion de la couleur dans la structure sculpturale. Dans les dernières oeuvres de George Segal, la couleur devint l'essentiel de nombre de ses figures.

De tous les artistes de la Côte Ouest qui travaillent dans le domaine de la sculpture colorée, le plus grand nombre vient de la région de la Baie [de San Francisco]. (Un autre groupe, composé d'artistes tels que DeWain Valentine, Peter Alexander et Larry Bell, tous de Los Angeles, forme encore une autre catégorie. Bien qu'on puisse correctement interpréter leurs oeuvres comme faisant partie du groupe de la sculpture en couleur telle que nous l'avons définie ici, en réalité, ces artistes travaillaient dans le verre et dans le plastique, à la limite du «Light and Space Mouvement» de Los Angeles, et ils s'intéressaient plus à la transparence, à la réflexion, à la lumière et à l'espace qu'à la couleur elle-même.) Kenneth Price, de Los Angeles, est le seul à employer la couleur structuralement, comme s'il s'agissait d'un solide.

Comment se fait-il que beaucoup d'entre les artistes compris dans cette exposition inclinent vers la peinture? Une bonne moitié des artistes dont les oeuvres sont présentées ici emploient la couleur comme faisant partie intégrale de leurs créations. Les autres sont plus purement des sculpteurs ou/et des constructivistes (ainsi que l'indique l'essai de Wortz). Comment expliquer que l'oeuvre de ces artistes, non contente de s'inquiéter de la ligne sculpturale traditionnelle, ait glissé vers la peinture, d'une manière presque discrète? La cause de cette évolution est en partie géographique. San Francisco a

toujours été une ville de prédilection des «peintres». On peut faire remonter, cette évolution au début, à la présence de ces «peintres des peintres» que furent Clyfford Still, Mark Rothko et Ad Reinhardt qui enseignèrent à l'Institut d'Art de San Francisco, pendant son «Age d'Or», de 1945 à 1950, puis ensuite à l'arrivée à l'école d'artistes de premier plan, tant maîtres qu'élèves, tels que les peintres Elmer Bischoff, Hassel Smith, Richard Diebenkorn, Joan Brown, Manuel Neri et bien d'autres.

Un autre centre important exista au California College of Arts and Crafts, au début des années cinquante, lorsque les peintres Richard Diebenkorn et Nathan Oliveira y enseignèrent (par la suite, Oliveira choisit Stanford comme base permanente, et Diebenkorn commença à enseigner à UCLA d'où il exerce une profonde influence sur la communauté des peintres de Californie du Sud.) Un autre point chaud de la sculpture et de la peinture, qui ajoute à son goût des couleurs vibrantes des qualités narratives eccentriques, se situe à l'Université de Californie à Davis, où il fleurit depuis le début des années soixante. L'Université de Californie à Davis a été très influencée par des artistes d'importance tels que Roy De Forest, Wayne Thiebaud et Robert Arneson et a formé un grand nombre d'artistes à tendance picturale qui travaillent la céramique.

Du fait que la région de la Baie [de San Francisco] est une ville de peintres, il est difficile, sinon impossible, de dresser une longue liste de «sculpteurs» purs travaillant selon les normes de l'école que Richard Shaw a appelée l'école «EH, BILL, VIENS M'DONNER UN COUP D'MAIN POUR TRANS—PORTER CETTE GROSSE POUTRE PAR ICI», (exception faite de Brian Wall, Pete Voulkos et de David Anderson et David Bottini, qui sont des sculpteurs plus jeunes). Le plupart des artistes de la Baie qui allèrent à l'une de ces écoles prestigieuses avec l'intention de devenir des sculpteurs devinrent des peintres, parce que la peinture était dans l'air. Personne ne les y força, ils prirent tout naturellement cette direction. Leurs oeuvres étaient eccentriques, «funky», hautes en couleurs et erratiques. Ils les recouvrirent de peinture d'une façon inconnue jusqu'alors. Ils travaillèrent aussi avec des matériaux non durables comme le plâte—en partie parce qu'il est si bon marché et aussi, et c'est important, parce qu'il se laisse manipuler comme la peinture. Si l'on voulait faire de la sculpture, le tout était de s'y prendre le plus possible comme un peintre. Il est clair qu'en Californie du Nord, à partir du milieu des années quarante, les peintres et les sculpteurs eurent tendance à se préoccuper de problèmes très similaires—problèmes ayant rapport directement au pouvoir de l'image plutôt qu'aux propriétés d'un matériau spécifique.

Le fait de savoir si les figures en marbre ou en plâtre polychrome de Manuel Neri étaient nées de la peinture figurative de Joan Brown, dans la région de la Baie, ou si c'était Joan Brown qui avait incorporé les figures de Neri dans sa peinture n'a aucune importance—ce qui compte, c'est leur symbiose. De même, les peintures de Nathan Oliveira, avec leurs personnages à la silhouette fantômatique, sont-ils les ancêtres poétiques de Neri comme de Brown. Neri a beaucoup plus de traits en commun avec ces deux artistes qu'avec les autres sculpteurs car son souci de la forme est parallèle au leur. De même, les oeuvres en céramique, brillamment colorées, humoristiques et ironiques de Robert Arneson ont beaucoup de points communs avec celles de ses maîtres et amis Roy De Forest et Wayne Thiebaud. Ils ont en commun un goût de la narration aux couleurs vives, basée en partie ou complètement sur la fantaisie. Tom Holland et Robert Hudson enseignent depuis longtemps au San Francisco Art Institute, héritier de l'Expressionnisme abstrait. Tous deux créent des sculptures d'importance majeure: Holland d'une façon vibrante, gestuelle, post-cubiste et Hudson d'une façon post-Kandinsky, héritière de la manière Dada. Il est intéressant de noter que tous deux sont aussi actifs comme peintres que comme sculpteurs. Ceci est vrai aussi de William Wiley. Il n'y a pas d'oeuvre représentant Wiley dans cette exposition, pour la seule raison qu'il ne crée pas d'oeuvres de grandes dimensions pouvant être présentées à l'extérieur (facteur déterminant pour cette exposition). Si ce n'était cela, il y figurerait. Richard Shaw est un autre sculpteur puissant qui fait surtout des oeuvres de petites dimensions. Il utilise la céramique et introduit la peinture en trompe-l'oeil dans ses sculptures, tout à fait à la manière des sculptures de Robert Hudson.

De tous les artistes que nous examinons, Sam Richardson est celui qui emploie la couleur de la manière la plus réservée et la plus délicate (ceci ne s'applique pas à l'image). Il est un des rares artistes réputés de la Baie qui semble ne pas avoir été influencé par l'Expressionisme abstrait. Toutefois, il s'intéresse à la peinture. Ses paysages miniatures délicats et ses ensembles de grandes dimensions sont dérivés de la peinture, mais de sa peinture à lui et non de celle d'un autre. En tant qu'artiste, ses concepts sont ceux d'un solitaire, bien que ses ensembles d'intérieur et ses oeuvres destinées au plein-air soient toujours exécutés avec l'aide d'une équipe.

Les «fourrés» d»un réalisme surprenant de Chuck Arnoldi, que, maintenant, il coule en bronze, dérivent des oeuvres en «brindilles» brillamment colorées qu'il a réalisées pendant plus d'une dizaine d'années. C'est alors qu'il était étudiant au Chouinard Art Institute de Los Angeles, à la fin des années soixante, qu'Arnoldi découvrit sa voie à une époque où la sensibilité aux «procédés et aux matériaux» était très forte. A ce moment-là, à Los Angeles, la peinture était «morte», et pour un jeune artiste, il ne semblait y avoir de possibilité que dans la sculpture. Ce n'est qu'au cours de ces dernières années, après avoir atteint une renommée nationale comme sculpteur, qu'Arnoldi s'est mis à la peinture, créant d'énormes peintures sculpturales, en bois, qu'il découpe à la scie mécanique. Par conséquent, ses oeuvres, comme celles des artistes de la baie, lui ont été inspirées par le lieu et les circonstances, toutefois, il y est parvenu, comme nous l'avons dit, d'une manière complètement différente.

Tout les artistes dont nous avons parlé ont élargi leur champ d'action et amplifié, à la fois, notre *perception* de l'oeuvre sculptée et son but ou sa signification. Les «sculptures colorées» qui figurent dans cette exposition ne sont pas seulement très représentatives du genre de travail qui s'exécute présentemment sur la Côte Ouest des Etats-Unis, elles suggèrent aussi le rôle de plus en plus vaste tenu par la figuration, la narration et l'humour dans la tradition de la sculpture du XXe sicle.

Jan Butterfield
décembre 1983

1. Ainsi que l'a fait remarquer Melinda Wortz dans ce catalogue, les autres six sculpteurs dont les oeuvres figurent dans cette exposition commencerent aussi leur carrière comme peintres, et, parmi eux, Fletcher Benton continue à peindre activement.

2. Barbara Haskell, "Two Decades of American Sculpture," *Two Hundred Years of American Sculpture*. New York: Whitney Museum of American Art, 1976, p. 187.

3. Lucy Lippard, "As Painting is to Sculpture: A Changing Ratio," *American Sculpture of the Sixties*, Los Angeles: Los Angeles County Museum of Art, 1967, p. 31.

4. Lucy Lippard, p. 33.

5. Lucy Lippard, pp. 106–09.

Bildhauerei ist wirklichkeitsnaher als Malerei

Bildhauerei, die in Kalifornien geschaffen wird, ist eine Ungereimtheit. Viel bei ihr ist andersartig in Farbe und Ausdruck als bei Werken aus fast allen anderen Teilen des Landes. Die Tatsache, daß ein großer Teil kalifornischer Bildhauerei expressionistisch und malerisch ist, scheint zunächst ein Widerspruch in sich zu sein, in Wirklichkeit aber eine interessante Ausdehnung beider Eigenheiten.

In der hiesigen Ausstellung repräsentieren Robert Arneson, Tom Holland, Robert Hudson, Manuel Neri, Sam Richardson und Chuck Arnoldi den malerischen Aspekt kalifornischer Bildhauerei—einen Aspekt, der sich mit äußerst farbigen und oft gebärdenhaften Arbeiten, häufig erzählerhaft in idiosynkratischer Weise, beschäftigt. Die größte Anzahl dieser Bildhauer ist eher in Nordkalifornien zu finden als im südlichen Teil des Staates, aus Gründen, die wir später noch untersuchen werden. Von all den Künstlern dieser Ausstellung, die expressionistisch und/oder mit Farbe arbeiten, lebt nur Chuck Arnoldi in Südkalifornien.

Obwohl diese Ausstellung die bekanntesten Bildhauer der Westküste hervorhebt, *begannen* drei von denen, die dem gebärdenhaften/figurenhaften Bereich angehören, als Maler (Holland, Neri und Richardson), zwei andere *wurden* Maler (Hudson und Arnoldi), und der letzte Bildhauer (Arneson) ist seit einigen Jahren in der Herstellung von Drucken und als Zeichner tätig. Daraus läßt sich ersehen, daß diese Faktoren im wesentlichen für ihre hervorragende Kenntnis von Oberfläche und Farbe in bezug auf ihre gegenwärtigen Skulpturen maßgebend sind.[1]

Die Eigenschaften einer Aussage, die einmal in einem zweidimensionalen Medium und zum anderen in einem dreidimensionalen Medium zum Ausdruck gebracht worden sind, verhalten sich recht unterschiedlich; jedoch scheinen die in diesem Aufsatz behandelten Künstler jenen Sprung intuitiv gemacht zu haben. Theoretisch ist der Entwicklungsprozeß eines größeren Künstlers einzigartig. Damit soll gesagt werden, daß der Prozeß, durch den er oder sie zu der Aussage kommt, die in reifer Arbeit verdinglicht ist, ein weitschweifiger ist, auf den wahrscheinlich kein anderer stoßen würde oder den kein anderer nachvollziehen würde. Warum also findet man derartig frappierende Parallelen in dem reifen Werk einer Anzahl von Künstlern? Zum einen scheint es klar, daß wir in den 80er Jahren Zeuge eines Auseinanderfalls und einer Auflösung der (willkürlichen) Grenzen zwischen Malerei und Bildhauerei sind. Diese Auflösung macht das Konzept gradliniger bildhauerischer Entwicklung null und nichtig. Zum andern ist zunehmend eindeutig geworden, daß Malerei, wenn sie auch als eine zweidimensionale Tätigkeit ausgeübt wird, in ihrem Konzept dreidimensional ist. Der Maler der 80er Jahre beschäftigt sich oft mit einem angenommenen Raum, der völlig dreidimensional ist und/oder der die Illusion dreier Dimensionen im tatsächlichen Werk enthält. Erstens wurde Clement Greenbergs kritischen Richtlinien zur Flachheit der Oberfläche und äußerster Trennung der Richtungen (um so besser für die Selbstkritik als auch für die Aufrechterhaltung der Skulpturhaftigkeit der Bildhauerei und der Malerhaftigkeit der Malerei) niemals viel Glaubwürdigkeit an der Westküste zuerkannt. Es ist fast, als ob Greenberg spürte, daß ein Eindringen in die genetische Struktur irgendwie die Reinrassigkeit verletzen würde. Tatsächlich war das einst unerlaubte Verschmelzen von Malerei und Bildhauerei ein glücklicher Zufall, denn es schuf eine bemerkenswerte Kreuzung—ein Hybrid, das eher eindeutig Bildhauerei als Malerei ist, wie wir sie kannten. In ihrem Gebrauch von Materialien und Bildern vebindet die neue Kreuzung die bemerkenswertesten Aspekte von beiden. Dadurch hat sie kraftvolle innovative Eigenschaften zur Gattung Bildhauerei beigetragen, die ihrerseits das Kommunikationsver-

mögen sehr verstärkt haben.

Bildhauerei erreichte erst spät die volle Reife und Neuerung, wie Barbara Haskell im folgenden bemerkt: «The creative atmosphere and international recognition achieved by Abstract Expressionist painting was not shared by American sculpture until the sixties. . . . By the early sixties American sculpture became as prominent and as vital as painting.»[2] (Die schöpferische Atmosphäre und internationale Anerkennung, die die Abstrakte Expressionistische Malerei erreichte, wurde bis zu den sechziger Jahren nicht von der amerikanischen Bildhauerei geteilt. . . . Um die frühen sechziger Jahre wurde amerikanische Bildhauerei ebenso bekannt und ebenso lebendig wie Malerei.[2])

Wenn es auch Vitalität Anfang der 60er Jahre in der Bildhauerei gab, war es doch erst Ende jener Jahre und Anfang der 70er, als eine wahre Neuorientierung aufkam—eine Neuorientierung, die die Bildhauerei jenseits der Grenzen der implizierten Bildhauerhaftigkeit trug und die verlangte, daß sie in einem neuen Kontext untersucht wurde. 1967 bemerkte Lucy Lippard: «Perhaps the most important aspect of sculpture today is its apparent potential as a vehicle of advance—both formal and evocative, or sensuous. This comprises its most crucial relationship to painting for it is only with the avant-garde's decreasing interest in painting that sculpture has come to the fore. This is a very literal period. *Sculpture, existing in real space and physically autonomous is realer than painting.*»[3] (Vielleicht der wichtigste Aspekt heutiger Bildhauerei ist ihre anscheinende Kapazität als Träger des Fortschritts—formal und evokativ oder sinnlich. Dieses umfaßt ihr entscheidendstes Verhältnis zur Malerei, denn nur durch das sich verringernde Interesse der Avantgardisten an Malerei trat die Bildhauerei in den Vordergrund. Dies ist eine sehr nüchterne Epoche. *Bildhauerei, die in realem Raum und physikalisch gesehen autonom existiert, ist wirklichkeitsnaher als Malerei.*[3])

Bilderhauerei *ist* «wirklichkeitsnaher» als Bildhauerei. Ende der 60er Anfang der 70er Jahre haben Künstler wie Smithson, Heizer und Christo unsere Vorstellungen von Maßstab und Größe grundlegend geändert, indem sie ortsspezifische «earth works» (Erdschöpfungen) machten, die in Konzept und Aussagegehalt so grandios waren, daß sie unser Vorstellungsvermögen provozierten. Zur gleichen Zeit schufen Robert Irwin, Maria Nordman, Doug Wheeler, Michael Ascher, Eric Orr und andere Stücke für den Innenraum in einer «Licht-und-Raum»-Naturhaftigkeit, die eine Neuuntersuchung unserer Wahrnehmungsprozesse aus phänomenologischer und empirischer Sicht zur Folge hatte. Größere Beiträge wurden auch in einer Kategorie, die wir «farbige Bildhauerei» nennen, geleistet (welche für unsere Zwecke als unterschiedlich von der «gemalten Bildhauerei» angesehen werden soll, wobei letztere die Farbe fast als einen geistigen Nachtrag gebraucht, und die erstere sie als einen Bestandteil des Aussagegehalts und der Oberfläche einschließt). Schon früh schloß diese Kategorie unterschiedliche Künstler wie John Chamberlain, Dan Flavin, Claes Oldenburg und George Segal an der Ostküste und Kenneth Price, William Geis, Robert Hudson und Robert Arneson im Westenein.

Lucy Lippard diskutiert in ihrem Essay in dem *American Sculpture of the Sixties* katalog die formale Rolle der Farbe in der Bildhauerei: «It [color] is used illusionistically to disperse and minimize volume, to separate shapes and space, making heavy forms seem weightless, light ones heavy, near forms farther away and far ones closer. And it is used to unify, to make a form more ‹real›, isolating it from the environment and asserting the piece as a self-contained whole.»[4] (Sie [die Farbe] wird illusionistisch verwandt, um Volumen aufzulösen und zu verringern, Formen im Raum voneinander zu trennen, schwere Formen schwerelos, leichte schwer, nahe Formen weiter weg und entfernte näher erscheinen zu lassen. Sie wird auch verwandt zu vereinheitlichen, eine Form «realer» zu machen, indem man es von der Umgebung isoliert und das Stück als eigenständiges Ganzes behauptet.[4] Ein Konflikt existierte jedoch zwischen diesem formalen Schritt zur Farbe und dem verhältnismäßigen Erfolg ihres tatsächlichen Verwendens oder ihrer Funktion. Trotz des Zusatzes von Farbe konzentrierte sich Bildhauerei (welche seit jeher im Grunde Nicht-Farbe gewesen ist—die «Nicht-Farbe» ihres Materials, sei es Marmor, Holz, Bronze etc.) weiterhin noch auf *Material* und *Struktur*. Lippard zitiert Clement Greenberg zu Anthony Caro in einer Geschichte, die diesen Zustand veranschaulicht: «Clement Greenberg's complaint about Anthony Caro's color could be applied to any number of other sculptors: ‹I know of no piece of his, not even an unsuccessful one, that does not *transcend* its color, or whose specific color or combination of colors does not detract from the quality of the whole (especially when there is more than one color). In every case I have the impression that the color is aesthetically (as well as literally) provisional— that it can be changed at will without affecting quality.› »[5] (Clement Greenbergs Beschwerde über Anthony Caros Farbe ließe sich auf eine jegliche Anzahl von anderen Bildhauern anwenden: ‹Ich kenne keine seiner Werke, auch kein nicht erfolgreiches, das nicht seine Farbe übersteigt oder dessen spezifische Farbe oder Farbkombinationen nicht von der Qualität des Ganzen ablenkt (besonders, wenn es mehr als eine Farbe gibt). In jedem Falle gewinne ich den Eindruck, daß die Farbe ästhetisch (wie auch buchstäblich) vorläufig ist—daß sie nach Belieben geändert werden kann, ohne dabei die Qualität zu beeinflussen.› »[5])

Die Eigenschaften der Dreidimensionalität und von Gewicht, Masse und Schwerkraft, die im klassischen Sinne als die Wesensmerkmale einer Skulptur betrachtet werden, wurden niemals mit Farbe in Verbindung gebracht. Tatsächlich war die Farbe in der Tradition westlicher Bildhauerei von zweitrangiger Erwägung, wenn nicht ein nachträglicher Gedanke. Sogar die polychromatische griechische Skulptur war lediglich ein Versuch, das Werk lebensnah erscheinen zu lassen, ohne einen wesentlichen Teil der Aussage aufs Spiel zu setzen. Sie hatte eher dekorative als strukturelle Funktion. In gleicher Weise war der primäre Zweck der vergoldeten Oberflächen vieler religiöser Kunstwerke des 14., 15. und 16. Jahrhunderts, den Religionsbezug und die Geistigkeit zu vermitteln und nicht der Absicht einer Formgebung oder einer Definition zu dienen. Erst in den späten 50er und frühen 60er Jahren fand die Farbe in der Bildhauerei ihre Eigenständigkeit. An der Ostküste (wie wir schon bemerkt haben) verblieb es den Bildhauern wie John Chamberlain, Dan Flavin, Claes Oldenburg und George Segal die Farbe zu einem hervorstechenden Merkmal zu machen, indem sie sie unlösbar mit der Form verbanden. Für Flavin bedeutete es, mit ihr zu «malen»—mit strahlend farbigem Licht, das sich über Wände und Decken ergoß. Für Oldenburg war es zuerst eine Frage des *Auftragens* der Farbe (wie er es früher mit Mörtel tat) und dann diese einerseits Stück für Stück in die Oberfläche des Werkes einzuarbeiten, andererseits sie auch als einen Bestandteil seiner ironischen Pop-Aussage zu benutzen.

Für die folgende Diskussion ist es vielleicht wesentlich zu bemerken, daß Oldenburg, der farbige Skulpturen schuf, zu dieser Feinfühligkeit über das *Zeichnen* kam, eine Voraussetzung, die er mit den Künstlern an der Westküste auf dieser Ausstellung gemeinsam hat. Tatsächlich waren seine frühen wunderschön gezeichneten «Monumente» niemals zur Ausführung gedacht—sie waren ganz einfach Spielereien des Auges und der Hand des Künstlers.

John Chamberlain, der in einer völlig anderen Art und Weise arbeitete, schuf Skulpturen aus intensiv bemalten Autoteilen und ermöglicht damit ein außerordentliches Beispiel des Einfließens von Farbe in die bildhauerische Struktur.

In George Segals späteren Arbeiten wurde die Farbe zum Mark vieler seiner Figuren.

Die größte Anzahl der Künstler der Westküste, die in der Arena farbiger Skulpturen arbeiten, kamen aus der Bay-Gegend. (Eine andere Gruppe, die sich aus Künstlern wie DeWain Valentine, Peter Alexander und Larry Bell, alle aus Los Angeles, zusammensetzte, gehört einer anderen Kategorie an. Obwohl deren Arbeiten ohne weiteres als in die Begriffsbestimmung von farbige Sculpturen passend, wie wir sie hier definiert haben, angesehen werden könnten, arbeiten diese Künstler in Wirklichkeit jedoch mit Glas und Plastik am Rande von Los Angeles' «Light and Space Movement» (Licht und Raumbewegung), und ihr Interesse galt mehr der Transparenz, der Reflektion, dem Licht und dem Raum als der Farbe an sich.) Nur Kenneth Price in Los Angeles benutzte Farbe strukturhaft, als wäre sie ein festes Ganzes.

Warum arbeiten viele der Künstler auf dieser Ausstellung malend? Die gute Hälfte der Künstler auf dieser Ausstellung verwendet Farbe als Bestandteil ihrer Aussage. Die verbleibenden Künstler sind mehr bildhauerhaft und/oder konstruktivistisch (wie Wortz' Essay besagt). Wie kommt es, daß zusätzlich zur gewöhnlichen Involviertheit mit linearen bildhauerischen Anliegen die Arbeit dieser Künstler in die Arena der Malerei überging? Ein Teil der Antworten wird durch den örtlichen Zusammenhang bestimmt. Schon immer war San Francisco eine «Stadt des Malers». Schon früh kann man das auf die Gegenwart solch wichtiger «Malers Maler» wie Clyfford Still, Mark Rothko und Ad Reinhardt zurückführen, die am San Francisco Art Institute in seiner «goldenen Ära» von 1945–1950 unterrichteten, und auf den späteren Zufluß zu der Schule von größeren Künstlern als Lehrer und Schüler—Maler wie Elmer Bischoff, Hassel Smith, Richard Diebenkorn, Joan Brown, Manuel Neri und viele andere.

In den früheren 50er Jahren gab es ein weiteres wichtiges Zentrum am California College of Arts and Crafts, als die Maler Richard Diebenkorn und Nathan Oliveira dort lehrten (später wählte Oliveira Stanford als seinen dauerhaften Sitz, und Diebenkorn begann an der UCLA zu lehren, wo er eine tiefe Wirkung auf die malende Gemeinde in Südkalifornien hatte.) Seit dem Beginn der 60er Jahre gibt es noch eine weitere Brutstätte von Malerei und Bildhauerei, eine mit ekzentrischen erzählenden Qualitäten zuzüglich zu ihrer Neigung zu intensiver Farbe, an der University of California, Davis. Die U.C. Davis wurde tief von der Gegenwart solch wichtiger Figuren wie Roy De Forest, Wayne Thiebaud und Robert Arneson beeinflußt und hat eine große Anzahl von bedeutenden malerhaften Künstlern hervorgebracht, die mit Keramik arbeiten.

Da die Bay-Gegend die Stadt der Maler ist, ist es schwierig, wenn nicht gar unmöglich, eine ausführliche Liste reiner «Bildhauer» anzufertigen, die in der Schule arbeiten, die Richard Shaw als die «YO HO BILL HELP ME TOTE THIS BIG HEAVY BEAM OVER HERE» (Hallo Bill hilf mir diesen großen schweren Balken nach hier zu schleppen) Schule bezeichnete (die wesentlichen Ausnahmen sind Brian Wall, Peter Voulkos und die jüngeren Bildhauer David Anderson und David Bottini). Zum größten Teil wurden alle diese Bay-Gegend-Künstler, die irgendeine dieser Schulen besucht haben, um Bildhauer zu werden, Maler, weil dort soviel Malerei in der Luft lag. Niemand erzwang es; die Künstler gaben einfach dieser Richtung nach. Ihre Werke waren ekzentrisch, funky, bunt bemalt und unberechenbar. Sie übermalten in einer Weise, wie es nie zuvor getan wurde. Sie arbeiteten auch mit schäbigem Material wie Mörtel—teils, weil es so erschwinglich war, aber auch, und das war der Hauptgrund, weil man damit wie mit Farbe arbeiten konnte. Wenn man schon Bildhauer sein mußte, so war man es so malerhaft wie möglich. Es scheint klar, daß seit Mitte der 40er Jahre die Maler und Bildhauer in Nordkalifornien sich mit sehr ähnlichen Problemen zu beschäftigen pflegten—Probleme, die direkt mit der Ausdruckskraft des Bildes zu tun hatten und nicht mit den technischen Eigenschaften eines bestimmten Materials.

Ob Manuel Neris Mörtel- oder marmorpolychromatisierte Figuren aus den bilderreichen Gemälden der Joan Brown Bay-Gegend hervortraten, oder ob Joan Brown Neris Figuren oft in ihre Gemälde miteinbezog, macht keinen Unterschied, den entscheidenden Punkt stellt ihre Symbiose dar. In ähnlicher Weise sind Nathan Oliveiras Gemälde mit ihren verwünschten, geisterhaften Figuren poetische Vorfahren von beiden. Mit jenen Künstlern hat Neri mehr gemeinsam, als mit anderen Bildhauern, da seine Beschäftigung mit der Figur deren parallel steht. Genauso haben die bunt bemalten humorvollen/ ironischen Keramikarbeiten von Robert Arneson viel gemeinsam mit den Arbeiten seiner Berufsfreunde Roy De Forest und Wayne Thiebaud. Sie teilen ein Interesse an einer bunt bemalten erzählerischen Darstellung, die teils oder ganz auf Laune beruht. Tom Holland und Robert Hudson unterrichten seit langem an dem San Francisco Art Institute, wo es ein großartiges historisches Erbe des abstrakten Expressionismus gibt. Beide schaffen sie hervorragende bildhauerische Arbeiten: Holland in erregender, gebährdenhafter, nachkubistischer Weise und Hudson in einer nach-Kandinskyscher Kind-des-Dada Weise. Beide sind tätig (und begabt) sowohl als Maler als auch als Bildhauer. Dies trifft auch auf William Wiley zu. Auf Wiley wird in diesen Ausführungen nicht näher eingegangen, aus dem einfachen Grunde, weil er keine großmaßstäbigen Kunstwerke schafft, die man unter freiem Himmel ausstellen kann (ein Gesichtspunkt, der als Voraussetzung dieser Ausstellung galt. Dennoch würde er sich qualifizieren. Richard Shaw ist ein weiterer ausdrucksstärftiger Bildhauer, der vorwiegend in kleineren Ausmaßen arbeitet, mit Keramik als seinem Werkstoff, und der die optische Täuschungsmalerei in seine Werke einbaut, ähnlich wie es Robert Hudson mit seinen Skulpturen tut.

Unter all den Künstlern, die wir behandeln, ist Sam Richardson der am zurückhaltendste und feinfühligste mit Farbe (wenn auch nicht mit Bildhaftigkeit). Er ist einer der wenigen Künstler der Bay-Gegend, der nicht vom abstrakten Expressionismus beeinflußt zu sein scheint. Er ist jedoch mit malerischen Anliegen beschäftigt. Seine feinen Miniatur-Landschaften und übergroßen Umwelt-Stücke kommen aus der Malerei, allein von Richardsons eigener Malerei und nicht aus irgendeiner anderen Quelle. Als Künstler stellt er im Prinzip einen Einzelgänger dar, wenn auch die komplexen, großangelegten Raum-Stücke, die während des letzten Jahrzehnts geschaffen wurden, immer mit Hilfe einer Arbeitsgruppe fertiggestellt worden sind.

Chuck Arnoldis unwahrscheinlich realistische «Dickichte», die nur in Bronze gegossen sind, finden ihren Ursprung in den buntfarbigen «Zweig-» Arbeiten, die er mehr als ein Jahrzehnt lang geschaffen hat. Als Student am Chouinard Art Institute in Los Angeles in den späten 60er Jahren wurde Arnoldi zu einem eigenständigen Künstler, zu einer Zeit, als das Gefühl für «Vorgang und Materialien» in vollem Schwung war. Während dieser Zeit war die Malerei in Los Angeles «tot», und der einzig einzuschlagende Weg schien in der Bildhauerei zu liegen. Es war erst in den letzten paar Jahren, nachdem er sich einen nationalen Ruf als Bildhauer machte, daß sich Arnoldi der Malerei zuwandte und gigantische bildhauerische

Gemälde aus Holz mit Hilfe einer Kettensäge schuf. Seine Werke sind daher gleichviel eine Funktion seiner Örtlichkeit wie jene der Bay-Geglend-Künstler, und doch gelangte er völlig unterschiedlich, wie wir gesehen haben, zu ihnen. Alle der ge-

Alle der genannten Künstler haben ihre Grenzen erweitert und haben unser *Gefühl* für das bildhauerische Objekt, seinen Zweck und seine Bedeutung, verstärkt. Die «farbige Skulptur», die in dieser Ausstellung mit eingeschlossen ist, gilt nicht nur als äußerst repräsentativ für die Art des Schaffens, wie sie zur Zeit an der Westküste getan wird, sondern sie schlägt auch einen ganz eindeutigen Weg zur sich immer erweiternden Rolle der Figuration, der Erzählung und des Humors innerhalb der bildhauerischen Tradition des 20. Jahrhunderts ein.

Jan Butterfield
Dezember 1983

Sensuous Constructivism in California Sculpture

Although the sculptors represented in this exhibition live in California, their work transcends regionalism. In the 1960s, when California began to be recognized as a "second" art center in America (second, of course, to New York), it was customary for critics such as John Coplans and Phil Leider to characterize Southern California art in particular according to its uniqueness vis-à-vis that of New York—its openness to untraditional technological materials and processes such as the use of resin, glass, plexiglas, vacuum forming, and di-electri-coating; its interest in breaking the traditional distinctions between painting and sculpture; its commitment to finely crafted execution; and its fascination with the subtle mysteries of projected and reflected light.

In the current work of Bruce Beasley, Fletcher Benton, Guy Dill, Jud Fine, Michael Todd, and DeWain Valentine, the commitment to fine craftsmanship remains. But several other premises of their work can be seen in the larger context of twentieth century art history, particularly the constructivist movement begat in Russia and its charge to incorporate techniques and materials of twentieth-century life into the rarified realm of art. Each of these artists works additively, constructing works from many parts and processes, rather than the more traditional monolithic or megalithic casting or carving from a single mass.

Bruce Beasley produced metal sculpture exclusively until 1966, achieving a high degree of visibility in this medium. As early as 1961, when he was still a student, his piece, *Lemures*, was purchased by The Museum of Modern Art, and in 1963 renowned French Minister of Culture André Malraux cited Beasley's *Icarus* with an award. In 1966, however, Beasley wanted to create "sculpture in which one could see forms through other forms." This was an interest shared by several other sculptors during this period, many of them—such as Peter Alexander, Larry Bell, and DeWain Valentine—also living in California. And like them, Beasley found that he had to develop his own transparent medium as none of the commercial products available would serve his purposes. Glass, for example, was not adaptable enough.

With his award prize, Beasley purchased an "autoclave," an eccentric-looking machine that he painted with Northwest Coast Indian designs, transforming the tools of his trade into artworks in their own rights. Proceeding by trial and error, he subjected liquid plastics (acrylic and lucite) to pressure and heat in the autoclave, a process resulting in polymerization, which fused the liquids into a hard, transparent, solid material. Eventually Beasley developed enough control of the heat and pressure to prevent clouding in the final product, even though DuPont advisors told him the kind of clarity he wanted would be impossible to achieve. His process remains a secret.

Beasley's forms are derived from mineral crystals. Metals, minerals, and alloys are defined as crystalline because their molecular structure is composed in regular, repeating patterns, as opposed to other types of solid matter whose molecular structure is amorphous. It is only in the crystalline state that matter exhibits some geometric structure. Such is not the case in liquid or gaseous states. Beasley uses the crystalline state's unique blend of organic and geometric forms as a source for the modular, repeated units of his acrylic sculpture and, more recently, monumental metal pieces as well. Whether executed in acrylic or stainless steel, the faceted modular units of these sculptures refract and reflect light in continuously shifting patterns according to weather and time of day. Beasley's largest acrylic work, *Apolymer* (1967–70), is permanently installed in Sacramento, California. The six and one-half tons of cast acrylic captures the natural light in such a way as to inspire critic Ed Hotaling to describe the work's effect as "the ocean brought to Sacramento." Beasley's largest metal sculpture to date is included in this exhibition.

Beasley's interest in creating crystalline sculptures in metal as well as transparent lucite developed naturally when he built molds for casting the lucite modules. In this case the modules are hexagonal and create negative spaces according to how they are fitted together, resulting in a shifting pattern of spaces through which the sky or surrounding landscape can be glimpsed. As with lucite, the surface of the stainless steel is highly reflective, making interaction with the light and motion of the environment an important facet of the work (a facet also demonstrated by Dill's and Valentine's pieces in this exhibition). The surface of Beasley's sculpture assumes coloration present in the landscape.

Fletcher Benton's first flush of national recognition in the middle 1960s was in response to his kinetic sculptures—moving planes of color centered in finely finished stainless steel frameworks—but he actually began his career as a painter. While still a teenager, he and a childhood friend set up a sign painting business in Ohio because the town's only two sign painters had left to serve in World War II. The occupational demand for well-defined forms and legible lettering reverberated two decades later in his precisely machined metal sculptures of recent years, with a vocabulary derived from geometry and often enlivened by three-dimensional letters of the alphabet. In other words, Benton's clearly constructed metal sculptures, many of them monumental in scale, incorporate primary structures not only in the Bauhaus sense of the three perfect forms—the cube or square, sphere or circle, cone or triangle (and their various manifestations)—but also in the basic building blocks that comprise the conceptual system of language.

As a mature artist Benton painted for many years before turning to sculpture in the 1960s. Likewise, many other constructivists produced paintings as well as sculpture. But Benton's involvement with painting, in which he achieved the most success with a series of gestural portraits of friends, was sensual and visual rather than theoretical. Thus, in his kinetic sculptures of the 1960s we see that his sophisticated engineering of color, shifting in layers to create a moving variety of tonalities and shapes, is about hedonistic lyricism more than about technological bravura.

By the 1970s Benton abandoned movement in his sculpture and, for a time, color as well, concentrating on a full expression of inherent characteristics of the materials—mostly steel and bronze. In recent years Benton has also experimented with articulations of scale, executing both monumental and intimate works. What are playful balancing acts in small scale become virtuoso performances in monumental size, such as *Balanced/Unbalanced Wheels* (1982) in this exhibition, which measures 28 feet high by 30 feet long by 7 feet wide. Originally worked out in a small "wooden sketch" or maquette whose largest dimension is 12 inches, the sculpture jumped immediately to the 28-foot scale. After the fact, it is now being reworked to a 7-foot scale. The piece juxtaposes two tower-like structures—one a giant "T" leaning at an angle, the other a vertical stack of cylinders and boxes—with a horizontal grouping of two steel, tube-like wheels, each 5 feet by 5 feet by 18 inches, and a long horizontal bar. In *Balanced/Unbalanced Wheels* Benton has returned to an earlier interest in movement, but with an ironic twist. Whereas the kinetic work incorporated literal movement activated by a hidden mechanism, the new piece looks like a crazy cart about to roll, tumble, or topple, but it is actually anchored securely.

This construction is one of Benton's most playful and complex. Even though its various components—triangles, circles, cylinders, boxes, et cetera—appear to be randomly assembled, their geometry and placement lend a kind of logic to the sculpture. The variety of colors—gray, white, red, and blue—are accented on a predominantly black work, contributing to the sense of play, as does the irrational use of form as "immovable movement." Benton's audience's inclination to climb into and through an object of this scale is anticipated; he deliberately designs circles to be jumped into and sat upon.

Guy Dill's piece in this exhibition is part of his *Egalmeh* or *Great Palace* series. The series format incorporates geometric elements lifted to lintels supported by wedge-shaped columns. In fact the artist's interest in this ancient post and lintel structure configuration stems from his desire to incorporate multi-dimensional time references in the series. While Dill refers to it in its entirety as the *Great Palace*, its individual manifestations are titled after Sumerian texts, which themselves incorporate a distant time reference. The work for this exhibition is entitled *Siduri* (1983), or "she who is the divine wine maker and brewer, dwells on the shore of the sea in the garden of the sun, and may be a form of Ishtar"—a reference to highly elevated romantic hedonism.

The lower section of this piece—two wedge-shaped columns supporting a lintel—evokes not only ancient monuments such as Stonehenge, but also the ritual uses (in terms of astronomical trackings) to which we impute them. In a more contemporary vein, the Post-Modern movement in architecture is also addicted to the quotation of historical architectural devices. Dill's avowed interest in making his sculpture more architectural in both form and content finds analogues in the sculptural approach to architecture that can be seen in the work of the most innovative contemporary architects, such as Luis Barragán, with whom Dill has sensed a kindred spirit for many years.

Both the large scale and the lush but subtle coloration of Dill's new work are the result of an extended period of experimentation with the technology of cast concrete. Since 1974 when he exhibited his first concrete sculpture at Pace Gallery in New York, Dill's use of the material has become increasingly scientific and controlled. The concrete amalgam is comprised of lava rock and custom-ground cement, which is fast-setting and strong but which has a soft surface. Dill's unique coloration of *Siduri's* components comes from the technique of mixing pure liquid pigment into the cement, whose alkalai sets and dries it. This process, says Dill, is opposite to the traditional manner of coloring sculpture by applying pigment onto a surface. In *Siduri* the color is inseparable from the structure—it emerges from within instead of merely coating.

Dill does not work from preparatory drawings in formulating these architectonic constructions. Over the years he has developed a tight vocabulary of form, not unlike Benton's, which includes the wedges/columns, lintels, and various permutations of triangles, bars, rectangles, and planks. This reductive modernist vocabulary becomes lyrical in spite of its size by means of its lovely coloration—varying and subtle tonalities of black and gray, barely discernable blushes of pink, strong blues, seductive lavenders, dusty greens, earthy reds. The strong linear shadows cast by the clean geometric forms modulate the surface color to additional nuances, which appear to be painted. When this work is seen indoors, the shadows cast on walls and floors create ethereal ghost images of their source, and Dill sometimes makes large-scale drawings of the piece after the fact by transferring the images to photographic paper. In outdoor settings the soft concrete is sensitive not only to the flickering light of the environment, but also to the amount of moisture in the air, so that the sculptural surface is continuously changing. It is as if *Siduri* is engaged in a courtship with her environs.

The structure of this work cannot be perceived all at once, nor can it be precisely remembered. And the implied processional, marker-like character of the post and lintel supports alludes to a faintly remembered ritual of ancient origin, a spiritual longing to establish a bond with the universe by the structure and placement of matter.

Jud Fine was enrolled in a doctoral program in American intellectual history at the University of California, Santa Barbara, when he switched his major to art. The change was precipitated by frustration with the research of minutia in order to prove a hypothesis that could be refuted by the same process. He sought a field in which he could "hypothesize a premise and prove it by force of conviction," an endeavor he decided could only be feasible in philosophy, literature, or art. He chose Cornell's graduate program (partly because it did not require a Bachelor's degree in studio art) and at first was intimidated by his lack of skills. Especially when compared to the rigorous demands of a doctoral pursuit, he was confused by the absence of definition in the practice of art. Rationalizing his change of course, he sought a way to "give art value and elevate the discipline." Beginning with a philosophical investigation of the decision-making process, he added the study of phenomenology and minimalism; his aesthetic attitude was predicated by both the conceptual and sensory aspects of information processing.

Returning to California in the early 1970s, Fine did not have the access to materials and tools that he had enjoyed at Cornell. Financial constraints dictated that he seek inexpensive and easily available materials. His earliest works were constructed of rocks, sand, and bamboo in both natural settings and in the studio—the kind of site/nonsite contextual contrasts that Robert Smithson also had found fascinating. At this time Fine was consciously trying to develop his physical (as opposed to cultural) sensibilities. During this experimental period he simply did as much work as possible without making value judgments about its quality. In conjunction with the process of making art, Fine has undertaken extensive research of ancient cultures. He found that "shime," or occupation marks, the earliest architectural forms in Eastern cultures, were constructed of "bunches of grasses wrapped with string," impermanently, with the apparent intent of allowing each generation to ritually construct its own shelter.

In considering the relatively high value placed on social interaction and lack of emphasis on creativity in Eastern cultures and, conversely, the relative lack of social structure and importance placed on individual creativity in the West, Fine sought a means of synthesizing the two in a tertiary conceptual mode. His solution, or transcendence of dualistic thinking in a new synthetic form, is exemplified by the long horizontal column, the newest version of which is presented in this exhibition.

Fine's 80-foot-long horizontal line looks Eastern in its minimalist, unobtrusive qualities, but is constructed with a steel core of Western technology. The vertical supports for the five sections are the link with gravity, the connection to the ground. As Fine says, "you can only project so far (both literally and metaphorically) without returning to the ground. You must have the vertical from which to extend the horizontal."

Although the column, with its sections of different surfaces—copper tubing, rubber innertubes, wrapped apple tree trimmings—remains strictly horizontal, it appears to be taller and shorter in reference to the alterations of ground level. In other words, it challenges our perceptions of our relationship to the earth we inhabit, sharpening our awareness of our environment as, we suspect, ancient artifacts were intended to do.

Michael Todd began his study of art as a printmaker, a student of John Paul Jones', and laughingly recalls the etching plate as his first contact with metal. He has also made paintings, along with sculpture, throughout his career. Living in New York in the mid 1960s, he was confronted with the minimalist challenge to create reductive forms in order to focus perception more acutely on previously unnoticed subtleties. His work of this period was included in the Jewish Museum's "Primary Structures" exhibition in the late 1960s. By then, however, he had tired of the reductive format. "My temperament is really more sensuous," he explains. Exposure to the sculpture of David Smith, while teaching at Bennington College in Vermont, encouraged his new preference to express more complexity in his own work.

Two events had such strong aesthetic impact on Todd that they precipitated the major stylistic change evident in his work of the last decade—open, welded, abstract steel sculpture. The first jolt came at an exhibition of Chinese calligraphy at The Metropolitan Museum of Art in New York, calligraphy that so haunted him that he longed to replicate its sense of gesture and randomness in a three-dimensional format. Subsequently, while visiting a temple in Japan, he was confronted and astounded by a very large steel vase, which held flowers also made of steel.

A teaching position at the University of California, San Diego, in the early 1970s fortuitously placed Todd in close proximity to a steel yard and offered access to the university's sculpture tools, student help, and yearly grants for materials. From this rich soil a ripe harvest of additive metal constructions ensued. In the course of a decade Todd has produced sculptures in three formats. The one he calls "screens" incorporates open metal grids as a primary compositional device. The "tables" hover playfully between function and decoration. The "circles" are based upon the motif of a relatively closed curve. The 18-foot-tall *Nataraja* (1982) included in this exhibition is an example of the third group.

The basically circular format of *Nataraja*, made from a hollow tube, is interrupted variously by bent rods, cut slabs, and the like. Similarly, the circle is punctuated both in and outside its contour by a long, calligraphically curving rod running diagonally from top to bottom (or vice versa), a grid, an X, a circle, and other bits of metal, which act as ornamentation. The slab-like form with a torn edge functions for Todd like a broad brush stroke, contrasting with the more delicate calligraphic sweep of the thinner rods and tubes. Todd thinks of his sculptural process as analogous to painting or drawing. in spite of—or even in contradiction to—its weight and scale. As is true of the work of other sculptors in the exhibition, Todd's *Nataraja* offers multiple references beyond its considerable formal strength—to Eastern restraint and assymetrical composition in conjunction with Western technology.

DeWain Valentine's work in the 1960s, like Todd's, consisted of large, simple forms, however cast in polyester resin from a patented formula of his own invention. He chose this demanding and treacherous medium because it afforded a means for achieving illusions of colored light suspended in space, to replicate indoors such natural phenomena as sunsets and rainbows.

For many years Valentine had wanted to work with glass but was discouraged by prohibitive fabrication costs. By the middle 1970s he had developed a technique for laminating glass, cut into thin modular strips, with silicon glue. The modular units facilitated the building of architectural forms—posts and lintels, arches, pyramids, windows—in potentially infinite variations. This process has facilitated not only the use of architectural references, but the scale of architecture as well.

In the last two years Valentine has been working with a number of materials new to him, whose properties do not include transparency: traditional materials such as bronze, granite, and marble. His latest projects combine these dense, opaque materials with colored glass in configurations that, as Dill's, allude to history and ritual. Valentine's sculpture in this exhibition consists of three components, which are combined in a basic post and lintel structure. The two 8-foot bronze columns are triangular, with 24-inch-long sides. Ten sheets of 3/4-inch blue-green glass, 36 inches high and 96 inches long, are laminated to form the lintel. Together they form an 8-inch-thick mass, which slips into slots in the bronze columns. The richness of the materials and their coloristic contrast—the blue-green glass sparkling against the warmer but duller patina of the bronze columns—invite associations of ritual and fantasy, such as the entrance to the Emerald City of Oz.

The toughness and durability of Valentine's new materials mean the work can be installed permanently out of doors, in contrast to the instability of resin when exposed to direct sunlight for extended periods of time. Thus, instead of a gallery's immaculate white walls, the new work is able to interact with the outdoor environment, whose marvels continue to influence the artist.

Melinda Wortz
December 1983

Constructivismo sensual en la escultura de California

Aunque los escultores representados en esta exposición residen en California, su labor transciende cualquier regionalismo. En los años 60, cuando California comenzó a ser reconocida como «segundo» centro artístico de América (segundo, por supuesto, después de Nueva York), ciertos críticos como John Coplans y Phil Leider solían caracterizar el arte de California del Sur en particular por su singuliaridad vis-à-vis con el de Nueva York—su receptividad hacia los materiales y procedimientos tecnológicos no tradicionales tales como el uso de resina, vidrio, plexiglas, moldeos al vacío, y laminados di-eléctricos; su interés en romper con las distinciones tradicionales entre pintura y escultura; su compromiso a la exquisita ejecución artesanal; y su fascinación por los sutiles misterios de la proyección y reflejo de la luz.

En la reciente obra de Bruce Beasley, Fletcher Benton, Guy Dill, Jud Fine, Michael Todd, y DeWain Valentine, permanece el compromiso con la fina artesanía. Pero se pueden observar varias otras premisas de su trabajo en el contexto más amplio de la historia del arte del siglo veinte, particularmente el movimiento constructivista iniciado en Rusia y su doeoo de incorporar a la enrarecida atmósfera artística, técnicas y materiales de la vida del siglo veinte. Cada uno de estos artistas trabaja integradoramente, creando obras a partir de multitud de piezas y procesos, en oposición al tallado y moldeado monolítico o megalítico más tradicionales a partir de un solo material.

Bruce Beasley esculpió en metal exclusivamente hasta 1966, alcanzando un alto grado de reconocimiento en este medio. Ya en el año 1961, cuando todavía era estudiante, su pieza, *Lemures*, fue adquirida por el Museo de Arte Moderno, y en 1963 el renombrado ministro francés de Cultura André Malraux otorgó un premio al *Icarus* de Beasley. Sin embargo, en 1966, Beasley deseaba crear «una escultura en la que se vieran formas a través de otras formas.» Este interés fue compartido por varios otros escultores de este período, muchos de los cuales—como Peter Alexander, Larry Bell, y DeWain Valentine—también residen en California. Y como ellos, Beasley se dio cuenta de que tenía que desarrollar su propio medio transparente, puesto que ninguno de los productos comerciales disponibles servirían a sus fines. El vidrio, por ejemplo, no era suficientemente adaptable.

Con su premio honorífico, Beasley compró una «autoclave,» una máquina de apariencia extravagante que pintó con diseños indígenas de la costa Noroeste, transformando los instrumentos de su oficio en obras artísticas legítimas. Mediante el método de tanteos sometió a plásticos líquidos (acrílico y lucita) bajo presión y caldeo en la autoclave, un proceso resultante en la polimerización, que fundía los líquidos transformándolos en un material duro, transparente y sólido. Más tarde Beasley desarrolló un alto control del calor y la presión para evitar el empañamiento en el producto final, aunque como le previnieron consejeros de DuPont sería imposible alcanzar el grado de claridad que él deseaba. Su proceso sigue siendo un secreto.

Las formas de Beasley se derivan de cristal mineral. Se definen como cristalinos los metales, minerales, y aleaciones debido a que su estructura molecular está compuesta por patrones regulares y repetidos, en oposición a otros tipos de materia sólida cuya estructura molecular es amorfa. Unicamente en estado cristalino exhibe la materia algún tipo de estructura geométrica. Este no es el caso de los estados líquidos o gaseosos. Beasley usa una mezcla única de estado cristalino para formas orgánicas y geométricas como fuente de su escultura acrílica, modular, de unidades repetidas y, más recientemente, también de piezas metálicas monumentales. Ya sean ejecutadas en acrílico o en acero inoxidable, las fa-

céticas unidades modulares de estas esculturas refractan y reflejan la luz en destellos que cambian continuamente según el tiempo atmosférico y la hora del día. La obra acrílica más voluminosa de Beasley, *Apolymer* (1967–70), está instalada permanentemente en Sacramento, California. Las seis toneladas y media de compuesto acrílico captan la luz natural de tal forma que inspiró al crítico Ed Hotaling a describir los efectos de la obra como «el océano traído a Sacramento.» La mayor escultura en metal de Beasley hasta la fecha también se presenta en esta exposición.

El interés de Beasley por crear esculturas cristalinas en metal así como en lucita transparente se desarrolló de forma natural cuando comenzó a construir moldes para la forja de módulos de lucita. En este caso los modulos son hexagonales y crean espacios negativos dependiendo de cómo son ensamblados, lo que resulta en patrones cambiantes de espacio a través de los cuales se vislumbra el cielo o el paisaje circundante. Como con la lucita, la superficie del acero inoxidable es altamente reflectante, interactuando con la luz y el movimiento del entorno como una importante faceta de la obra (una faceta también demostrada por las piezas de Dill y Valentine que se muestran en esta exposición). La superficie de la escultura de Beasley adquiere el color presente en el paisaje.

La primera señal de reconocimiento nacional hacia Fletcher Benton a mediados de los años 60 constituyó una respuesta a sus esculturas kinéticas—planos dinámicos de color centrados en marcos de acero inoxidable finamente acabados—pero en realidad su carrera comenzó en la pintura. Cuando aún era un adolescente él y sus amigos de la niñez iniciaron un negocio de pintura de letreros en Ohio debido a que los dos únicos pintores de letreros de la ciudad tuvieron que incorporarse a filas en la Segunda Guerra Mundial. La demanda laboral de formatos bien definidos y de letreros legibles tuvo su eco dos décadas más tarde precisamente en sus esculturas labradas en metal de años más recientes, con un vocabulario derivado de la geometría y a menudo realzado por letras del alfabeto tridimensionales. En otras palabras, las esculturas de Benton claramente construídas en metal, muchas de ellas de tamaño monumental, incorporan estructuras primarias no sólo en el sentido de las tres formas perfectas del Bauhaus—el cubo o el cuadrado, la esfera o el círculo, el cono o el triángulo (y sus varias manifestaciones)—sino también en las cuadras de edificios básicas que comprenden el sistema conceptual del lenguaje.

En su madurez artística Benton se dedicó a pintar durante muchos años antes de cambiar a la escultura en los años 60. De la misma forma, muchos otros constructivistas produjeron tanto pintura como escultura. Pero la dedicación de Benton a la pintura, en la cual alcanzó su mayor éxito con una serie de retratos gestuales de amigos, fue más sensual y visual que teórica. Por ello, sus esculturas kinéticas de los años 60 reflejan que su sofisticada composición de color, en capas cambiantes que crean una dinámica variedad de tonos y formas, está más relacionado con un lirismo hedonista que con una osadía tecnológica.

Hacia los años 70, Benton abandonó el movimiento en sus esculturas y, por algún tiempo, también el color, concentrándose en una plena expresión de las características inherentes de sus materiales—especialmente el acero y el bronce. En años recientes, Benton también ha experimentado con tamaños articulados, ejecutando obras tanto monumentales como intimistas. Lo que son actos de equilibrio caprichoso a pequeña escala se convierten en realizaciones virtuosas de tamaño monumental, como las *Balanced/Unbalanced Wheels* (1982) que se muestra en esta exposición, que mide 28 pies de altura por 30 pies de largo por 7 pies de ancho. Diseñada originalmente en un pequeño «esbozo de madera» o maqueta cuya dimensión mayor es de 12 pulgadas, la escultura saltó inmediatamente a la escala de 28 pies. Después de todo, en la actualidad está siendo convertida a una escala de 7 pies. La pieza yuxtapone dos estructuras en forma de torre—una de ellas es una «T» gigante apoyada angularmente, y la otra un conglomerado vertical de cilindros y cajas—con un agrupamiento horizontal de dos ruedas de acero en forma de tubo, cada una de ellas de 5 pies por 5 pies por 18 pulgadas, y una larga barra horizontal. En *Balanced/Unbalanced Wheels* Benton ha retornado a su anterior interés por el movimiento, pero con un efecto irónico. Mientras que su obra kinética incorporaba el movimiento preciso activado por un mecanismo oculto, la nueva pieza se asemeja a una carreta loca a punto de volcar, rodar o tambalearse, pero que en realidad está firmemente anclada.

Esta es una de las construcciones mas caprichosas y complejas de Benton. A pesar de que sus diversos componentes—triángulos, círculos, cilindros, cajas, etcétera—parecen estar ensamblados al azar, su geometría y colocación prestan a la escultura una cierta lógica. La variedad de colores—gris, blanco, rojo y azul—resultan en una obra predominantemente negra, lo que contribuye al sentido lúdico, como también lo hace el uso irracional de la forma como «movimiento estático.»

La pieza de Guy Dill que aparece en esta exposición es parte de su serie *Egalmeh* o el *Gran Palacio*. El formato de la serie incorpora elementos geométricos elevados a dinteles apoyados en columnas enforma de cuña. En efecto, el interés del artista en esta configuración estructural de pilar y dintel antiguos proviene de su deseo de incorporar a esta serie referencias temporales multidimensionales. Mientras que Dill se refiere a ello enteramente como el *Gran Palacio*, sus manifestaciones individuales se han titulado según textos sumerios, que a su vez pertenecen a lejanas referencias temporales. La obra que se muestra en esta exposición se titula *Siduri* (1983), o «ella que es la diosa del vino y de la cerveza, mora en las playas del mar del jardín solar, quizá una forma de Ishtar»— referencia ésta a un elevado hedonismo romántico.

La sección inferior de esta pieza—dos columnas cuneiformes apoyando un dintel—evoca no sólo antiguos monumentos como el de Stonehenge, sino también las costumbres rituales con ellos asociadas (de acuerdo con sus localizaciones astronómicas). En una vena más contemporánea, el movimiento post-modernista en arquitectura también se somete a referencias de recursos arquitectónicos históricos. El marcado interés de Dill por hacer su escultura más arquitectónica tanto en forma como en contenido es análogo a la aproximación escultural a la arquitectura que se refleja en los arquitectos contemporáneos más innovadores como Luis Barragán, con el que Dill ha compartido un sentido fraternal durante muchos años.

Tanto la gran escala como el exuberante pero sutil colorido de la nueva obra de Dill son el resultado de un extenso período de experimentación con la técnica de cemento forjado. Desde 1974 en el que expuso su primera escultura de cemento en la Galería Pace de Nueva York, Dill ha incrementado el uso de este material de una forma cada vez mas científica y controlada. La amalgama de cemento se compone de lava rocosa y de cemento prefabricado que cuaja rápidamente y de gran dureza pero cuyo superficie es suave. El singular colorido que Dill dota a los componentes de *Siduri* proviene de la técnica de mezclar pigmento líquido puro con el cemento cuyos álcalis lo hacen asentarse y secar. Este procedimiento, señala Dill, es el contrario de la forma tradicional de colorear esculturas aplicando el pigmento a la superficie. En *Siduri* el color es inseparable de la estructura—surge del interior en lugar de ser mero revestimiento.

Dill no parte de esbozos previos para formular estas construcciones arquitectónicas. En el transcurso de los años ha desarrollado un apretado vocabulario de formas, no muy diferente al de Benton, que incluye cunas/columnas, dinteles y diversas permutaciones de triángulos, barras, rectángulos y planchas. Este reducido vocabulario modernista deviene lírico a pesar de su tamaño por medio de su exquisito colorido— variadas y sutiles tonalidades de negro y gris, atisbos de rosa apenas discernibles, azules intensos, seductoras lavándulas, polvorientos verdes y terrosos rojos. Las fuertes sombras lineales proyectadas por las limpias formas geométricas modulan el color de la superficie hacia matices adicionales que parecen pintados. Cuando esta obra es contemplada en el interior, las sombras proyectadas en paredes y suelos crean imágenes etéreas y fantasmagóricas por sí mismas, y Dill, a veces, crea dibujos a gran escala de la pieza después de su realización, al transferir las imágenes a papel fotográfico. Al aire libre el blando cemento es sensible no sólo a la oscilante luz del ambiente sino también a la cantidad de humedad del aire, de tal forma que la superficie escultural está en constante mutación. Es como si *Siduri* hubiera entablado una relación amorosa con su entorno.

Jud Fine estuvo inscrito en un programa doctoral sobre la historia intelectual de América en la Universidad de California en Santa Bárbara, donde cambió su especialidad a arte. El cambio fue precipitado por su frustración con la investigación de minucias para demostrar una hipótesis que podía ser refutada por el mismo proceso. Buscaba un campo en el cual pudiera «hipotetizar una premisa y demostrarla por fuerza de convicción,» una tarea, se dio cuenta, solo podría ser posible en filosofía, literatura o arte. Escogió el programa graduado de la Universidad de Cornell—(en parte porque no exigía una licenciatura en arte de estudio) y al principio le intimidaba su falta de preparación. Especialmente en comparación con las rigurosas exigencias de una carrera doctoral, él estaba perplejo por la ausencia de una definición en la práctica del arte. Racionalizando su cambio de rumbo, buscó un camino para «dar valor al arte y elevar la disciplina.» Comenzando con una investigación filosófica sobre el proceso de toma de decisiones, le añadió el estudio de la fenomenología y el minimalismo; su actitud estética fue dictada por los aspectos tanto conceptuales como sensoriales de la informática.

A su vuelta a California a principios de los años 70, Fine no tuvo acceso a los materiales e instrumentos de los que disfrutaba en Cornell. La búsqueda de materiales económicos y fácilmente disponibles estaba mediatizada por sus limitaciones financieras. Sus obras primerizas fueron hechas de rocas, arena y bambú tanto en un marco natural como en el estudio—el tipo de contraste contextual de presencia/ausencia de emplazamiento que tanto había fascinado también a Robert Smithson. Por ese tiempo Fine estaba dedicado a un desarrollo consciente de sus sensibilidades físicas (en oposición a las culturales). Durante este período experimental sencillamente trabajó tanto como pudo sin realizar juicios de valor sobre su calidad. En conjunción con el proceso de ejecución artística, Fine ha llevado a cabo extensas investigaciones de culturas antiguas. Descubrió que el «shime» o señas ocupacionales, las formas arquitectónicas más antiguas de las culturales orientales, fueron construídas con «ramos de hierbas atadas con una cuerda,» transitoriamente y con la intención aparente de permitir que cada generación construyera ritualmente su propio cobijo.

Al considerar el alto valor relativo que poseía la interacción social y la falta de énfasis en la creatividad en las culturas orientales e, inversamente, la relativa falta de estructura social e importancia de la creatividad individual en el Oeste, Fine buscó el medio de sintetizar las dos de un modo conceptual terciario. Su solución, o transcendencia del pensamiento dualista en una nueva forma sintética, queda ejemplificada por la larga columna horizontal, la versión más reciente de la cual se presenta en esta exposición.

La línea horizontal de 80 pies de largo de Fine parece oriental en sus cualidades minimalistas y moderadas pero está construída con un interior de acero de tecnología occidental. Los soportes verticales para las cinco secciones constituyen el nexo con la gravedad, su conexión con el suelo. Como dice Fine, «sólo se puede proyectar hasta una cierta distancia (tanto literal como metafóricamente) sin que la proyección vuelva al suelo. Sólo a partir de la línea vertical puede extenderse la horizontal.»

Aunque la columna, con sus secciones de diferentes superficies—tuberías de cobre, tubos interiores de goma, adornos de manzano envueltos—permanece estrictamente horizontal, parece más alta o más baja en referencia a las alteraciones del nivel del suelo. En otras palabras, desafía las propias percepciones de nuestra relación a la tierra que habitamos, agudizando la conciencia de nuestro medio ambiente como, sospechamos, ocurría con los antiguos artefactos.

Michael Todd comenzó sus estudios de arte como impresor y discípulo de John Paul Jones, y riendo recuerda el grabado en lámina como su primer trabajo con el metal. También realizó pinturas, junto con esculturas, a lo largo de su carrera. Cuando vivía en Nueva York a mediados de los años 60, se enfrentó al reto minimalista de crear formas reductivas con el propósito de concentrar su percepción más agudamente en sutilezas previamente desapercibidas. Su trabajo de este período fue incluído en la exposición «Estructuras Primarias» del Museo Judío a finales de los años 60. Por esa época, sin embargo, se había cansado del formato reductivo. «Tengo un temperamento verdaderamente más sensual,» explica. La entrada en contacto con la escultura de David Smith mientras enseñaba en el Bennington College de Vermont le animó a expresar su nueva preferencia con mayor complejidad en su propio trabajo.

Lo que precipitó este total cambio estilístico evidente en su trabajo de la última década fueron dos acontecimientos que tuvieron un fuerte impacto estético en Todd—la escultura abierta, soldada y abstracta en acero. El primer impacto llegó en una exposición de caligrafía china en el Museo Metropolitano de Arte de Nueva York, caligrafía que le inquietó de tal forma que deseó reproducir el sentido de gesto y de azar en un formato tridimensional. Subsiguientemente, mientras visitaba un templo en Japón, se enfrentó con asombro a una enorme vasija de acero que contenía flores también de acero.

Fue un puesto docente en la Universidad de California en San Diego lo que, a principios de los años 70, colocó a Todd fortuitamente en la proximidad inmediata de un taller de acero y le ofreció acceso a los instrumentos de escultura de la universidad, asistencia estudiantil y becas anuales para materiales. De este fértil terreno surgió una madura cosecha de metales y construcciones integradoras. En el transcurso de una década ha producido esculturas en tres formatos. A una la llama «screens (pantallas)», que incorporan parrillas abiertas de metal como dispositivo de composición primaria. Las «tables (mesas)» oscilan lúdicamente entre lo funcional y lo decorativo. Los «circles (círculos)» se basan en el motivo de una curva relativamente cerrada. El *Nataraja* (1982) de 18 pies de altura incluído en esta exposición es un ejemplar del tercer grupo.

El formato básicamente circular de *Nataraja* hecho con un tubo hueco, está interrumpido variablemete por medio de varillas dobladas, losas cortadas, y materiales similares. De la misma forma el círculo está perforado tanto por dentro como por fuera de su contorno por una larga varilla caligráficamente curva, que va diagonalmente de la parte superior a la inferior (o viceversa), una rejilla, una X, un círculo, y otros trozos de metal usados como ornamento. El objeto en forma de losa con una arista rota funciona para Todd como una amplia brochada, contrastando con la pincelada más delicadamente caligráfica de las varillas y tubos más delgados. Todd cree que este proceso escultural es análogo a la pintura o al dibujo, a pesar de—o incluso en contradicción con—su peso y su escala. Como ocurre con la obra de otros escultores en esta exposición, el *Nataraja* de Todd ofrece múltiples referencias más allá de su considerable impacto formal—conjuga la moderación y asimetría de composición orientales con la tecnología occidental.

La obra de DeWain Valentine en los años 60, al igual que la de Todd, consistía en formas grandes y simples, aunque estaban forjadas en resina de poliéster formada con una fórmula patentada de su propia invención. El escogió este medio exigente y traicionero porque proporcionaba un medio de producir ilusiones de luz coloreada suspendida en el espacio, con el fin de reproducir en interiores fenómenos tan naturales como la puesta del sol y el arco iris.

Valentine había deseado trabajar con vidrio durante muchos años, pero no pudo debido a los prohibitivos costes de fabricación. Hacia la mitad de los años 70 había desarrollado una técnica para laminar vidrio cortado en tiras modulares finas con pegamento de silicona. Las unidades modulares facilitaban la construcción de formas arquitectónicas—pilares y dinteles, arcos, pirámides, ventanas—en variaciones potencialmente infinitas. Este proceso no sólo ha permitido el uso de referencias arquitectónicas, sino también la escala arquitectónica.

En los últimos dos años Valentine ha estado trabajando con un conjunto de materiales nuevos para él, cuyas propiedades no comprenden la transparencia: materiales tradicionales como el bronce, el granito, y el mármol. Sus proyectos más recientes combinan los materiales densos y opacos con vidrio coloreado en configuraciones que, como ocurre con Dill, aluden a la historia y al ritual. La escultura de Valentine que se presenta en esta exposición consiste en tres componentes combinados en una estructura básica de pilar y dintel. Las dos columnas de bronce de 8 pies son triangulares, con aristas de 24 pulgadas de largo. Las diez láminas de vidrio azul verdoso de 3/4 pulgadas, 36 pulgadas de alto y 96 pulgadas de largo, están laminadas formando el dintel. Juntas forman una masa con un grosor de 8 pulgadas que se desliza en hendiduras de las columnas de bronce. La riqueza de los materiales y su colorista contraste—el vidrio azul verdoso destellando contra la más acogedora pero monótona patena de las columnas de bronce—invitan a la asociación del ritual y la fantasía, como la entrada a la Ciudad Esmeralda de Oz.

La firmeza y durabilidad de los nuevos materiales de Valentine permiten que la obra pueda ser instalada permanentemente al aire libre, en contraste con la inestabilidad de la resina cuando está expuesta a la luz solar directa durante extensos períodos de tiempo. De esta forma, en lugar de permanecer entre las inmaculadas paredes blancas de una galería, la nueva obra es capaz de interactuar con el medio ambiente exterior, cuya maravillosidad sigue influyendo al artista.

Melinda Wortz
Diciembre 1983

Le constructivisme voluptueux de la sculpture californienne

Bien que les sculpteurs représentés dans cette exposition vivent en Californie, leurs oeuvres transcendent le régionalisme. Dans les années soixante, quand la Californie commença à être reconnue comme le «second» centre artistique en Amérique (après New York, bien sûr), les critiques tels que John Coplans et Phil Leider avaient l'habitude de définir en particulier l'art de la Californie du Sud en termes de son originalité vis-à-vis de celui de New York—disant son acceptation de matériaux et de procédés non-traditionnels tels que l'emploi de la résine, du verre, du plexiglace et du moulage sous vide; son effort pour faire cesser les distinctions traditionnelles entre la peinture et la sculpture et sa fascination envers les mystères subtils de la lumière projetée et réfléchie.

Dans les oeuvres actuelles de Bruce Beasley, Fletcher Benton, Guy Dill, Jud Fine, Michael Todd et DeWain Valentine le souci de l'ouvrage bien fini demeure. Mais d'autres particularités de leur travail peuvent s'inscrire dans le contexte plus large de l'histoire de l'art du vingtième siècle, en particulier dans celui du mouvement Constructiviste, né en Russie, et qui tenta d'incorporer les techniques et les matériaux de la vie au vingtième siècle dans le domaine de l'art où l'air commençait à se raréfier. Chacun de ces artistes travaille d'une façon additive, construisant l'oeuvre à partir de morceaux et de procédés nombreux plutôt qu'en moulant ou en sculptant une pièce dans son ensemble, à la manière traditionnelle.

Bruce Beasley travailla dans la sculpture sur métal seulement jusqu'à 1966, et son oeuvre fut très acclamée. Dès 1961, alors qu'il était encore étudiant, sa pièce appelée *Lemures* fut acquise par le Museum of Modern Art et, en 1963, le Ministre français de la Culture, André Malraux décerna un prix à son *Icarus*. En 1966, toutefois, Beasley voulait créer une «sculpture dans laquelle on puisse voir des formes à travers d'autres formes.» Cet intérêt, d'autres sculpteurs de l'époque le partageaient et beaucoup d'entre eux, tels que Peter Alexander, Larry Bell et DeWain Valentine—vivaient en Californie. Beasley, comme ses collègues, découvrit qu'il lu faudrait deviser son propre matériau transparent car aucun des produits trouvés dans le commerce n'était utilisable. Le verre, par exemple, n'était pas assez adaptable.

Avec l'argent de son prix, Beasley acheta une «autoclave», machine aux formes eccentriques qu'il peignit de motifs indiens de la côte de Nord-Ouest, transformant les outils de sa profession en objets d'art à leur façon. Procédant à tâtons, il soumit des plastiques liquides (plastique acrylique et lucite) à la pression et à la chaleur dans l'autoclave, traitement qui eut pour résultat la polymérisation de ses plastiques qui fondit les liquides en un matériau dur, transparent et solide. Finalement, Beasley parvint à contrôler suffisamment la chaleur et la pression pour empêcher qu'à la fin de l'opération le produit ne s'obscurcisse, bien que—DuPont l'en avait prévenu—il n'aie jamais obtenu la pureté dont il rêvait. Son procédé est demeuré secret.

Les formes inventées par Beasley sont dérivées des cristaux des minéraux. Les métaux, les minéraux et les alliages sont appelés cristallins parce que leur structure moléculaire est constituée d'ensembles qui se répètent selon une disposition régulière alors que, dans d'autres types de matière solide, la structure moléculaire est amorphe. C'est seulement à l'état cristallin que la matière laisse apparaître une structure géométrique. Ce n'est pas le cas des états gazeux ou liquides. Beasley tire parti de l'unique mélange de formes organiques et géométriques de l'état cristallin et y puise l'inspiration des unités modulaires de sa sculpture acrylique, et, dernièrement, de pièces monumentales aussi. Qu'elles soient exécutées en plastique acrylique ou en acier inoxydable, les facettes de ses unités modulaires réfractent et réfléctent la lumière en produi-

sant des effets qui changent constamment selon le temps qu'il fait ou l'heure de la journée. La plus haute des oeuvres en plastique acrylique de Beasley, *Apolymer* (1967–70), est installée à Sacramento, en Californie, da façon permanente. Les six tonnes et demie de plastique acrylique moulé capturent la lumière naturelle d'une telle manière qu'elles ont inspiré cette remarque au critique Ed Hotaling qui essayait de décrire l'effet produit: «C'est l'océan transporté à Sacramento». La plus grande sculpture métallique faite par Beasley jusqu'à ce jour est inclue dans l'exposition.

L'intérêt de Beasley pour la création de sculptures cristallines en métal, comme en lucite transparente, lui vint tout naturellement quand il construisait des moules destinés à la fonte des modules de lucite. Dans ce cas, les modules sont hexagonaux et créent des espaces négatifs selon la façon dont ils sont assemblés, ce qui a pour effet de produire des motifs changeants à travers lesquels on peut apercevoir le ciel ou le paysage environnant. Comme dans le cas de la lucite, la surface de l'acier inoxydable est très réfléchissante, en sorte que l'intéraction de la lumière et du mouvement de l'environnement sont un aspect important de l'oeuvre (aspect important aussi pour comprendre les oeuvres de Dill et de Valentine présentées dans l'exposition). La surface des sculptures de Beasley prend la coloration du paysage alentour.

Fletcher Benton fut reconnu nationalement pour la première fois au mileu des années soixante. On aima ses sculptures cinétiques—surfaces mouvantes et colorées centrées dans des cadres d'acier inoxydable au fini soigneux—mais en fait, il avait commencé sa carrière comme peintre. Lorsqu'il n'était encore qu'un adolescent, il s'associa avec un camarade pour ouvrir une affaire de peinture d'enseignes commerciales en Ohio, parce que les deux seuls peintres de la ville étaient partis servir pendant la Deuxième Guerre Mondiale. Les exigences professionnelles qui leur avaient enseigné à créer des formes précises et des lettres lisibles portèrent leurs fruits deux décades plus tard: on retrouve le même souci de la précision dans les sculptures de métal de Benton, un vocabulaire dérivé de la géométrie et souvent animé de lettres de l'alphabet en trois dimensions. En d'autres termes, les sculptures en métal de Benton, construites avec précision, la plupart de taille monumentale, incorporent des formes primaires, non seulement au sens bauhausien des trois formes parfaites, le cube ou le carré, la sphère ou le cercle, le cône ou le triangle (et leurs variantes)—mais aussi dans les blocs de base qui incluent le système conceptuel du langage.

Dans sa maturité, Benton fit longtemps de la peinture, avant de se tourner vers la sculpture dans les années soixante. De même, de nombreux autres constructivistes produisirent des tableaux aussi bien que des sculptures. Mais en peinture l'approche de Benton, dont on apprécia surtout une série de portraits gestuels de ses amis, fut surtout sensuelle et visuelle, plutôt que théorique. De même, dans ses sculptures cinétiques des années soixante, nous voyons que ses agencements sophistiqués de couleurs, disposées en couches changeantes de façon à créer une variété mouvante de tonalités et de formes tenait plus du lyrisme hédoniste que de l'audace technologique.

Pendant les années soixante-dix, Benton abandonna le mouvement dans ses sculptures et, pour un temps, la couleur, concentrant ses efforts sur l'expression des caractéristiques inhérentes aux matériaux—essentiellement l'acier et le bronze. Au cours des dernières années, Benton a aussi fait des expériences avec des modèles articulés, exécutant des oeuvres monumentales ainsi que des oeuvres plus intimes. Ce qui est un simple jeu avec les lois de l'équilibre lorsque l'on travaille à petite échelle devient une performance de virtuose lorsq'on travaille à l'échelle monumentale, comme dans l'oeuvre appelée *Balanced/Unbalanced Wheels* (1982) présentée dans cette exposition, oeuvre qui mesure 28 pieds de haut par 30 pieds de long et 7 pieds de largeur. Partant d'une maquette en bois de 12 pouces tout au plus, la sculpture passa d'un bond à 28 pieds. Benton y travaille après-coup pour la ramener à une échelle de 7 pieds. Deux pièces, ressemblant à des tours s'y trouvent juxtaposées—l'une un «T» géant, penché, l'autre une pile de cylindre et de boîtes—avec un groupe horizontal de deux roues en acier, ressemblant à des tubes, mesurant chacune 5 pieds par 5 pieds par 18 pouces, et une longue barre horizontale. Dans *Balanced/Unbalanced Wheels*, Benton est revenu à son ancien intérêt pour le mouvement, mais avec une pointe d'ironie. Tandis que l'oeuvre cinétique était mue, pour de bon, par un mécanisme caché, l'oeuvre nouvelle ressemble à une charrette en folie, sur le point de rouler ou de se renverser, mais, en fait, elle est solidement arrimée.

Cette construction est l'une des plus amusantes et des plus complexes faites par Benton. Bien que ses éléments—triangles, cercles, cylindres, boîtes et caetera . . . semblent avoir été assemblés au hasard, leur géométrie et leur position prêtent une sorte de logique à la sculpture. La variété des couleurs—gris, blanc, rouge et bleu—se remarque davantage sur le fond noir et contribue à donner à l'oeuvre un aspect ludique, comme d'ailleurs le fait l'emploi irrationnel de la forme «mouvement immobile».

L'oeuvre de Guy Dill exposée ici fait partie de sa série *Egalmeh* ou *Great Palace*. Le format de la série comprend des éléments géométriques posés sur des linteaux soutenus par des colonnes en forme d'équerre. En fait, l'intérêt de l'artiste pour cette structure ancienne est né de son désir d'incorporer des références temporelles multidimensionnelles à la série. Tandis que Dill appelle la série dans sa totalité *the Great Palace*, ses composantes sont nommées d'après des textes sumériens qui, eux-mêmes, apportent une référence temporelle très ancienne. L'oeuvre présentée dans le cadre de l'exposition s'appelle *Siduri* (1983), ou «celle qui est la divine faiseuse de vin et brasseuse, qui demeure sur le rivage de la mer, dans le jardin du soleil, et qui est peut-être une incarnation d'Ishtar»—référence à un hédonisme hautement romanesque.

La partie inférieure de cette pièce—deux colonnes en forme d'équerre soutenant un linteau évoque non seulement d'anciens monuments tels que Stonehenge, mais aussi les emplois rituels (tel que celui d'observatoire astronomique) auxquels nous imaginons qu'ils étaient destinés. Dans une veine plus contemporaine, le mouvement dit «Post-Modern», en architecture, partage cette manie de faire des références à l'histoire au moyen d'artifices architecturaux. Le désir avoué de Dill de rendre sa sculpture plus architecturale trouve un écho dans l'approche sculpturale que l'on détecte chez certains architectes contemporains tels que Luis Barragán, avec qui Dill se sent des affinités depuis de longues années.

Les grandes dimensions et la coloration abondante mais subtile de la nouvelle oeuvre de Dill résultent d'une longue période passée à expérimenter avec la technologie du béton. Depuis 1974, année où il exposa ses premières sculptures en béton à la Pace Gallery de New York, Dill en est venu à employer ce matériau d'une façon de plus en plus scientifique et contrôlée. L'amalgame qui forme le béton se compose de lave et de ciment dont la finesse a été obtenue sur mesure et qui prend rapidement mais qui a une surface très douce. La coloration unique employée par Dill dans les éléments de *Siduri* est le résultat d'une technique qui consiste à verser du pigment liquide pur dans le ciment. L'alcali ensuite le sèche. Ce procédé, dit Dill, est contraire à la manière traditionnelle de colorer une sculpture en appliquant le pigment à la surface. Dans *Siduri*, la couleur est inséparable de la structure—elle en émerge au lieu de simplement la couvrir.

Dill ne travaille pas d'après des ébauches préparatoires de ses constructions architectoniques. Au fil des années, il a mis au point un vocabulaire de formes rigoureux, qui n'est pas sans ressembler à celui de Benton, et qui comprend des équerres, des colonnes, des linteaux et diverses sortes de triangles, des barres, des rectangles et des surfaces. Ce vocabulaire moderniste devient lyrique en dépit de sa taille à cause de sa coloration—tonalités variées et subtiles de noir et de gris, touches de rose à peine discernables, bleus profonds, tons lavande séduisants, verts poussiéreux, rouges argileux. Les puissantes ombres linéaires jetées par les formes géométriques nettes modifient la couleur des surfaces en ajoutant des nuances qui semblent y avoir été peintes. Quand cette sorte d'oeuvre est vue dans une pièce, les ombres qu'elle projette sur les murs et le plancher créent des images ressemblant au fantôme éthéré de leur source. En plein air, le béton doux est sensible non seulement aux changements d'intensité de la lumière mais aussi au degré d'humidité de l'air, en sorte que la surface sculpturale change constamment. *Siduri* a l'air de flirter avec l'environnement.

Jud Fine était inscrit dans un programme de doctorat en histoire intellectuelle des Etats-Unis, à l'université de Santa Barbara, quand il décida de changer de spécialité et choisit l'art. Ce qui l'incita à changer de discipline fut la frustration qu'il éprouva à faire des recherches minutieuses pour prouver une hypothèse qui pouvait être réfutée de la même façon. Il se chercha une spécialité où il pourrait «poser une hypothèse et la prouver par la force de sa conviction», entreprise qui, décida-t-il, ne pouvait être menée à bien qu'en philosophie, en littérature ou en art. Il choisit le programme d'études de troisième cycle à Cornell (en partie parce qu'il n'était pas nécessaire, pour y entrer, d'avoir un diplôme de deuxième cycle en art) et, tout d'abord, fut intimidé par son manque de technique. L'absence de règles en art, comparée aux exigences rigoureuses des études que demande la préparation d'un doctorat, le troublait. Rationalisant, il chercha «à donner à l'art une valeur et à élever la discipline.» Il étudia la phénoménologie et le Minimalisme.

De retour en Californie, au début des années soixante-dix, Fine n'avait accès ni aux matériaux ni aux outils dont il avait pu se servir à Cornell. L'état de ses finances lui imposait de chercher des matériaux peu coûteux et faciles à trouver. Ses premières oeuvres furent faites de rocs, de sable et de bambou, dans leur habitat naturel et en studio—c'était cette sorte de contraste, in situ/non in situ, que Robert Smithson avait trouvé fascinant. A cette époque, Fine était consciemment en train d'essayer de développer sa sensibilité physique (opposée à sa sensibilité culturelle). Pendant cette période expérimentale, il réalisa le plus d'oeuvres qu'il était possible sans prononcer de jugements de valeur sur leur qualité. En conjonction avec la poursuite de son art, Fine avait entrepris de vastes recherches sur les anciennes cultures. Il découvrit que les «shime», symboles professionnels, qui sont les formes architecturales les plus anciennes dans les cultures asiatiques, étaient fabriqués d'«herbes gerbées entourées d'une cordelette», fabrications éphémères, construites avec l'intention apparente de permettre à chaque génération de construire son propre abri, rituellement.

En considérant la valeur relativement importante accordée aux rapports sociaux et le manque d'insistance placé sur la créativité dans les cultures orientales et, vice-versa, le manque relatif de structure sociale et l'importance donnée à la créativité individuelle à l'Occident, Fine chercha un moyen de faire la synthèse des deux dans un mode conceptuel tertiaire. Sa solution, ou transcendance d'une pensée dualiste en une nouvelle forme synthétique, est illustrée par la longue colonne horizontale, dont la version la plus récente est présentée dans cette exposition.

La barre de plus de 100 pieds de long de Fine a l'air orientale par ses qualités minimalistes, par sa discrétion, mais elle est construite avec un noyau d'acier, produit de la technologie occidentale. Les supports verticaux des cinq sections ré-représentent la gravité, la relation au sol. Ainsi que le dit Fine: «Il arrive un moment où l'on ne peut plus aller plus avant (littéralement et métaphoriquement) sans retomber au sol. Il faut une verticale pour soutenir une horizontale.»

Bien que la barre, avec ses sections de surfaces différentes—tubes de cuivre, tube intérieur en caoutchouc, garnitures enroulées, en bois de pommier—reste parfaitement horizontale, elle semble être placée à des hauteurs différentes selon les accidents de terrain. En d'autres termes, elle défie notre perception de la terre que nous habitons, nous rend plus conscients de notre environnement ainsi que, du moins le supposons-nous, devaient le faire les objets des anciennes cultures.

Michael Todd commença ses études d'art dans la gravure, il fut étudiant de John Paul Jones, et il rappelle en riant que la plaque du graveur fut son premier contact avec le métal. Outre la sculpture, il a aussi fait de la peinture, tout au long de sa carrière. Alors qu'il vivait à New York au milieu des années soixante, il fut confronté par le défi minimaliste qui désirait créer des formes réduites afin de centrer la perception intensément sur des subtilités que l'on n'avait pas remarquées avant. L'oeuvre qu'il réalisa à cette période fut présentée dans l'exposition de «Primary Structures» du Jewish Museum, à la fin des années soixante. Cependant, à cette date, il s'était fatigué du format réduit. «Je suis, en réalité, d'un tempérament plus sensuel que cela», explique-t-il. La découverte de la sculpture de David Smith lorsqu'il enseignait à Bennington College, dans le Vermont, l'encouragea à exprimer plus de complexité dans son propre travail.

Deux évènements eurent un tel impact stylistique sur Todd qu'ils précipitèrent le majeur changement de style évident dans ses oeuvres des dix dernières années—c'est à dire dans ses sculptures en acier, ouvertes, soudées, abstraites. Le premier fut une exposition de calligraphie chinoise au Metropolitan Museum of Art de New York. Cette calligraphie le hanta au point qu'il rêvait d'en reproduire le mouvement et la liberté dans un format tri-dimensionnel. Le second fut la découverte qu'il fit, lors de la visite d'un temple, au Japon, d'un très large vase en métal contenant des fleurs en métal aussi, et qui l'abasourdit.

Un poste d'enseignant à l'université de Californie, à San Diego, au début des années soixante-dix, plaça, par hasard, Todd à proximité d'un dépôt de ferraille et lui permit d'avoir accès aux outils de sculpture de l'université, aux services financiers d'aide aux étudiants ainsi qu'à des bourses annuelles pour acheter des matériaux. En l'espace de dix ans, Todd a produit des sculptures en trois formats. Celles qu'il appelle les «écrans» comprennent des grilles ouvertes, de métal, comme composants essentiels. Les «tables» hésitent plaisamment entre l'utile et le décoratif. Les «cercles» sont basés sur le motif d'un cercle relativement fermé. La *Nataraja* de 18 pieds (1982) qui fait partie de cette exposition est un exemple du troisième groupe.

La forme essentiellement circulaire de *Nataraja*, qui est fait d'un tube creux, est interrompue de diverses façons par des baguettes courbées, par des plaques coupées et cetera. . . . De même, le cercle est ponctué, à la fois à l'intérieur et à

l'extérieur, par une longue baguette courbée calligraphiquement, qui court en diagonale, du haut en bas (ou vice-versa), par une grille, un X, un cercle et d'autres débris de métal servant de décoration. La forme qui ressemble à une dalle au rebord déchiqueté remplit pour Todd la fonction d'un coup de pinceau audacieux, contrastant avec la touche calligraphique plus délicate des baguettes et des tubes de moindre épaisseur. Todd pense ses sculptures en peintre ou en dessinateur, en dépit de, ou même en proportion inverse de leur poids et de leurs dimensions. Comme c'est le cas pour d'autres sculptures de l'exposition, le *Nataraja* de Todd, outre sa puissance considérable, suggère de maintes façons la retenue et la composition assymétrique des oeuvres orientales, alliées à la technologie de l'Occident.

Dans les années soixante, le travail de DeWain Valentine, comme celui de Todd, consistait en formes simples, de grandes dimensions, bien qu'elles aient été moulées en résine de polyester, selon une formule patentée qu'il avait inventée. Il choisit ce matériau exigeant et traître parce qu'il permettait de créer l'illusion de lumière colorée suspendue dans l'espace, de reproduire, en chambre, des phénomènes naturels tels que le coucher du soleil et l''arc-en-ciel.

Depuis des années, Valentine voulait travailler dans le verre, mais le coût prohibitif de la fabrication l'en avait découragé. Au milieu des années soixante-dix, il avait mis au point une technique pour laminer le verre découpé en fines bandes modulaires, tenues ensemble par une colle au silicium. Les unités modulaires facilitaient la construction de formes architecturales—poteaux et linteaux, arches, pyramides, fenêtres— qu'il pouvait combiner presque à l'infini. Cette technique lui facilita non seulement l'emploi de références architecturales, mais encore lui donna plus de flexibilité dans le choix des dimensions.

Depuis ces deux dernières années, Valentine emploie, pour la première fois, des matériaux non-transparents, nouveaux pour lui: matériaux traditionnels tels que le bronze, le granite et le marbre. Ses oeuvres les plus récentes combinent ces matériaux denses, opaques avec le verre de couleur pour créer des ensembles qui, comme ceux de Dill, évoquent l'histoire et le rituel. La sculpture de Valentine présentée dans cette exposition consiste en trois éléments arrangés de façon à former une structure en forme de poteau et de linteau. Les deux colonnes de bronze de 8 pieds sont triangulaires, avec des côtés de 24 pouces. Dix feuilles de verre bleu-émeraude de 3/4 de pouce, hautes de 36 pouces et longues de 96 pouces sont laminées pour former le linteau. Ensemble, elles forment une masse épaisse de huit pouces qui se glisse dans dans des fentes des colonnes de bronze. La richesse des matériaux et leur coloris forment un puissant contraste—le verre bleu-émeraude étincelle à côté de la patine plus chaude mais plus terne des colonnes de bronze—évoque un rituel ou fait naître des visions de fantaisie. On se croirait à la porte de la ville émeraude d'Oz.

La résistance et la durabilité des nouveaux matériaux employés par Valentine signifient que ses oeuvres peuvent être installées dehors à titre permanent, au contraire de la résine qui subit des variations lorsqu'elle est exposée au soleil pour de longues périodes. Ainsi, au lieu de se détacher sur les murs blancs immaculés d'une galerie, les nouvelles oeuvres sont elles en mesure de réagir avec l'environnement dont les merveilles continuent à influencer l'artiste.

Melinda Wortz
décembre 1983

Empfindsamer Konstruktivismum in kalifornischer Bildhauerei

Wenn auch die Bildhauer, die in dieser Ausstellung vertreten sind, in Kalifornien leben, überschreitet ihr Schaffen regionale Grenzen. In den 60er Jahren, als Kalifornien anfing, als «zweites» Kunstzentrum in Amerika angesehen zu werden (als «zweites» selbstverständlich gegenüber New York), war es üblich für Kritiker wie John Coplans und Phil Leider, südkalifornische Kunst im besonderen wegen ihrer Einzigartigkeit im Vergleich zu der von New York zu charakterisieren—ihre Aufgeschlossenheit gegenüber untraditionellen technologischen Materialien und Arbeitsweisen wie Harz, Glas, Plexiglas, das Formen im Vakuum und Galvanisieren; ihr Interesse, die traditionellen Unterschiede zwischen Malerei und Skulptur zu durchbrechen; sich feiner kunstvoller Ausführung zu widmen; ihre Faszination mit dem subtilen Rätsel von projeziertem und reflektiertem Licht.

Im derzeitigen Schaffen von Bruce Beasley, Fletcher Benton, Guy Dill, Jud Fine, Michael Todd und DeWain Valentine verbleibt die Widmung zu kunstvollem Werken. Einige andere Prämissen ihrer Arbeit können jedoch im großen Kontext der Kunstgeschichte des 20. Jahrhunderts gesehen werden, besonders in dem in Rußland aufgekommenen Konstruktivismus und dessen Aufforderung, Techniken und Materialien des Lebens im 20. Jahrhundert in den esoterischen Bereich der Kunst einzugliedern. Jeder dieser Künstler arbeitet in additiver Weise, indem er Kunstwerke aus vielen Teilen und Prozessen konstruiert und nicht das traditionellere monolithische oder megalithische Gießen oder Meißeln aus einer einzelnen Masse anwendet.

Bruce Beasley schuf bis 1966 ausschließlich Metallskulpturen, wodurch er ein besonderes Maß an Aufmerksamkeit mit diesem Stoff erregte. Schon 1961, als er noch Student war, wurde sein Stück *Lemures* vom Museum of Modern Art angekauft, und 1963 wurde Beasleys *Icarus* von dem bekannten französischen Kultusminister André Malraux mit einem Preis bedacht. 1966 jedoch wollte Beasley eine «sculpture in which one could see forms through other forms» (Skulptur, in welcher man Formen durch andere Formen sehen kann) schaffen. Dieses Interesse wurde von einigen anderen Bildhauern dieser Periode geteilt; viele von ihnen wie Peter Alexander, Larry Bell und DeWain Valentine leben auch in Kalifornien. Wie diese, fand Beasley heraus, daß er seinen eigenen transparenten Stoff entwickeln mußte, da keine der vorhandenen kommerziellen Produkte seinen Zwecken dienen würden. Glas beispielsweise war nicht anpassungsfähig genug.

Mit der Dotierung seines Preises kaufte Beasley einen «autoclave», eine ekzentrisch aussehende Maschine, die er mit indianischen Motiven von der Nordwestküste bemalte, wobei er sein Handwerkszeug zum Kunstwerk seinerselbst verwandelte. Indem er schrittweise voranging, unterwarf er flüssige Kunststoffe (Akryl und Lucit) Druck und Hitze in dem Autoklav, ein Vorgang, der in Polymerisation resultierte und der die Flüssigkeiten in starkes, durchsichtiges und festes Material verschmolz. Mit der Zeit entwickelte Beasley ein Gefühl dafür, Hitze und Druck so zu kontrollieren, daß Trübung im Endprodukt vermieden wurde, obwohl ihm die DuPont Fachleute gesagt hatten, daß die von ihm gewünschte Reinheit unmöglich zu erreichen sei. Sein Verfahren bleibt ein Geheimnis.

Beasleys Formen werden von mineralischen Kristallen abgeleitet. Metalle, Mineralien und Legierungen werden als kristallin beschrieben, weil ihre molekulare Struktur in regelmäßigen, sich wiederholenden Mustern angelegt ist, verglichen mit anderen Arten von Feststoffen, deren molekulare Struktur amorph ist. Nur im kristallinen Zustand zeigen sich geometrische Strukturen in diesem Stoff. Dies ist nicht der Fall im flüssigen oder gasförmigen Zustand. Beasley benutzt die einzigartig Mischung organischer und geometrischer Formen des kristallinen Zustandes als Grundlage für die sich wiederholenden Bausteine seiner Akryl-Skulptur und in letzter Zeit auch monumentale Metallstücke. Ob in Akryl oder rostfreiem Stahl

ausgeführt, die facettenhaften Bausteine dieser Skulpturen brechen und reflektieren Licht in fortwährend sich wandelnden Mustern, dem Wetter und der Tageszeit entsprechend. Beasleys größtes Akrylkunstwerk, *Apolymer* (1967–1970) hat seinen festen Sitz in Sacramento, Kalifornien. Die sechseinhalb Tonnen gegossenen Akryls fangen das natürliche Licht in der Weise ein, daß es den Kritiker Ed Hotaling inspiriert hat, die Wirkung des Kunstwerks als «the ocean brought to Sacramento» (den Ozean nach Sacramento gebracht) zu beschreiben. Beasleys bisher größte Metallskulptur findet sich auf dieser Ausstellung.

Beasleys Interesse für das Schaffen kristalliner Skulpturen entwickelte sich von selbst, als er Formen für das Gießen der Lucitteile baute. In diesem Falle sind die Teile hexagonal und bilden Hohlräume der Art und Weise ihrer Zusammenfügung entsprechend, was in einem sich verändernden Muster von Lücken resultiert, durch die man den Himmel oder die Umgebung sehen kann. Gleich dem Lucit ist die Oberfäche des rostfreien Stahls stark reflektierend, was die Wechselwirkung zwischen Licht und Bewegung der Umgebung zu einem wichtigen Aspekt des Werkes werden läßt (ein Aspekt, der auch durch die Stücke von Dill und Valentine auf dieser Ausstellung gezeigt wird). Die Oberfläche der Skulptur von Beasley fängt die Färbung ein, die in der Landschaft vorhanden ist.

Fletcher Bentons erste Welle von nationaler Anerkennung in der Mitte der 60er Jahre war eine Antwort auf seine kinetischen Skulpturen—bewegliche Farbflächen in einem Gerüst aus hochpoliertem rostfreiem Stahl zentriert—aber seine eigentliche Karriere begann er als Maler. Als Teenager gründeten er und ein Jugendfreund eine Schildermalerei in Ohio, weil die beiden einzigen Schildermaler der Stadt im II. Weltkrieg dienen mußten. Die berufliche Forderung nach präzisen Formen und lesbaren Schriftzeichen hallte zwei Jahrzehnte später in den mit der Maschine fein bearbeiteten Metallskulpturen der letzten Jahre, mit einem von der Geometrie abgeleiteten Vokabular und oft belebt durch dreidimensionale Buchstaben des Alphabets wider. Mit anderen Worten, Bentons klar konstruierte Metallskulpturen, viele von ihnen in übergroßem Ausmaß, verkörpern Grundstrukturen nicht nur im Bauhaus-Sinn der drei perfekten Formen—Würfel oder Quadrat, Kugel oder Kreis, Kegel oder Dreieck (und ihre verschiedenen Darstellungen)—sondern auch im Sinn der grundlegenden Bausteine, die das konzeptuelle System der Sprache beinhalten.

Als reifer Künstler malte Benton viele Jahre lang, ehe er sich in den 60er Jahren der Skulptur zuwandte. In ähnlicher Weise schufen viele andere Konstruktivisten Gemälde ebenso wie Skulpturen. Bentons Verbindung mit der Malerei, wo er den größten Erfolg mit einer Serie von Gebärden-Portraits von Freunden erzielte, war jedoch eher sinnlicher und visueller Natur als theoretischer. So sehen wir an seinen kinetischen Skulpturen der 60er Jahre, daß sein sophistischer Gebrauch der Farbe, die sich in Schichten abwechselt, um eine bewegliche Vielfalt an Farbtönen und Formen zu schaffen, mehr einen hedonistischen Lyrizismus als eine technologische Bravour darstellt.

Anfang der 70er Jahre kam Benton vom Ausdruck der Bewegung in seinen Skulpturen, und für eine Weile auch von der Farbe, ab, und konzentrierte sich auf einen Ausdruck materialeigener Charakteristika—meistens Stahl und Bronze. In den letzten Jahren hat Benton auch mit dem Ausdruck verschiedener Größen experimentiert, wobei er sowohl monumentale als auch intime Werke schuf. Wie werden spielerische Balanceakte in kleinem Maßstab zu virtuosen Aufführungen monumentaler Größe, wie beispielsweise die *Balanced/Unbalanced Wheels* (1982) auf dieser Ausstellung, die 28 ft. hoch, 30 ft. breit und 7 ft. lang ist? Ursprünglich in einem kleinen Holzentwurf ausgearbeitet, dessen größte Dimension 12 in. beträgt, springt die Skulptur sofort auf einen 28-ft-Maßstab. Hiernach wird sie auf einen 7-ft.-Maßstab umgearbeitet. Das Kunstwerk stellt zwei turmähnliche Strukturen gegenüber—eine ein riesiges «T», das im Winkel liegt, die andere ein senkrechter Stapel von Zylindern und Kästen—mit einer horizontalen Gruppierung zweier Stahl-, röhrenähnlicher Räder, jedes 5 ft. × 5 ft. × 18 in. und eine lange horizontale Stange. Mit *Balanced/Unbalanced Wheels* kehrte Benton zu einem früheren Interesse an Bewegung zurück, allerdings mit einem ironischen Dreh. Wo das kinetische Kunstwerk wirkliche Bewegung einschloß, in Gang gesetzt durch einen versteckten Mechanismus, sieht das neue Stücke wie ein verrückter Karren aus, der im Begriff ist, zu rollen, zu fallen oder sich zu überschlagen; in Wirklichkeit aber ist er fest verankert.

Diese Konstruktion ist eine von Bentons spielerischsten und komplexesten. Trotzdem seine verschiedenen Komponenten—Dreiecke, Kreise, Zylinder, Kästen usw.—aufs Geratewohl angesammelt zu sein scheinen, verleihen ihre Geometrie und Plazierung der Skulptur eine Art von Logik. Die Vielfalt an Farben—grau, weiß, rot und blau—sind auf einem vorwiegend schwarzem Kunstwerk betont und tragen zu der Aussagekraft des Spiels bei, so wie der Gebrauch von Form als «immovable movement» (unbewegliche Bewegung). Die Neigung der Betrachter von Bentons Kunst, in und durch ein Objekt dieser Größe zu klettern, wird erwartet. Mit Absicht entwirft er Kreise zum Hineinspringen und Draufsitzen.

Guy Dills Stück auf dieser Ausstellung ist ein Teil seiner *Egalmeh* oder *Great Palace* Serie. Das Serienformat schließt geometrische Elemente ein, die, getragen von keilförmigen Säulen, zum Sturz erhoben sind. Tatsächlich rührt das Interesse des Künstlers in diese altertümliche Pfosten- und Sturzstrukturanordnung von seinem Streben her, multidimensionale Zeitbeziehungen in die Serie einzuschließen. Während Dill zu ihr in ihrer Ganzheit als *Great Palace* verweist, werden ihre individuellen Darstellungen nach sumerischen Texten benannt, die ihrerseits einen entfernten Zeitbezug beinhalten. Das Werk für diese Ausstellung trägt den Titel *Siduri* (1983) oder «she who is the divine wine maker and brewer, dwells on the shore of the sea in the garden of the sun, and may be a form of Ishtar» (sie, die die göttliche Küferin und Brauerin ist, lebt an den Ufern des Meeres im Garten der Sonne und könnte eine Form von Ishtar sein)—ein Bezug zu hochveredeltem romantischen Hedonismus.

Der untere Teil dieses Stücks—zwei keilförmige Säulen, welche den Sturz tragen—ruft nicht nur altertümliche Denkmäler wie Stonehenge hervor, sondern auch die rituellen Anwendungen (in Ausdrücken astronomischer Geschehnisse), denen wir sie zuschreiben. In heutiger Zeit ist die postmoderne Bewegung innerhalb der Architektur auch der Anführung historischer Architektur-Gerätschaften verfallen. Dills eingestandenes Interesse, seine Skulptur in sowohl Form als auch Inhalt architektonischer zu gestalten, findet Analogien in der bildhauerischen Annäherung an die Architektur, die im Werk der innovativsten zeitgenössischen Architekten wie Luis Barragán, mit dem sich Dill seit Jahren geistig verwandt fühlt, gesehen werden kann.

Sowohl der große Maßstab als auch die üppige aber subtile Farbengebung von Dills neuer Arbeit sind das Resultat einer ausgedehnten Versuchsperiode mit der Technik von Gußbeton. Seit 1974, als er seine erste Betonskulptur in der Pace Gallery in New York ausstellte, ist Dills Anwendung des Materials zunehmend wissenschaftlicher und gebundener geworden. Die Betonmischung besteht aus Bimstein und spezial gemahlenem Zement, die sich schnell erhärtet, aber eine weiche Oberfläche hat. Dills einzigartige Farbengebung der *Siduri*-Teile kommt von der Technik, reine, flüssige Farbstoffe in den Mörtel zu geben, dessen Laugen es binden und trocknen. Dieses Verfahren, sagt Dill, steht im Gegensatz zu der herkömmlichen Methode, Skulpturen mit Farbe zu versehen, bei der man die Farbe *auf* die Oberfläche aufträgt. In *Siduri* ist die Farbe untrennbar von der Struktur—sie geht aus dem Innern hervor anstatt bloß aufgestrichen zu sein.

Dill arbeitet nicht nach vorgefertigten Zeichnungen, wenn er diese architektonischen Konstruktionen ausarbeitet. Im Laufe der Jahre hat er ein straffes Formovokabular entwickelt, Bentons nicht unähnlich, das Keile/Säulen, Sturze, und mannigfaltige Variationen von Dreiecken, Stangen, Rechtecken und Balken einschließt. Dieses reduktive modernistische Vokabular wird lyrisch trotz seiner Größe mittels seiner hübschen Farbgebung—sich verändernde und subtile Tonalitäten von schwarz und grau, kaum erkennbare Schattierungen von rosa, starke Blautöne, verführerische Lavendeltöne, staubige Grüntöne und erdfarbene Rottöne. Die staklinearen Schatten, die durch die rein geometrischen Formen geworfen werden, verändern die Farbe der Oberfläche zu zusätzlichen Nuancen, die gemalt erscheinen. Wenn dieses Werk in einem Raum betrachtet wird, schaffen die an Wände und Boden geworfenen Schatten ätherische geisterhafte Abbilder ihrer Herkunft. Dill macht manchmal hinterher großangelegte Zeichnungen von dem Stück, indem er die Abbilder auf Photopapier überträgt. Unter freiem Himmel ist der weiche Beton nicht nur für das flackernde Licht der Umgebund empfänglich, sondern auch für den Grad an Luftfeuchtigkeit, sodaß sich die Oberfläche der Skulptur in dauernder Veränderung befindet. Es ist, als ob sich *Siduri* in einem gegenseitigen Werben mit ihrer Umgebung befindet.

Jud Fine war als Doktorand in amerikanischer Geistesgeschichte an der University of California in Santa Barbara immatrikuliert, als er Kunst zu seinem Hauptfach machte. Der Wechsel hierzu wurde durch die Frustration bei der Forschung nach Minutiösem, um ein Hypothese zu belegen, die durch den gleichen Vorgang widerlegt werden konnte, ausgelöst. Er suchte ein Gebiet, in dem er «hypothesize a premise and prove it by force of conviction» (eine Prämisse annehmen und durch die Gewalt der Überzeugung beweisen) konnte, ein Unternehmen, wie er entschied, das nur in Philosophie, Literatur oder Kunst ausführbar sei. Er wählte Cornells «Graduate Program» (zum Teil, weil es keines Bakkalaureats in Studiokunst bedurfte) und war zuerst durch seinen Mangel an Fähigkeiten eingeschüchtert. Besonders im Vergleich zu den harten Anforderungen einer Promotion war er durch die Abwesenheit von Begriffsbestimmung im Ausüben der Kunst verwirrt. Indem er den Richtungswechsel rationalisierte, suchte er nach einem Weg «[to] give art value and elevate the discipline» (der Kunst Wert zu geben und die Disziplin zu veredeln). Er begann mit einer philosophischen Untersuchung des Entscheidungsfällungsvorganges; er fügte das Studium der Phenomenologie und des Minimalismus hinzu; seine ästhetische Anschauung gründete sich auf beiden, den konzeptuellen und Sinnesaspekten der Informationsverarbeitung.

Als er in den frühen 70er Jahren nach Kalifornien zurückkehrte, hatte Fine nicht den Zugang zu den Materialien und dem Handwerkszeug, die ihm an Cornell zur Verfügung standen. Finanzielle Einschränkungen zwangen ihn, nach billigen und leicht zugänglichen Materialien zu suchen. Seine frühesten Werke schuf er aus Steinen, Sand und Bambus, sowohl in natürlicher Umgebung als auch im Studio—die Art und Weise von Platz/Nicht-Platz Zusammenhangskontrast, den Robert Smithson auch faszinierend gefunden hatte. Zu dieser Zeit versuchte Fine bewußt, seine physischen (im Gegensatz zu kulturellen) Empfindsamkeiten zu entwickeln. Während dieser Experimentierphase arbeitete er einfach soviel wie möglich, ohne Werturteile über Qualität abzugeben. Im Zusammenhang mit dem künstlerischen Arbeiten hat Fine eine ausführliche Erforschung altertümlicher Kulturen unternommen. Er fand heraus, daß «shime» oder Berufsschilder die frühesten architektonischen Formen östlicher Kulturen aus «bunches of grasses wrapped with string» (Grasbüschel umwickelt mit Schnur) konstruiert waren, nicht dauerhaft, mit der augenscheinlichen Absicht, jeder Generation zu erlauben, eigenes Obdach rituell zu errichten.

Unter Berücksichtigung des relativ hohen Wertes, der auf das soziale Gefüge und auf den Mangel an Betonung der Kreativität in östlichen Kulturen gelegt wird, und umgekehrt des beträchtlichen Mangels an Wertbetonung im sozialen Gefüge und individueller Kreativität im Westen, suchte Fine nach Mitteln, diese zwei auf tertiäre faßbare Weise zusammenzubringen. Seine Lösung oder Transzendenz dualistischen Denkens in einer neuen künstlichen Form wird exemplifiziert durch die lange waagerechte Säule, deren jüngste Version auf dieser Ausstellung vertreten ist.

Fines 80-Fuß langer horizontaler Gegenstand sieht in seinen minimalistischen unaufdringlichen Eigenschaften fernöstlich aus, ist aber mit einem Stahlkern westlicher Technologie konstruiert. Die senkrechten Stützen für die fünf Teile sind das Bindeglied zur Schwerkraft, die Verbindung mit der Erde. Wie Fine sagt: «you can only project so far (both literally and metaphorically) without returning to the ground. You must have the vertical from which to extend the horizontal.» (. . . man kann nur soweit hinausgehen—wörtlich und metaphorisch—ohne zum Boden zurückzugelangen. Man muß die Senkrechte haben, von der man die Horizontale dehnt.)

Obwohl die Säule mit ihren Teilen verschiedener Oberflächen—Kupferröhren, Gummischläuche, eingewickelte Apfel-Ornamente—streng horizontal bleibt, erscheint sie höher und kürzer in Bezug auf die Veränderungen des Bodens. Mit anderen Worten, es fordert unser Verständnis für das Verhältnis zu der Erde, die wir bewohnen, heraus, indem es das Bewußtsein für unsere Umgebung schärft, so wie es die altertümlichen Kunstwerke wahrscheinlich tun sollten.

Michael Todd begann sein Kunststudium als Drucker. Er war Schüler von John Paul Jones und bezeichnet lächelnd die Radierplatte als seinen ersten Kontakt mit Metall. Während seiner Karriere malte er auch neben seiner Bildhauerei. Als er Mitte der 60er Jahre in New York lebte, wurde er von der minimalistischen Herausforderung konfrontiert, reduktive Formen zu schaffen, um die Wahrnehmung schärfer auf die vorher nicht beachteten Kleinigkeiten hinzuleiten. Sein Werk aus dieser Periode war in den späten 60er Jahren auf der «Primary Structures»-Ausstellung des Jewish Museums zu sehen. Dann jedoch war er von dem reduktiven Format abgekommen. «My temperament is really more sensuous,» (Meine Natur ist in Wirklichkeit empfindsamer), gab er zur Erklärung. Während er am Bennington College in Vermont lehrte, war er der Bildhauerei von David Smith ausgesetzt. Das bestärkte sein neues Bestreben, mehr Komplexität in seinem Werk zum Ausdruck zu bringen.

Zwei Ereignisse waren von solch starker ästhetischer Wirksamkeit auf Todd, daß sie den eigentlichen stilistischen Richtungswechsel, der in seinen Werken des letzten Jahrzehnts offensichtlich war, auslösten—offene, geschweißte, abstrakte Stahlskulpturen. Der erste Anstoß kam auf einer Ausstellung chinesischer Kalligraphie im Metropolitan Museum of Art in New York. Diese Kalligraphie verfolgte ihn so, daß er das Verlangen hatte, deren Eindruck von Gebärdenspiel und Zufälligkeit in dreidimensionalem Format wiederzugeben. Im Anschluß daran, als er einen Tempel in Japan besuchte, fiel ihm zu seinem Erstaunen eine große Stahlvase ins Auge, die ebenfalls aus Stahl geformte Blumen enthielt.

Ein Lehrauftrag an der University of California, San Diego, Anfang der 70er Jahre brachte Todd durch Zufall in die Nähe eines Schrottplatzes und bot Zugang zu Bildhauereiwerkzeugen, studentischer Hilfe und jährlichen Unterstützungsbeträgen für Materialien. Diesem reichen Boden entsprang eine reiche Ernte von additiven Metallkonstruktionen. Im Verlaufe eines Jahrzehnts schuf Todd Skulpturen in drei Formaten. Das eine, das er «screens» (Gemesch) nennt, besteht aus einem offenen Metallgitter als primärer Kunstgriff. Die «tables» (Tische) schweben verspielt zwischen Funktion und Ausschmückung.

Die «circles» (Kreise) fußen auf dem Motiv einer fast geschlossenen Krümmung. Die 18-Fuß hohe *Nataraja* (1982) auf dieser Ausstellung ist ein Beispiel der dritten Gruppe.

Das grundsätzlich kreisförmige Format von *Nataraja*, das aus einer hohlen Röhre gemacht ist, wird gelegentlich von gebogenen Stangen, geschnittenen Blöcken und ähnlichem unterbrochen. In gleicher Weise wird der Kreis innerhalb und außerhalb seiner Kontur durch eine lange kalligraphisch gebogene Stange, welche sich diagonal von oben nach unten (oder umgekehrt) erstreckt, ein Gitter, ein X, einen Kreis und andere Metallstückchen, die als Ornamente dienen, unterstrichen. Die blockähnliche Form mit einer zerrissenen Kante fungiert für Todd wie ein breiter Pinselstrich, der im Kontrast zu dem delikateren kalligraphischen Schwung der inneren Stangen und Röhren steht. Todd denkt sich seinen bildhauerischen Vorgang als dem des Malens und Zeichnens analog, trotz—oder sogar im Widerspruch zu—dessen Gewicht und Ausmaß. Genauso wie es auf andere Bildhauer auf der Ausstellung zutrifft, bietet Todds *Nataraja* vielfache Bezüge jenseits seiner beträchtlichen formalen Stärke—zu fernöstlicher Zurückhaltung und asymmetrischer Anordnung in Verbindung mit westlicher Technologie.

Wie bei Todd bestand DeWain Valentines Werk in den 60er Jahren aus großen, einfachen Formen, die jedoch aus Kunstharz nach patentierter Formel eigener Entdeckung gegossen worden sind. Er wählte diesen anfordernden und tückischen Stoff, weil er ein Mittel bot, Eindrücke von farbigem Licht im Raum hängend zu gewinnen, um im Innenraum solche Naturphänomene wie Sonnenuntergänge und Regenbögen nachzubilden.

Viele Jahre lang schon wollte Valentine mit Glas arbeiten, wurde aber durch die unerschwinglichen Herstellungskosten entmutigt. Um die Mitte der 70er Jahre hatte er eine Technik entwickelt, wobei er dünne, zugeschnittene Glasstreifen mit Silikon-Klebstoff zusammenschichtete. Diese zugeschnittenen Stücke erleichterten das Schaffen architektonischer Formen wie Pfosten und Sturze, Bögen, Pyramiden und Fenster,—in prinzipiell unendlichen Variationen. Dieser Vorgang hat nicht nur den Gebrauch architektonischer Bezüge begünstigt, sondern ebenso das Ausmaß der Architektur.

In den letzten beiden Jahren hat Valentine mit einer Anzahl an Materialien, die ihm neu waren und deren Eigenschaften keine Transparenz aufwiesen, gearbeitet: traditionelle Materialien wie Bronze, Granit und Marmor. Seine jüngsten Projekte verbinden diese dichten und opaken Stoffe mit buntem Glas zu Konfigurationen, welche genau wie bei Dill auf Geschichte und Ritual anspielen. Valentines Skulptur auf dieser Ausstellung besteht aus drei Komponenten, die in einer grundlegenden Pfosten- und Sturzstruktur verbunden sind. Die zwei 8-Fuß bronzenen Säulen stellen ein Dreieck mit zwei 24-inch langen Seiten dar. Zehn 3/4-inch dicke blau-grüne Glasscheiben, 36-inch hoch und 96-inch lang werden zusammengeschichtet, den Sturz zu bilden. Zusammen ergeben sie eine 8-inch dicke Masse, die in Schlitze in den bronzenen Säulen hineingleitet. Die Reichhaltigkeit des Materials und ihr farblicher Kontrast—das blau-grüne Glas glitzert gegen die wärmere aber dumpfe Patina der Bronzesäulen—rufen Assoziationen mit Ritual und Fantasie, wie z.B. der Eingang zur Emerald City von Oz, hervor.

Die Widerstandsfähigkeit und Dauerhaftigkeit von Valentines neuem Material bedeutet, daß das Werk auf ewige Zeit draußen aufgestellt werden kann, im Gegensatz zur Unbeständigkeit des Harzes, wenn es direktem Sonnenlicht für einen ausgedehnten Zeitraum ausgesetzt wird. In dieser Weise, statt mit den fleckenlosen weißen Wänden der Gallerie, kann das neue Werk auf die Außenwelt einwirken, deren Wunder den Künstler weiterhin beeinflussen.

Melinda Wortz, Dezember 1983

The Artists

43-50 **Robert Arneson**

51-58 **Charles Arnoldi**

59-66 **Bruce Beasley**

67-74 **Fletcher Benton**

75-82 **Guy Dill**

83-90 **Jud Fine**

91-98 **Tom Holland**

99-106 **Robert Hudson**

107-114 **Manuel Neri**

115-122 **Sam Richardson**

123-130 **Michael Todd**

131-138 **DeWain Valentine**

Born: Benicia, California, 1930
Resides: Benicia, California

Robert Arneson

Robert Arneson

From Cecile N. McCann in *Contemporary Artists* (New York: St. Martin's Press, 1977):
Robert Arneson's explicitly autobiographical sculptures confront his pleasures and embarrassments with a wry, self-deprecating humor that touches a responsive chord for most viewers. . . . Beyond the clearly personal comments, the work contains wide-ranging art-historical references. Arneson has so thoroughly studied the history of ceramics that he has made both the concepts and techniques of the past accessible for his own uses. At one time he created a series of irreverent small sculptures that used imagery resembling fruit stand souvenirs, and made them of exquisitely finished, celadon-glazed porcelain as seductive as a Sung bowl. One homage to ancient Rome took the form of a self-portrait bust set head-high on an accurately reproduced classical column, the calm austerity of the piece punctured by male genitals protruding from the smooth cylinder at the appropriate position and bare toes lifting the column's base as if it were the hem of a toga. Pomposity and self-importance are not permitted to linger in this artist's work. [P. 39]

From Robert Arneson in *Craft Horizons*:
The self-portrait is a portrait of the mind . . . fragments of my mind at various stages. . . . I'm not looking at the past whatsoever. I'm just making a brick. When you are making a brick, you are not working in the past; you are making a form, a shape. The consciousness of it was simply that it was the most heroic of ceramics. [No. 6, December 1977/31]

From Robert Arneson cited by Beth Coffelt in the *San Francisco Sunday Examiner & Chronicle*:
I never did consider myself an "artist." We just called ourselves "clay people." Sounds like we came in from under the earth, don't it? [8 April 1979]

From Dennis Adrian in *Art in America*:
The whimsy and intellectual caperings of Arneson's pieces, seen singly or in the context of a group show, have suggested to many of us that he is primarily a fringe-Pop gagster, sticking with his ancient and homely craft out of the *faux-naif* doggedness that is the plague of much California art. . . . However, the true foci of Arneson's interest are not easy gags of Funk conceits, but persistently varied investigations of ambiguities in the materials, processes and rationales of artistic activity itself. [September/October 1974/80–83]

From Alfred Frankenstein in *Artnews:*
Of all of the [University of California at] Davis group, which includes Wayne Thiebaud, William T. Wiley, Manuel Neri, Roy De Forest and Roland Petersen, a good case could be made for Robert Arneson as the most widely influential. He is almost single-handedly responsible for the fact that ceramic is now a major sculptor's medium, particularly in California. . . . He began ceramics under the influence of Voulkos and the Abstract Expressionist movement. His early pieces—around 1959–60—are rugged vessels full of accident and agony. [No. 75, January 1976/48–50]

From Beth Coffelt in the *San Francisco Sunday Examiner & Chronicle*:
. . . it is the self-portraits—or rather the works of sculpture which use Arneson's head and features as their *point d'appui*—that have made him famous as the progenitor of an unprecedented school of polychrome clay sculpture. He has taken his own intransigent selfhood and molded it into breath-taking contraventions of content and form. He is a virtuoso colorist, an artist who can take a viscid shrimp pink glaze, dab it on one of his heads, and end up with a finish of such freshness and elegance that it makes celadon look dull. If his content threatens to overwhelm his form, the vivacity of his color, the depth and luminosity of his glaze bring it all back together as a work of art. When you see one of those heads you think, not what a genius Arneson is, but, oh, what a work of art is man. [8 April 1979]

From Jonathan Fineberg, *Robert Arneson* (New York: Allan Frumkin Gallery, 1983):
The . . . new sculpture and drawings by Robert Arneson aren't funny. The predominant theme is nuclear holocaust and the images are unpleasant. But the power of these works to rupture the psychological barriers we keep to shield ourselves from such visions has once again to do with their extreme literalness. On one level this series represents a sense of political responsibility in that the artist has used his creative powers to convey the unspeakable possibilities of nuclear proliferation. The base of *Holy War Head* has a quite graphic description of the effects of the radiation, right down to the smell of rotting flesh. But the text is badly defaced as if to imply that the terrible blast not only obliterated human life but that it also ironically erased the moral message of its own history.

Ground Zero, 1984
Bronze
26 × 80 × 80"
66 × 203 × 203 cm
Lent by the artist

**De Cecile N. McCann, *Artistas Contemporáneos*
(Nueva York: St. Martin's Press, 1977):**

Las esculturas explícitamente autobiográficas de Robert
Arneson confrontan sus gustos y turbaciones con un seco
humor auto-irónico que toca la cuerda sensible de la mayoría
de los espectadores. . . . . Más allá de los comentarios claramente personales, la obra contiene referencias artístico-histó-
ricas de gran alcance. Arneson ha estudiado tan profunda-
mente la historia de la cerámica que tanto los conceptos y las
técnicas del pasado se han hecho accesibles a sus propios
usos. Una vez creó una serie de estatuillas irreverentes usando
imagenes que asemejaban souvenirs de puestos de fruta, y
las modeló con porcelana barnizada con celedón exquisitamente acabadas y seductoras como un tazón de Sung. Como
homenaje a la Roma antigua creó un busto de auto-retrato co-
locado en lo alto de una columna clásica reproducida minucio-
samente, y la calmada austeridad de la pieza queda desbara-
tada por los genitales masculinos que sobresalen del suave ci-
lindro en su apropiada posición y los pies desnudos que elevan
la base de la columna como si fueran la bastilla de una toga.
En la obra de este artista no hay lugar para la pomposidad y
la vanidad personales. [pág. 39]

De Robert Arneson en *Horizontes Artesanales*:

El auto-retrato es un retrato de la mente . . . fragmentos de m
mente en varios niveles . . . de ninguna manera miro hacia el
pasado. Simplemente estoy creando un ladrillo. Cuando se
construye un ladrillo no se trabaja con el pasado; se hace una
forma, un contorno. Es la conciencia del ladrillo como la más
heróica de las cerámicas. [No. 6, diciembre de 1977/31]

**De Robert Arneson citado por Beth Coffelt en el
San Francisco Sunday Examiner & Chronicle:**

Nunca me consideré un «artista.» Nos llamábamos sencillamente «trabajadores de la arcilla.» Suena como si saliéramos
de la tierra, ¿verdad? [8 de abril de 1979]

Pablo Ruiz with Itch, 1980, glazed ceramic
29.5 x 22 x 22", 76 x 56 x 56 cm (bust)
58 x 27.5 x 15", 147 x 71 x 38 cm (pedestal)

De Dennis Adrian en *Arte en América*:

Las caprichosas cabriolas intelectuales de las piezas de
Arneson, vistas individualmente o en el contexto de una exposición de grupo, nos han sugerido a muchos de nosotros que
él es primordialmente un comediante rozando el arte Pop, des-
tacando con su artesanía antigua y sencilla de entre la obsci-
nación *faux-naif* que es la plaga de mucho del arte de California. . . . No obstante, los verdaderos puntos de interés de
Arneson no son los trucos fáciles de una presunción Funk,
sino variadas y persistentes investigaciones de las ambigüeda-
des de los materiales, procesos y de la lógica de la actividad
artística misma. [septiembre/octubre de 1974/80–83]

De Alfred Frankenstein en *Artnews*:

De todo el grupo de [la Universidad de California en] Davis,
que incluye a Wayne Thiebaud, William T. Wiley, Manuel
Neri, Roy De Forest y Roland Petersen, cabe señalar el caso
de Robert Arneson como el de más amplia influencia. A él,
casi exclusivamente, le corresponde el mérito de que la cerámica sea hoy día un medio principal en la escultura, sobre
todo en California. . . . En sus primeros trabajos de la cerámica sufrió la influenciá de Voulkos y del Movimiento Expresionista Arbstracto. Su obra temprana—de los años 1959-60—
está constituida por rugosas vasijas que exhuman accidente y
agonía. [No. 75, enero de 1976/48–50]

**De Beth Coffelt en el *San Francisco Sunday Examiner
& Chronicle*:**

. . . son los auto-retratos—o más bien las esculturas que utilizan la cabeza y los rasgos de Arneson como su punto de
apoyo—los que le hicieron famoso como el prócer de una
escuela de escultura con arcilla policromada sin precedentes.
Arneson ha tomado su propia personalidad intransigente y la
ha moldeado en impresionantes infracciones de la forma y del
contenido. Es un colorista virtuoso, un artista que puede to-
mar un viscoso barniz rosado de crustáceo, salpicarlo en uno
de sus bustos y alcanzar un acabado de tal frescura y elegancia capaz de eclipsar al celedón. Si su contenido amenaza
con abrumar a su forma, la viveza de su color, la profundidad
y luminosidad de su brillo se encargan de recomponerlo como
obra de arte. Cuando vea uno de esos bustos, pensará, no
en lo genial de Arneson, sino, oh, en lo artístico que es el
hombre. [8 de abril de 1979]

**De Jonathan Fineberg, *Robert Arneson* (Nueva York:
Galería Allan Frumkin, 1983):**

La . . . nueva escultura y dibujos de Robert Arneson no son
graciosos. El tema predominante es el holocausto nuclear y las
imágenes son desagradables. Pero el poder de estas obras al
romper las barreras psicológicas con las que nos protegemos
de tales visiones refleja de nuevo su extremada literalidad. En
un cierto nivel esta serie representa un sentido de responsabilidad política en la que el artista ha usado sus poderes crea-
dores para transmitir las inefables posibilidades de la prolifera-
ción nuclear. La base del busto *Holy War Head* (Cabeza de
Guerra Santa) posee una descripción bastante gráfica de los
efectos de la radiación, llegando a sugerir incluso el hedor de
la carne putrefacta. Pero el texto está altamente deformado
como para implicar que la terrible explosión no sólo destruyó
la vida humana sino que también borró, irónicamente, el
mensaje moral de su propia historia.

Cecile N. McCann, *Contemporary Artists* (New York: St. Martin's Press, 1977):

Les sculptures explicitement autobiographiques de Robert Arneson évoquent les joies et les ennuis de l'artiste avec un humour un peu pincé et critique qui ne manque pas de faire vibrer une corde sensible chez la plupart de ceux qui les voient. Outre les allusions personnelles, l'oeuvre contient de vastes, références à l'histoire de l'art. Arneson a si complètement étudié l'histoire de la céramique qu'il s'est approprié les concepts ainsi que les techniques du passé. Il lui arriva de créer une série de petites sculptures irrévérencieuses en employant l'imagerie qui sert à décorer les compotiers vendus en guise de souvenirs. Il les fit d'une porcelaine au fini exquis de céladon, aussi attrayante que celle d'une coupe Song. Il rendit hommage à la Rome antique en sculptant son propre buste qu'il jucha, tête haute, sur une colonne ancienne, fidèlement reproduite, le calme et l'austérité de la pièce ponctués seulement par la présence d'un organe génital mâle faisant saillie du cylindre lisse, à l'endroit attendu, et par des orteils nus soulevant la base de la colonne, comme s'il s'agissait de l'ourlet d'une toge. Il n'y a de place ni pour l'emphase ni pour la suffisance dans l'oeuvre de cet artiste. [p. 39]

Robert Arneson, paru dans *Craft Horizons*:

Ce portrait de l'artiste par lui-même est un portrait spirituel . . . saisissant les différentes étapes de ma pensée . . . ce qui ne veut pas dire que je suis tourné vers le passé. Je fais tout simplement une brique. Quand vous faites une brique, vous ne travaillez pas dans le passé, vous êtes occupé à façonner un objet, à lui donner forme. Je n'étais conscient que du fait que c'était là de la céramique sous sa forme la plus héroique. [No. 6, 31 décembre 1971]

Robert Arneson, cité par Beth Coffelt dans le *San Francisco Sunday Examiner & Chronicle*:

Je ne me suis jamais considéré comme un «artiste». En parlant de nous, nous disions «les gens de l'argile». Ça sonne un peu comme si nous étions sortis des entrailles de la terre, n'est-ce pas? [8 avril 1979]

Dennis Adrian dans *Art in America*:

Les fantaisies et les pirouettes intellectuelles des oeuvres d'Arneson, que celles-ci soient prises à part ou examinées dans le contexte d'une exposition d'ensemble, ont donné à penser à beaucoup d'entre nous que leur auteur était surtout un créateur de gags à la limite de l'art Pop, fidèle à ses anciennes techniques artisanales sans élégance, par un attachement obstiné au *faux naïf* qui, pour une large part, est la plaie de l'art californien. . . . Toutefois, ce qui intéresse Arneson, ce ne sont pas les gags faciles nés d'idées saugrenues, mais l'étude variée et constante des ambiguïtés des matériaux, des méthodes et des modes de raisonnement de l'activité artistique elle-même. [septembre/octobre 1974/80–83]

Alfred Frankenstein dans *Artnews*:

De tous les membres du groupe de l'université de Californie à Davis, groupe qui comprend Wayne Thiebaud, William T. Wiley, Manuel Neri, Roy De Forest et Roland Petersen, il ne serait pas faux de dire que Robert Arneson est probablement celui qui a le plus d'influence. C'est presque à lui seul que la céramique doit d'être aujourd'hui un medium majeur de la sculpture, particulièrement en Californie. . . . Il commença à travailler dans la céramique sous l'influence de Voulkos et du mouvement Expressioniste abstrait. Ses premières oeuvres—qui remontent aux années 1959–60—sont des vases frustes, raboteux et torturés. [No. 75, janvier 1976/48–50]

Beth Coffelt dans le *San Francisco Sunday Examiner & Chronicle*:

. . . ce sont les portraits de l'artiste par lui-même—ou plutôt les sculptures qui prennent la tête et les traits d'Arneson comme point d'appui—qui l'ont établi comme le créateur d'une école de sculpture sur argile polychrome sans précédent. Il a pris son moi intransigeant et l'a moulé dans des formes et des volumes d'un inédit à vous couper le souffle. C'est un coloriste virtuose, un artiste capable de prendre un vernis rose crevette visqueux, d'en mettre une touche sur l'un de ses bustes et d'aboutir à un fini d'une telle fraîcheur qu'il fait pâlir même le céladon. Si chez lui le volume tend à écraser la forme, l'éclat de ses couleurs, la profondeur et la luminosité de son vernis rétablissent l'unité et transforment l'oeuvre en oeuvre d'art. En voyant l'un de ces bustes, on ne se dit pas: «Quel génie, cet Arneson!» mais «Quelle oeuvre d'art qu'est l'homme!» [8 avril 1979]

Jonathan Fineberg, *Robert Arneson* (New York: Allan Frumkin Gallery, 1983):

Les . . . nouvelles sculptures et les nouveaux dessins de Robert Arneson n'ont pas pour but d'amuser. Leur thème dominant est celui de l'holocauste nucléaire et les images font mal à voir. Le pouvoir qu'ont ces oeuvres de briser les barrières psychologiques que nous élevons pour nous protéger de telles visions tient une fois de plus à leur extrême littéralité. A un certain niveau, cette série communique un sens de responsabilité politique en ce que l'artiste a employé ses talents créateurs pour décrire les horreurs sans nom que risque d'entraîner la prolifération nucléaire. A la base de la pièce intitulée *Holy War Head* [i.e., Sainte Ogive] se trouve une description très graphique des effets des radiations qui va jusqu'à évoquer la puanteur de la chair en putréfaction. De plus, le texte est partiellement oblitéré comme pour impliquer que la terrible explosion n'a pas seulement anéanti la vie humaine mais a aussi, ironiquement, effacé le message moral contenu dans sa propre histoire.

California Artist, 1982, glazed ceramic
78 x 28 x 21", 198 x 71 x 53 cm

Aus Cecile N. McCann, *Contemporary Artists* (New York: St. Martin's Press, 1977):

Robert Arnesons ausgesprochen autobiographische Skulpturen verbinden seine Vergnügen und Verlegenheiten mit einem trockenen, selbstkritischen Humor, der bei den Betrachtern auf Resonanz stößt . . . Jenseits der rein persönlichen Bemerkungen enthält das Werk weitrangige, kunsthistorische Bezüge. Arneson hat die Geschichte der Keramik so gründlich studiert, daß er sich sowohl die Konzepte als auch die Techniken der Vergangenheit zu eigen gemacht hat. Einmal schuf er eine Serie von unehrerbietigen kleinen Skulpturen, die Bilder verwandten, die Obststandsouveniers ähnlich waren, und machte sie aus äußerst fein gearbeitetem Seladonit-glasiertem Porzellan verführerisch wie eine Sung-Schale. Eine Huldigung des antiken Roms nahm die Form einer Selbstportrait-Büste an, die in Augenhöhe auf eine originalgetreue klassische Säule gesetzt wurde, die friedliche Nüchternheit wurde von männlichen Genitalien durchbrochen, die aus dem glatten Zylinder in entsprechender Position hervortreten, und nackten Zehen, die den Sockel der Säule hochheben, als ob er der Saum einer Toga wäre. Prunk und Selbstherrlichkeit dürfen in dem Werk dieses Künstlers nicht verweilen. [p. 39]

Von Robert Arneson in *Craft Horizons*:

Das Selbstportrait ist ein Abbild der Erinnerung . . . Teilstücke meiner Erinnerung in verschiedenen Stadien. . . . Ich blicke auch in keinerlei Vergangenheit. Ich stelle einen Ziegel her. Wenn man einen Ziegel herstellt, arbeitet man nicht in der Vergangenheit; man schafft eine Form, eine Gestalt. Das Bewußtsein davon war einfach, daß es äußerst heldenhaft in der Töpfereikunst war. [No. 6, Dezember 1977/31]

Von Robert Arneson von Beth Coffelt im *San Francisco Sunday Examiner & Chronicle* zitiert:

Ich habe mich selbst nie als «Künstler» angesehen. Wir nannten uns selbst einfach «Tonleute». Es hört sich an, als kämen wir aus der Erde, nicht wahr? [8. April 1979]

Von Dennis Adrian in *Art in America*:

Die Laune und intellektuellen Kapriolen von Arnesons Stücken, als Einzelstück oder im Kontext einer Gemeinschaftsausstellung gesehen, haben vielen von uns verraten, daß er in erster Linie ein sich am Rande des Pops befindlicher Gagspezialist ist, der an der alten und herkömmlichen Kunst mit einer *faux-naif* Hartnäckigkeit, die die Plage vieler kalifornischer Kunst ist. . . . Die wahren Schwerpunkte des Arnesonschen Interesses sind jedoch keine einfachen Improvisationen von Funkspielereien,

Portrait of the Artist as an Old Dog, 1982, glazed ceramic
34" high, 86 cm

sondern ein andauernd andersartiges Erforschen der Ambiguität in den Werkstoffen, Arbeitsvorgängen und logischen Grundlagen der künstlerischen Arbeit selbst. [September/Oktober 1974/80-83]

Von Alfred Frankenstein in *Artnews*:

Von allen der (University of California) Davis-Gruppe, die Wayne Thiebaud, William T. Wiley, Manuel Neri, Roy De Forest and Roland Petersen einschließen, gilt dies insbesondere für Robert Arneson als dem weitaus einflußreichsten. Er ist beinahe allein verantwortlich für die Tatsache, daß Keramik heute ein wesentlicher Stoff des Bildhauers ist, besonders in Kalifornien. . . . Er begann mit der Keramik unter dem Einfluß Voulkos und der Abstrakten Expressionistischen Bewegung. Seine frühen Stücke—um 1959-60—sind rauhe Gefäße von Zufall und Agonie. [No. 75, January 1976/48-50]

Von Beth Coffelt im *San Francisco Sunday Examiner & Chronicle*:

. . . es sind die Selbstportraits—oder vielmehr die bildhauerischen Arbeiten, die Arnesons Kopf und Züge als ihren *point d'appui* benutzen,—die ihn als den Vorfahren einer beispiellosen Schule polychromer Tonskulpturen machten. Er hat sein eigenes unnachgiebiges Selbst genommen und es in einen atemberaubenden Widerspruch von Inhalt und Form verschmolzen. Er ist ein virtuoser Farbengeber, ein Künstler, der eine zähflüssige, krebsrote Glasur nehmen kann, einen seiner Köpfe damit betupfen und mit einem letzten Schliff von solcher Frische und Eleganz enden, daß es Seladonit matt erscheinen läßt. Wenn sein Inhalt seine Form zu überwältigen droht, bringt es die Lebendigkeit seiner Farbe, die Tiefe und der Glanz seiner Glasur wieder alles zusammen zu einem Kunstwerk. Wenn man einen seiner Köpfe erblickt, denkt man nicht, was Arneson für ein Genie ist, sondern, ach, welch ein Kunstwerk der Mensch ist. [8. April 1979]

Aus Jonathan Fineberg, *Robert Arneson* (New York: Allan Frumkin Gallery, 1983):

Die . . . neue Bildhauerei und Zeichnungen von Robert Arneson sind nicht komisch. Das hervortretende Thema ist der nukleare Holocaust und die Bilder sind unangenehm. Aber die Kraft dieser Werke, die psychologischen Barrieren zu durchbrechen, die wir aufrechterhalten, um uns vor solchen Schreckensbildern zu schützen, hat wieder einmal mit ihrer extremen Buchstäblichkeit zu tun. Auf einer Ebene repräsentiert diese Serie einen Sinn für politische Verantwortlichkeit dadurch, daß der Künstler seine Schaffenskraft benutzt hat, die unaussprechlichen Möglichkeiten nuklearer Prolifikation zu übermitteln. Die Grundlage des *Holy War Head* hat eine ausgesprochen graphische Beschreibung der Strahlenwirkung einschließlich dem Geruch verwesenden Fleisches. Aber der Text ist schlimm entstellt, um durchblicken zu lassen, daß die schreckliche Explosion nicht nur menschliches Leben ausgelöscht hat, sondern daß sie ironischerweise auch die moralische Botschaft ihrer eigenen Geschichte ausradiert hat.

Born: Dayton, Ohio, 1946
Resides: Venice, California

Charles Arnoldi

Charles Arnoldi

From Charles Arnoldi cited by Henry Hopkins in _Artnews_:

I have become interested in wood as an alternative to painting. I especially like tree branches, which have a very distinct line quality. They feel hand-drawn, they have a certain gestural quality, a naturalness. They feel seductive. At the same time I recognize that my work demands to be part of a well-defined pictorial tradition. _Volcano—Log Jam_, in combining different kinds of information, represents a synthesis of these concerns. It provides a solution to my desire for subject matter. . . . [No. 1, January 1982/73]

From Charles Arnoldi cited by Jan Butterfield, _Charles Arnoldi, Laddie John Dill_ (Fullerton: California State University, Fullerton, 1983):

When I think of art, I always think in terms of great paintings, not sculpture. So I started making the tree branch paintings because when I was in art school you couldn't make paintings. Painting was dead! So I was looking for an alternative way to make a painting. I used tree branches because they looked like hand-drawn lines, but I didn't have to draw them. That attitude was totally consistent with the late 1960s and early 1970s mentality. Here was this beautiful gestural line, but I didn't draw it. It was "prefabricated." I'd simply take the branches and make a picture with their line. [P. 6]

From Miles Beller in _Artweek_:

Charles Arnoldi's pieces, like his earlier works, are completely constructed from sticks and branches, forming irregular lattices in an overall, roughly rectangular shape. Whether the branches transcend their "real" function is a question that I found difficult to answer, for I never completely forgot I was looking at parts of a tree. [No. 31, 18 September 1976/3]

From Suzanne Muchnic in the _Los Angeles Times_:

Charles Arnoldi, one of the area's most celebrated younger-generation artists . . . distinguished himself a few years ago with squarish wall pieces composed of tree branches. They were open, angular structures that bent natural materials into formal abstractions. Later he painted fields of colored twigs, emulating the sculpture's branching currents but never catching their spirit or tensile strength. It seemed the branching sculptures weren't meant to be translated. . . . Now Arnoldi is back with the same old notes and brand new music. He is working with branching volumes, painted blocks of wood and wall pieces that juxtapose flat canvases with reliefs of branches. In two free-standing sculptures—roughly cubical and extending about 8 feet in every direction—he has massed together forests of painted diagonals, thus pulling former reliefs off the wall and stretching paintings into real space enclosed by linear structures. A thick slab of branches, resting on the floor and suspended upright by ceiling wires, is painted on one side, natural on the other. [3 October 1980]

From Jan Butterfield, _Charles Arnoldi, Laddie John Dill_ (Fullerton: California State University, Fullerton, 1983):

In 1978 . . . Arnoldi's branch works came off the wall and began to take shape as fully three-dimensional works. In them, the tender, carefully chosen branches intertwined and were woven like those of a young thicket in the winter, short of its spring leaves. In these unpainted sculptures, whose branches are in a natural state, the viewer half expects to encounter a startled deer bolting from its interior. This naturalism has romantic overtones to it as well, as critic Charles Kessler noticed: "Arnoldi's branches are never a neutral subject—they carry connotations of the organic, the nature-directed romantic. . . ." Arnoldi also _painted_ these thickets, giving them still another dimension. The Pollockian attributes evidenced in some of the earlier paintings now come to the fore in full force as colors weave in and out in an exquisitely determined pattern, stitching the composition together with flashes of light, as critic Peter Frank noticed: "They have been arranged with careful regard for the interaction of their various hues and textures, so that the busy networks they form seem almost to have been generated organically. The invariably square perimeter of each sculpture, however, testifies to the role of a human mind and hand." [P. 14] . . . Charles Arnoldi's work has always been formal, elegant, and deceptively simple. It is no longer so. Powerful, vibrant, gigantic, it overwhelms with its raw-boned power and intense coloration. His painstakingly whittled and painted twigs of fifteen years ago have given way to enormous paintings hewn fiercely out of thick plywood with a chain saw. So too has Arnoldi, the precocious youngster with the innate Italian sense of style and macho, given way to a thoughtful, mature artist who is in full command of his statement, and whose recognition has been international. Arnoldi's development, like that of his crony and fellow traveler Laddie Dill, represents an important chapter in the history of a maturing West Coast art scene. [P. 5] . . . Importantly, the most recent sculptures have been executed in bronze. The bronze process is a complicated one which allows Arnoldi an almost unlimited combination of elements. As a result of it, each sculpture is a unique piece created from a reservoir of bronze branches, two-by-fours, four-by-fours, and plywood shapes, individually cast at the foundry. Arnoldi chose some twenty-five of the most unique branches he could find and had each one of them cast many many times. Put together much like the natural branches in the paintings, the bronze twigs are then welded at the joints. The end result, which is stunning, powerful, and permanent, not only gives the works a patina of time, but allows them to be seen in a new context—allowing Arnoldi to be seen as a true inheritor of developments in modernist sculpture. [P. 14]

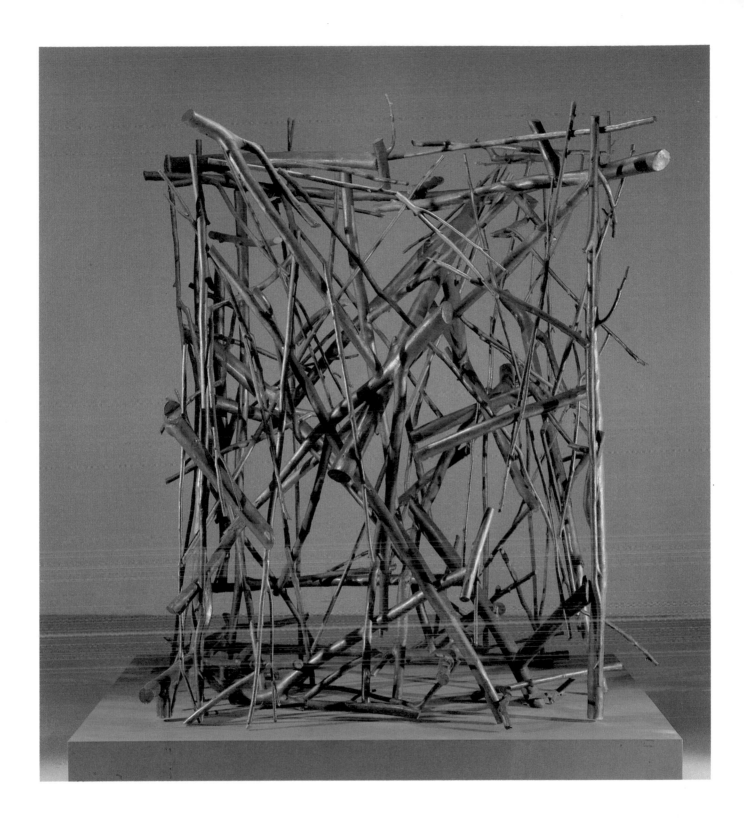

Not Marble nor Gilded Monument, 1982
Cast and welded bronze
102 × 78 × 86"
259 × 198 × 218 cm
Lent by James Corcoran Casting, Inc.

De Charles Arnoldi citado por Henry Hopkins en *Artnews*:

He llegado a cobrar interés por la madera como alternativa a la pintura. En especial me gustan las ramas de los árboles que poseen una cualidad lineal muy distintiva. Se sienten esbozadas a mano, poseen una cierta cualidad gesticulante, una cierta naturalidad. Sentimos la seducción. Al mismo tiempo reconozco que mi obra exige formar parte de una tradición pictórica bien definida. *Volcano—Log Jam*, en cuanto que combina diferentes tipos de información, representa una síntesis de estas preocupaciones. Aporta una solución a mi deseo de encontrar nuevos temas. . . . [No. 1, enero de 1982/73]

De Charles Arnoldi citado por Jan Butterfield, *Charles Arnoldi, Laddie John Dill* (Fullerton: Universidad Estatal de California, Fullerton, 1983):

Cuando pienso en el arte siempre lo asocio con grandes pinturas, no con esculturas. Por ello comencé a pintar ramas de árboles, porque cuando estaba en la escuela de Bellas Artes no se podían hacer pinturas. ¡La pintura había muerto! Por lo tanto estaba buscando una forma diferente de hacer pintura. Usé ramas de árboles porque se asemejaban a trazos hechos a mano y así no era necesario dibujarlas. Esta actitud era completamente coherente con la mentalidad de finales de los años 60 y principios de los 70. He aquí una hermosa línea gestual que no tenía que dibujar. Estaba «prefabricada.» Simplemente recogía las ramas y contruía un cuadro con su perfil. [pág. 6]

De Miles Beller en *Artweek*:

Las obras de Charles Arnoldi, como sus primeras obras, están construidas en su totalidad con palos y ramas, formando enrejados irregulares de forma cuasi-rectangular. Tanto si las ramas trascienden su función «real» o no, es una cuestión de difícil respuesta, ya que nunca olvidé por completo que estaba comtemplando partes de un árbol. [No. 31, 18 de septiembre de 1976/3]

De Suzanne Muchnic en *Los Angeles Times*:

Charles Arnoldi, uno de los artistas de esta zona más celebrados de la nueva generación . . . se distinguió hace algunos años con piezas murales cuadrangulares compuestas con ramas de árboles. Eran estructuras abiertas, angulares, que forjaban abstracciones formales a partir de materiales naturales. Más tarde pintó campos de ramaje llenos de colorido,

Untitled, 1972, wood branches
37 x 34", 94 x 86 cm

emulando las corrientes de escultura ramificante sin capturar en modo alguno su espíritu o fuerza de tensión. Es como si las esculturas ramificantes no hubieran sido hechas para ser traducidas. . . . Ahora Arnoldi ha vuelto con las mismas viejas notas pero con música nueva. Trabaja con volúmenes en ramificación, bloques de madera pintados y murales que yuxtaponen lonas lisas a bajorrelieves de ramas. En dos esculturas autónomas—más o menos cúbicas y de aproximadamente 8 pies de extensión en cada dirección—Arnoldi ha utilizado masivamente enjambres de diagonales pintadas, y con ello arrancando del mural anteriores relieves y estirando las pinturas al espacio real demarcado por estructuras lineales. Una losa gruesa de ramas, que está pintada en una cara del conjunto, pero está al natural en la otra cara, yace en el suelo suspendida verticalmente del techo por medio de cables. [3 de octubre de 1980]

De Jan Butterfield, *Charles Arnoldi, Laddie John Dill* (Fullerton: Universidad Estatal de California, Fullerton, 1983):

En 1978 . . . las obras sobre ramas de Arnoldi comenzaron a salir de la pared y a configurarse como obras plenamente tridimensionales. En ellas, las tiernas, cuidadosamente escogidas ramas se entretejían y trenzaban como las de un verde matorral en invierno, sin hojas primaverales todavía. Ante estas esculturas no pintadas, cuyas ramas se encuentran en estado natural, el espectador medio espera encontrar un ciervo asustado que salta inesperadamente del interior. Este naturalismo tiene también matices románticos, como lo ha apuntado el crítico Charles Kessler: «Las ramas de Arnoldi nunca son un tema neutral—poseen connotaciones de lo orgánico, de lo romántico encuazado hacia la naturaleza. . . .» Arnoldi tambien *pintó* estos matorrales, dándoles aún otra dimensión. Los atributos pollockianos evidentes en algunas de sus pinturas anteriores ahora se nos presentan con plena fuerza a medida que los colores se entrelazan por dentro y por fuera con un esquema exquisitamente determinado, que unifica la composición con rayos de luz, como notó el crítico Peter Frank: «Han sido dispuestas con cuidadoso esmero hacia la interacción de sus variados tonos y texturas de tal manera que las sobrecargadas redes que forman casi parecen haberse generado orgánicamente. El perímetro cuadrado invariable de cada escultura, sin embargo, da testimonio del papel de la mente y de la mano humana.» [pág. 14] . . . La obra de Charles Arnoldi siempre ha sido formal, elegante, y engañosamente simple. Ya no lo es. Poderosa, vibrante, gigantesca, abruma con su poderío crudo y su intenso colorido. Sus ramitas talladas y pintadas concienzudamente realizadas hace quince años han dado paso a pinturas enormes fieramente cortadas con sierra eléctrica de gruesa madera terciada. Así también Arnoldi, el precoz jovenzuelo con el sentido innato de los italianos hacia el estilo y el machismo, dió paso al pensativo artista maduro en pleno contról de su producción y cuyo reconocimiento se ha extendido internacionalmente. El desarrollo de Arnoldi al igual el de su compinche y compañero de viajes Laddie Dill, representa un importante capítulo en la historia de la maduración de una atmósfera artística en la Costa Oeste. [pág. 5]

Charles Arnoldi, cité par Henry Hopkins, paru dans *Artnews*:

Je me suis intéressé au bois comme alternative à la peinture. J'aime tout particuliérement les branches des arbres, qui ont une qualité de ligne très distincte. Elles semblent dessinées à la main, elles ont une certaine qualité gestuelle, du naturel. Elles séduisent. En même temps, je reconnais que mon travail demande à être intégré dans une tradition pictoriale bien définie. *Volcano—Log Jam*, en rassemblant des informations de sortes différentes, fait la synthèse de ces proccupations et fournit une solution à ma quête d'un sujet. . . . [No. 1, janvier 1982/73]

Charles Arnoldi, cité par Jan Butterfield, *Charles Arnoldi, Laddie John Dill* (Fullerton: California State University, Fullerton, 1983):

Quand je pense à l'art, je pense toujours à de grands tableaux et pas à la sculpture. J'ai commencé à faire des tableaux représentant des branches d'arbres parce que, quand j'étais à l'école des beaux-arts, vous ne pouviez décemment pas peindre la peinture était morte! Aussi cherchai-je un autre moyen de faire des tableaux. J'ai employé des branches d'arbres parce que leurs lignes semblaient dessinées à la main sans que j'aie eu besoin de les dessiner moi-même. Cette attitude cadrait tout à fait avec la mentalité de la fin des années soixante et du début des années soixante-dix. Et voilà, j'obtenais cette belle ligne gestuelle, mais je ne l'avais pas tracée! Elle était, en quelque sorte, «préfabriquée». Je ne faisais que choisir des branches et composer un tableau avec leurs lignes. [p. 6]

Miles Beller, paru dans *Artweek*:

Les oeuvres de Charles Arnoldi, comme ses oeuvres précédentes, sont entièrement construites de brindilles et de branches qui forment un treillis irrégulier dans un cadre d'ensemble à peu près rectangulaire. Les branches transcendent-elles leur «vraie» fonction? Voilà une question à laquelle je trouve qu'il est difficile de répondre, car, en les regardant, je n'ai jamais complètement réussi à oublier qu'elles venaient d'un arbre. [No. 31, le 18 septembre 1976/3]

Untitled, 1972, wood branches
37 x 34", 94 x 86 cm

Suzanne Muchnic, paru dans le *Los Angeles Times*:

Charles Arnoldi, l'un des plus célèbres parmi les artistes locaux de la nouvelle génération . . . se fit remarquer, il y a quelques années par ses compositions de pièces murales de forme un peu carrée, composées de branches d'arbres. Il s'agissait de structures ouvertes et angulaires qui tiraient de matériaux naturels des jeux de formes abstraites. Plus tard, il peignit des champs de brindilles de couleur, imitant les écoles de sculpture qui utilisaient des branches, mais il ne put jamais capter l'esprit de cet art ou sa force de tension. Peut-être les sculptures de branches n'étaient-elles pas faites pour être adaptées. . . . Maintenant, voici qu'Arnoldi réapparaît, jouant sur de vieilles notes une musique toute neuve. Il travaille avec des volumes faits de branches, de blocs de bois peint et de pièces murales où se juxtaposent des toiles plates et des reliefs de branches. Dans deux sculptures placées debout et libres de toute attache—presque cubiques, elles atteignent 2m50 dans toutes les directions—il a massé des forêts de diagonales peintes, faisant ainsi descendre son art du mur et lui permettant d'occuper un espace réel, délimité par des structures linéaires. Une masse épaisse de branches, posée à même le plancher et suspendue au plafond, en position verticale, par des fils, est peinte d'un côté et laissée telle quelle de l'autre. [3 octobre 1980]

Jan Butterfield, *Charles Arnoldi, Laddie John Dill* (Fullerton: California State University, Fullerton, 1983):

En 1978 . . . les oeuvres faites de branches d'Arnoldi cessèrent d'être des pièces murales et commencèrent à assumer trois dimensions. En elles, s'entrelaçaient de tendres branches choisies avec soin, mêlées comme les rameaux d'un jeune fourré en hiver, qui n'a pas encore reçu son feuillage de printemps. Dans ces sculptures non peintes, les branches sont laissées au naturel et la personne qui les regarde s'attend à demi à en voir bondir un cerf apeuré. Aussi bien ce naturalisme a-t-il des sous-entendus romanesques, ainsi que l'a remarqué le critique Charles Kessler: «Les branches d'Arnoldi ne sont jamais un sujet neutre—elles ont une signification organique, un romanesque orienté vers la nature. . . .» Arnoldi a *peint* aussi certains de ces fourrés, leur donnant encore une autre dimension. L'influence de Pollock, évidente dans quelques-uns de ses tableaux précédents, est maintenant prépondérante. On la remarque dans la façon dont les couleurs tissent le motif choisi de façon exquise, piquant la composition d'éclairs de lumière, ainsi que l'a fait observer le critique Peter Frank: «Il [Arnoldi] a disposé les couleurs en donnant un soin tout particulier à l'interaction de leurs diverses teintes et textures, de sorte que leurs réseaux serrés semblent presque avoir été produits organiquement. Toutefois, le périmètre invariablement carré de chaque sculpture atteste le rôle joué par l'esprit et la main de l'homme.» [p. 14] . . . Le travail de Charles Arnoldi avait toujours été précis, élégant et d'une simplicité qui n'était qu'apparente. Il n'en est plus ainsi. Puissant, vibrant, gigantesque, il écrase par sa force à vif et par son coloris intense. Les brindilles soigneusement parées et peintes d'il y a quinze ans ont cédé la place à d'énormes tableaux découpés violemment dans du contre-plaqué à la scie mécanique. Arnoldi aussi a changé. L'adolescent précoce, doué d'un sens tout italien du style et du machisme, est devenu un artiste réfléchi et mûr qui sait ce qu'il veut dire et dont le renom est international. L'évolution d'Arnoldi, comme celle de son vieil ami et compagnon de route Laddie Dill, représente un chapitre important dans l'histoire du mûrissement artistique de la Côte Ouest [des Etats-Unis]. [p. 5] . . . Il est important de

**Von Charles Arnoldi zitiert von Henry Hopkins in
Artnews:**

Ich gewann Interesse an Holz als einer Alternative zur Malerei.
Ich mag besonders Äste, die eine sehr ausgeprägte Linien-
qualität haben. Sie fühlen sich handgezeichnet an, sie haben
eine gewisse gebärdenhafte Eigenschaft, eine Natürlichkeit.
Sie fühlen sich verführerisch an. Zur gleichen Zeit wird mir bewußt, daß meine Arbeit danach verlangt, Teil einer wohldefi-
nierten bildhaften Tradition zu sein. *Volcano—Log Jam*, indem
es verschiedene Arten von Informationen verbindet, repräsentiert eine Synthese dieser Aspekte. Es liefert eine Lösung für
mein Verlangen nach Gegenstandsstoff. . . . [No. 1, Januar
1982/73]

**Von Charles Arnoldi zitiert von Jan Butterfield in
Charles Arnoldi, Laddie John Dill (Fullerton:
California State University, Fullerton, 1983):**

Wenn ich an Kunst denke, denke ich immer in Begriffen von
großartigen Gemälden, nicht von Bildhauerei. Deshalb fing ich
an, Baumast;Gemälde zu machen, denn als ich auf der Kunst-
akademie war, konnte man keine Gemälde schaffen. Malerei
war tot! Daher suchte ich nach einem anderen Weg, ein Gemälde zu schaffen. Ich benutzte Äste, denn sie sahen wie ge-

zogene Linien aus, aber ich brauchte sie nicht zu zeichnen.
Diese Anschauung war völlig mit der Mentalität der späten
60er und frühen 70er Jahre vereinbar. Hier gab es diese
schöne, gebärdenhafte Linie, aber ich hatte sie nicht gezeichnet. Sie war «vorgefertigt.» Ich brauchte einfach die Äste zu
nehmen und ein Bild mit ihren Linien zu machen. [p. 6]

Von Miles Beller in *Artweek*:

Charles Arnoldis Stücke, wie seine früheren Arbeiten, sind voll-
ständig aus Zweigen und Ästen angefertigt. Sie bilden unregel-
mäßige Gitter in einer annähernd rechteckigen Form. Ob die
Äste ihre «eigentliche» Funktion übersteigen, ist eine Frage, die
ich schwer zu beantworten wußte, da mir nicht ganz aus dem
Kopf ging, daß ich auf Teile eines Baumes schaue. [No. 31,
18. September 1976/3]

Von Suzanne Muchnic in der *Los Angeles Times*:

Charles Arnoldi, einer der meistgefeierten Künstler jüngerer
Generation dieser Gegend, zeichnete sich vor ein paar Jahren
durch ziemlich eckige Wandstücke, die aus Baumästen gestal-
tet waren, aus. Es waren offene, winkelige Strukturen, die
natürliche Materialien in formale abstrakte Kunstwerke bogen.
Später malte er ganze Felder bunter Zweige, die mit den verzweigenden Strömungen der Skulptur wetteifern, aber ihrem
Geist oder ihrer Spannkraft nie gleichkommen. Es schien, daß

Installation shot
Sculpture: Branches and acrylic paint
Painting: Acrylic on canvas

die Astskulpturen nicht dazu gedacht waren, übertragen zu
werden. . . . Jetzt ist Arnoldi wieder mit denselben alten No-
ten da und brandneuer Musik. Er arbeitet mit verzweigenden
Massen, bemalten Holzklötzen und Wandstücken, die flache
Leinwände mit Reliefs von Ästen nebeneinanderstellen. In
zwei freistehenden Skulpturen—in etwa kubisch und sich
ungefähr 8 Fuß nach allen Seiten ausbreitend—hat er einen
Wald von bemalten Diagonalen zusammengehäuft, dadurch
frühere Reliefs von der Wand gerissen und Gemälde in realem
Raum, eingeschlossen von linearen Strukturen, ausgesteckt.
Ein dicker Haufen von Ästen, der auf dem Boden ruht und
durch Deckendrähte aufrecht gehalten wird, ist auf einer Seite
bemalt und auf der anderen im natürlichen Zustand.
[3. Oktober 1980]

**Aus Jan Butterfield, *Charles Arnoldi, Laddie John Dill*
(Fullerton: California State University, Fullerton, 1983):**
1978 . . . kamen Arnoldis Astschöpfungen von der Wand
herunter und fingen an, die Form dreidimensionaler Werke
anzunehmen. In ihnen verflochten sich die zarten, sorgsam
ausgewählten Äste und wurden wie jene eines jungen
Dickichts im Winter noch ohne Frühlingsgrün verwoben. Von
diesen umbemalten Skulpturen, deren Äste im natürlichen
Zustand sind, erwartet der Betrachter fast ein aufgescheuchtes
Reh, das von dessen Innern herausbricht. Dieser Naturalismus
hat auch romantische Obertöne, wie der Kritiker Charles
Kessler bemerkte: «Arnoldi's branches are never a neutral subject—they carry connotations of the organic, the nature-
directed romantic.» (Arnoldis Äste sind niemals ein neutraler
Gegenstand—sie sind verbunden mit Andeutungen von organischer, naturbezogener Romantik.) . . . Arnoldi bemalte diese
Dickichte auch, und gab ihnen damit noch eine andere
Dimension. Die Pollockschen Attribute, die in einigen der früheren Gemälde nachgewiesen sind, treten nun mit aller Macht
in den Vordergrund, während sich die Farben in fein ersonne-
nem Muster verflechten und die Schöpfung mit Lichtblitzen
zusammenheften, so wie der Kritiker Peter Frank bemerkte:
«They have been arranged with careful regard for the interaction of their various hues and textures, so that the busy networks they form seem almost to have been generated organically. The invariably square perimeter of each sculpture, however, testifies to the role of a human mind and hand.» [p. 14]
(Sie wurden mit sorgfältiger Beachtung der Wechselwirkung
der verschiedenen Farbtöne und Muster angeordnet, so daß
das geschäftige Geflecht, welches sie bilden, fast organisch
geschaffen zu sein scheint. Der unveränderlich quadratische
Umfang einer jeden Skulptur jedoch bezeugt die Rolle eines
menschlichen Sinnes und einer menschlichen Hand.) [p. 14]
. . . Charles Arnoldis Werk war immer formal, elegant und
täuschend einfach. Es ist nicht länger so. Kraftvoll, lebend, gi-
gantisch, überwältigt es mit seiner ungezügelten Kraft und intensiver Farbgebung. Seine gewissenhaft geschälten und bemalten Zweige von vor 15 Jahren haben den gewaltigen
Gemälden, aus dickem Sperrholz mit einer Kettensäge wild
herausgehauen, Platz gemacht. So hat auch Arnoldi, der früh-
reife Junge mit dem eingeborenen italienischen Sensus für
Stil und Macho, einem beschaulichen, reifen Künstler Platz
gemacht, der im völligen Besitz seiner Ausdrucksfähigkeit ist,
und dessen Anerkennung international ist. Arnoldis Entwicklung wie die seines Kollegen und Mitreisenden Laddie Dill,
stellt ein wichtiges Kapitel in der Geschichte der heranreifen-
den Kunst-Szene der Westküste dar. [p. 5]

Born: Los Angeles, California, 1939
Resides: Oakland, California

Bruce Beasley

Bruce Beasley

From _Time_:
Beasley maintains that he shifted to translucent sculptures primarily because he wanted to use "light as an element. I can't escape my work being elegant. . . . " he concedes readily that his work "looks like today. It doesn't look like any other time in history." [3 February 1968/45]

From Henry J. Seldis in the _Los Angeles Times_:
Bruce Beasley, a San Francisco artist in his early 20's, is the sort of rare, precocious talent that achieves mastery of content and technique at a remarkably early stage in a more than promising career. . . . The cast aluminum pieces are anchored to heavier metal bases but intrinsically they seem to have a floating grace without loss of a feeling of massiveness.
[3 June 1963]

From _Time_:
Newest arrival on the clear plastic scene is San Francisco's Bruce Beasley, 28, whose opulent, crystalline _Polomon_ flows sideways like a wind-whipped icicle. Beasley says he cast _Polomon_ in Du Pont's acrylic resin, Lucite, when chemical engineers said it couldn't be done—particularly not by an amateur working with two secondhand baking ovens in his Oakland backyard. So impressed was Du Pont by _Polomon_ that it has agreed to provide Beasley with a partial supply of free Lucite. [9 February 1968/45]

From Thomas Albright in the _San Francisco Chronicle_:
In Sacramento next week, a $50,000 State-commissioned sculpture of truly Michaelangelesque stature is scheduled to be raised in the center of the plaza between the new State office buildings near the Capitol. The six-and-one-half ton transparent Lucite abstraction by Oakland sculptor Bruce Beasley is as Renaissance in its heroic scale and dazzling grandeur as it is contemporary in form and material. It may well be the most magnificent public sculpture in Northern California, and is certainly among the finest anywhere. As the product of a collaboration between art and technology, architects and dispensers of public funds, it is also a milestone in the new renaissance of public art that is still in its infancy. [8 February 1970]

From _DuPont Magazine_:
"It's rare," points out Paul Mills, "when a major architectural commission coincides with a major technological advance. But Bruce Beasley's achievement in 'Lucite' is such a rarity. It's not only a brilliant esthetic accomplishment, but it also signals an important change in materials available to the artist for monumental sculpture, and a significant advance in the technical know-how of acrylic casting. . . ." The work, Beasley explains, was inspired by an artistic vision of something both massive and clear that would dramatize permutations of light and color. _Apolymon_ does exactly that with dazzling grandeur. Natural light plunges into the polished surfaces of the piece, seems to swim for a time within its lucid bulk, then bursts free from other surface areas in splashes of refracted brilliance and color. [No. 5, September/October 1970/12]

From Andree Marechal-Workman in _Artweek_:
. . . the new work is part of a universal gestalt. Made of organic material, the wood sculptures become one with the universe, like cosmic icons of the macrocosm. Governed by the natural laws of process and growth, they take on a dimension of spirituality that places them on the level of ancient arts and their philosophies, thereby bringing them within the realm of the art historical continuum. [No. 22, 20 June 1981/6]

Artemon, 1984
Stainless steel
192 × 384 × 120″
488 × 975 × 305 cm
Lent by the artist

Del semanario _Time_:

Beasley defiende que se ha pasado a las esculturas traslúcidas principalmente porque quería usar «la luz como elemento. No puedo evitar que mi trabajo sea elegante.» . . . admite fácilmente que su trabajo «parece el presente. No se asemeja a ningun otro período en la historia.» [3 de febrero de 1968/45]

De Henry J. Seldis en el _Los Angeles Times_:

Bruce Beasley, un artista veinteañero de San Francisco es el tipo de talento singular y precoz que logra el dominio del contenido y la técnica a una edad notablemente temprana hacia una carrera más que prometedora. . . . Las piezas de aluminio forjado están asentadas en bases de metal más pesado pero parecen tener una intrínseca gracia flotante sin pérdida del sentido de lo masivo. [3 de junio de 1963]

Del semanario _Time_:

La irrupción más reciente en la diáfana escena plástica es Bruce Beasley de San Francisco, de 28 años, cuyo _Polomon_ opulento y cristalino fluye oblicuamente como un carámbano castigado por el viento. Beasley dice que él forjó el _Polomon_ con resina acrílica Du Pont, lucita, cuando los ingenieros químicos afirmaban que esto no podía llevarse a cabo—en particular no por un aficionado que trabaja con dos hornos de cocción de segunda mano en su patio de Oakland. Tan impresionada estaba la compañía Du Pont con su _Polomon_ que acordó suministrar a Beasley una cantidad parcial de lucita gratuitamente. [9 de febrero de 1968/45]

De Thomas Albright en el _San Francisco Chronicle_:

La próxima semana en Sacramento, está programado que una escultura de 50.000 dólares subvencionada por el estado de calidad realmente miguelangelesca sea elevada en el centro de la plaza que está entre la nueva oficina del Estado cerca del Capitolio. Esta abstracción de lucita transparente de seis toneladas y media de peso del escultor de Oakland Bruce Beasley es tanto renacentista en su escala heróica y grandiosidad deslumbradora como contemporáneo en forma y material. Es posible que sea la escultura pública más grandiosa del Norte de California y es ciertamente una de las más hermosas. Producto de la cooperación entre arte y tecnología, entre arquitectos y administradores de fondos públicos, es un hito en el nuevo renacimiento del arte público que todavía se encuentra en eclosión. [8 de febrero de 1970]

De _DuPont Magazine_:

«Es raro,» señala Paul Mills, «que una comisión arquitectónica de primer orden coincida con un avance tecnológico importante. Pero el logro de Bruce Beasley en su ‹Lucita› constituye una rareza semejante. No sólo se trata de un brillante logro estético, sino que también marca el camino de un importante cambio en los materiales disponibles al artista para el trabajo con esculturas monumentales y un significativo avance en la manipulación técnica de la forja acrílica. . . .» La obra, explica Beasley, fué inspirada por una visión artística de algo tanto masivo como diáfano que dramatizaría las permutaciones de luz y color. El _Apolymon_ alcanza exactamente eso con inigualable grandeza. La luz natural se sumerge en las pulidas superficies de la pieza y parece nadar temporalmente en su reluciente masa, luego se libera de otras superficies salpicando brillo y color refractados. [No. 5, septiembre/octubre de 19/0/12]

De Andree Marechal-Workman en _Artweek_:

. . . la nueva obra es parte de una Gestalt universal. Hecha de material orgánico, la escultura de madera se funde con el universo, como iconos cósmicos del macrocosmos. Gobernadas estas esculturas por las leyes naturales del proceso y del crecimiento, adquieren una dimensión de espiritualidad que las coloca al nivel del arte antiguo y de su filosofía, llevándolas de este modo al dominio del continuum del arte histórico. [No. 22, 20 de junio de 1981/6]

Vascone, 1965 , cast aluminum
43" high, 109 cm

Extrait du *Time*:

Beasley soutient qu'il s'est mis à faire des sculptures translucides surtout parce qu'il voulait utiliser «la lumière comme élément. Je ne peux empêcher que mon travail soit élégant. . . .» Il concède volontiers que son oeuvre «ressemble à notre époque. Elle n'évoque aucune autre période de l'histoire.» [3 février 1968/45]

Henry J. Seldis dans le *Los Angeles Times*:

Bruce Beasley, un artiste de San Francisco d'une vingtaine d'années, offre l'exemple d'un talent précoce parvenu à maîtriser le fond et la technique de son art très tôt dans une carrière qui s'annonce plus que prometteuse. . . . Les pièces coulées en aluminium sont amarrées à des bases de métal plus lourd, mais intrinsèquement, elles semblent douées d'une sorte de grâce qui les fait flotter sans pour autant cesser d'être massives. [3 juin 1963]

Extrait du *Time*:

Bruce Beasley, 28 ans, est un nouveau venu sur la scène du plastique transparent à San Francisco. Son *Polomon* opulent, cristallin coule latéralement comme un glaçon auquel le vent aurait donné sa forme. Beasley dit qu'il a coulé *Polomon* en Lucite, une résine acrylique produite par Du Pont alors que les ingénieurs chimistes avaient déclaré que la chose était impossible à réaliser, en particulier par un amateur travaillant avec deux fours achetés d'occasion, dans son jardin à Oakland. Du Pont fut si impressionné par *Polomon* que la firme a accepté de fournir gratuitement une partie de la Lucite dont Beasley a besoin. [9 février 1968/45]

Thomas Albright dans le *San Francisco Chronicle*:

A Sacramento, le semaine prochaine, une sculpture de 50.000 dollars commandée par l'Etat [de Californie] et de dimensions proprement «michelangelesques» va être installée sur la place située entre les nouveaux bâtiments du gouvernement, à côté du Capitole. Cette sculpture abstraite de six

tonnes et demie, exécutée en Lucite transparente par le sculpteur d'Oakland Bruce Beasley, évoque la Renaissance par sa taille héroïque et son éblouissante splendeur, aussi bien que notre époque par sa forme et le matériau dont elle est composée. C'est peut-être la sculpture publique la plus magnifique en Californie du Nord et elle est à classer parmi les plus belles où que ce soit. En tant que produit de la collaboration entre l'art et la technologie, entre les architectes et les répartisseurs des fonds de la caisse publique, elle représente aussi une nouvelle étape de la récente renaissance de l'art populaire, qui en est encore aux balbutiements de l'enfance. [8 février 1970]

Apolymon, 1967–70 , cast acrylic
108 x 180", 274 x 457 cm
Collection: State of California

Extrait de *DuPont Magazine*:

«Il est rare,» souligne Paul Mills, «qu'une commande architecturale majeure coïncide avec un progrès technique majeur, cependant, c'est ce que Bruce Beasley est parvenu à réaliser. Son oeuvre n'est pas seulement une brillante réussite esthétique, elle marque un tournant important dans le choix des matériaux dont disposent les artistes de sculptures monumentales et un progrès significatif accompli dans la technique du moulage acrylique. . . .» Ce travail, explique Beasley, lui fut inspiré par la vision artistique de quelque chose devant être à la fois massif et transparent et qui mettrait en valeur les permutations de lumière et de couleur. *Apolymon* accomplit cela de façon éblouissante. La lumière du jour plonge dans les surfaces polies de la pièce, semble se baigner pour un temps dans sa masse lumineuse, puis ressurgit plus loin en éclaboussures de lumière réfractée et de couleur. [No. 5, septembre/octobre 1970/12]

Andrée Maréchal-Workman dans *Artweek*:

. . . cette oeuvre nouvelle fait partie d'une «gestalt» uni verselle. Etant faites d'un matériau organique, les sculptures en bois en viennent à n'en faire plus qu'un avec l'univers, comme si elles étaient des icônes cosmiques du macrocosme. Gouvernées par les lois naturelles de gestation et de croissance, elles y gagnent une dimension de spiritualité qui les met au niveau des arts anciens et de leurs philosophies, s'intégrant ainsi au continuum historique de l'art. [No. 22, 20 juin 1981/6]

Aus *Time*:
Beasley besteht darauf, daß er in erster Linie auf lichtdurch-
lässige Skulpturen umgesattelt ist, weil er «Licht als Element»
benutzen wollte. «Ich kann nicht vermeiden, daß mein Werk
elegant ist. . . .» Er gibt bereitwillig zu, daß sein Werk «wie
das Heute aussieht. Es sieht nicht wie ein anderer Zeitpunkt in
der Gesichichte aus.» [3. Februar 1968/45]

Von Henry J. Seldis in der *Los Angeles Times*:
Bruce Beasley, ein San Francisco Künstler, Anfang 20, ist
eines dieser seltenen frühreifen Talente, die Meisterschaft des
Inhalts und der Technik in einem bemerkenswert frühen Sta-
dium einer vielversprechenden Karriere erreichen. . . . Die
Guß-Aluminium Stücke sind in schweren Metall-Sockeln verankert, aber im wesentlichen scheinen sie eine fließende
Grazie zu haben ohne Verlust eines Gefühls des Massiven.
[3. Juni 1963]

Aus *Time*:
Der letzte Ankömmling auf der klaren-Plastik-Szene ist San
Franciscos Bruce Beasley, 28, dessen luxuriöser, kristalliner
Polomon seitwärts fließt wie ein im Wind gepeitschter Eis-
zapfen. Beasley sagt, er goß *Polomon* in Du Ponts Akryl-Harz,
Luzit, als Chemiker sagten, das ließe sich nicht machen—vor
allem nicht von einem Amateur, der mit zwei gebrauchten
Brennöfen in seinem Oakland Hinterhof arbeitete. De Pont war
so beeindruckt von *Polomon*, daß sie zugestimmt haben,
Beasley mit einer unentgeltlichen Lieferung von Luzit zu
versehen. [9. Februar 1968/45]

Von Thomas Albright im *San Francisco Chronicle*:
Nächste Woche soll in Sacramento eine $50000-, vom Staat
in Auftrag gegebene Skulptur von wahrhaft Michelangelo-
Ausmaßen im Zentrum des Platzes zwischen den neuen
Staatsverwaltungsgebäuden in der Nähe des Capitols errichtet
werden. Die sechseinhalb Tonnen schwere transparente Luzit-
Abstraktion von Oaklands Bildhauer Bruce Beasley ist genauso
eine Renaissance in ihren heroischen Ausmaßen und blendender Herrlichkeit, wie sie zeitgenössisch ist in Form und Material. Es mag wohl die prachtvollste öffentliche Skulptur in
Nordkalifornien sein und ist gewiß eine der schönsten überhaupt. Als Produkt einer Zusammenarbeit von Kunst und
Technologie, Architektur und Verteilern von öffentlichen
Geldern ist es auch ein Meilenstein in der neuen Renaissance von öffentlicher Kunst, die noch in den Kinderschuhen
steckt. [8. Februar 1970]

Aus *DuPont Magazine*:
«Es ist selten,» hebt Paul Mills hervor, «daß eine größere architektonische Aufgabe mit einem größeren technologischen
Fortschritt zusammenfällt. Aber Bruce Beasleys Leistung in
«Lucite» ist eine derartige Seltenheit. Es ist nicht nur eine bril-
liante ästhetische Vollendung, sondern kündigt auch einen
wichtigen Wechsel in den vorhandenen Materialien an, die
dem Künstler für monumentale Skulpturen zur Verfügung
stehen, und einen bedeutsamen Fortschritt in technischem
Wissen über Akrylguß. . . .» Das Werk, erklärt Beasley, wurde
von einer künstlerischen Vision von etwas Massivem und
Klaren inspiriert, die beide Permutationen von Licht und Farbe
dramatisieren. *Apolymon* tut genau das mit blendender Herrlichkeit. Tageslicht stürzt in die polierte Fläche des Stückes,
scheint eine Zeit lang innerhalb seiner leuchtenden Masse zu
schwimmen und bricht dann frei von den anderen Oberflächen
in Lichtflecken von gebrochener Brillanz und Farbe. [No. 5,
September/Oktober 1970/12]

Von Andree Marechal-Workman in *Artweek*:
. . . das neue Werk ist Teil einer universalen Gestalt. Aus orga-
nischem Material gemacht, werden die Holzskulpturen eins mit
dem Universum wie kosmische Figuren des Makrokosmos.
Beherrscht von natürlichen Gesetzen von Vorgang und Wachs-
tum, nehmen sie eine Dimension von Spiritualität an, die sie
auf die Ebene antiker Kunst und deren Philosophie stellt und
sie damit in das Reich des kunsthistorischen Kontinuums
bringt. [No. 22, 2&. Juni 1981/6]

Scalar Gyration, 1972, cast acrylic
23" high, 54 cm

Born: Jackson, Ohio, 1931
Resides: San Francisco, California

Fletcher Benton

Fletcher Benton

From press release, The Oakland Museum:
"Every artist works within certain limits," Benton says, "and these are mine. I've got to cut into the shapes, deal with them—and an arc is always there, or a straight edge. I find those challenges exciting. . . . It would be too easy for me not to have limits and just stick pieces of metal together, but that's not something I'm interested in. . . ."

From Peter Selz, _Fletcher Benton_ (La Jolla: La Jolla Museum of Contemporary Art, 1972):
His moving objects have somehow remained in that borderland between painting and sculpture, if, indeed, these traditional classifications have much meaning in an art which transpires in time. Whether he works with disks that revolve to create changing geometric designs (as in his early pieces), or with moiré patterns which he sees as visual equivalents to Doppler's sound effect, or with transparent color overlays, Fletcher Benton essentially remains on the plane, even if the framework of his crystalline pieces has consistently become more sculptural.

In much of his work he uses moving transparent plexiglass panels of color, which slide past each other and overlap, producing constantly changing and totally unexpected mixtures of color. Making use of sophisticated technology and, in fact, emphasizing the technical aspect in the appearance of his shiny stainless steel pieces, Fletcher Benton fuses color and movement into unique windows of joy and delight.

From Diane Ghiraro Burke, _Fletcher Benton, Selected Works 1964-74_ (Santa Clara: deSaisset Art Gallery and Museum, 1974):
Indeed, Benton could be considered the colorist of the Kinetic Movement. His early color works . . . are strikingly similar to the works of the colorists Morris Louis, Gene Davis, and Kenneth Noland, but with the important difference that in Benton's works, color change is not virtual but actual. Benton indicates that he was also influenced by the color studies of [Josef] Albers, and by the work of Malevich. The influence of the latter is perhaps most apparent in Benton's new paintings, shown here for the first time, which combine Malevich's Constructivist use of space with Benton's own Constructivist tendencies. . . . Despite the obvious three-dimensionality of the sculpture body in the early transparent works, Benton considers them almost more painting than sculpture, because they are viewed from essentially only one perspective.

From Jan Butterfield in _Art International_:
In 1978 Benton "discovered" stainless steel—an interesting phenomenon in and of itself, since he had been utilizing it all along as a casting for his kinetic works where, clean and machined, it served as a framing device for his technological art. Now, looking at the material with new eyes, Benton began to attack the steel, cutting, gouging, and burnishing it, handling it roughly and directly, rather than with kid gloves as he had previously done with the bronze. The result is the remarkable new _Folded Square_ or _Alphabet Series_ sculptures which represent a major breakthrough.

Bold, strong, the new works have an impeccable sense of balance and gravity. Their geometric, linear and curvilinear elements extend out of, fold into and zig zag around their sculptural forms, lending a delicate, drawing-like quality to some of their angles which provides the harmony for their full orchestration. [No. 3-4, November-December 1980/ 126–128]

From Allan Temko in the _San Francisco Sunday Examiner & Chronicle_:
The Oakland Museum's show of "folded circles" and "folded squares" (the squares are not pure abstractions, but alphabetic letters found in the geometry) reveal Benton as a superb metalsmith, as well as an extraordinary polisher, grinder, and painter of metal surfaces. . . . Nothing in this part of the world excels the machined brilliance of these objects. . . . But Platonic perfection on that order is not the intent of Benton's art. He is interested in the nature of forms for their own sake, and in the delightful surprises—literally unexpected spatial treasures—that he can extract from cut-up metal sheets. [30 March 1980/36]

Balanced/Unbalanced Wheels, 1982
Painted steel
360 × 336 × 84"
914 × 853 × 213 cm
Lent by the artist

Del boletín del Museo de Oakland:

«Todo artista trabaja dentro de ciertos límites,» indica Benton, «y éstos son los mios. Tengo que cortar las formas, manejarlas—y siempre hay un arco o un borde recto a desafiar. Estos desafíos los encuentro emocionantes. . . . Sería demasiado fácil para mí no tener límites y simplemente juntar piezas de metal, pero no estoy interesado en eso. . . .»

De Peter Selz, *Fletcher Benton* (La Jolla: Museo de Arte Contemporáneo de La Jolla, 1972):

Sus objetos en movimiento han permanecido de alguna manera en al frontera entre la pintura y la escultura, si es cierto que estas clasificaciones tradicionales tienen algún significado en un arte que transciende el tiempo. Ya trabaje con discos giratorios para crear diseños geométricos cambiantes (como sus primeras obras), o con estructuras moaré que él vislumbra como equivalentes visuales a los efectos sonoros de Doppler, o con capas de colores transparentes, Fletcher Benton permanece esencialmente en el plano, aunque el marco de sus piezas cristalinas se haya hecho consistentemente más escultórico.

En muchas de sus obras usa paneles de plexiglás coloreado transparentes y en movimiento, que se deslizan y se sobreponen unos a otros, creando mezclas de color totalmente inesperadas y constantemente cambiantes. Haciendo uso de una tecnología sofisticada y, de hecho, enfatizando el aspecto técnico en la presencia de sus brillantes piezas de acero inoxidable, Fletcher Benton funde el color y el movimiento en efusiones únicas de alegría y de encanto.

De Diane Ghiraro Burke, *Fletcher Benton, Obras Escogidas 1964–74* (Santa Clara: Galería y Museo deSaisset, 1974):

En efecto, Benton podría ser considerado el colorista del Movimiento Kinético. Su obra temprana . . . es sorprendentemente similar a las obras de los coloristas Morris Louis, Gene Davis, y Kenneth Noland, pero con la importante diferencia de que en las obras de Benton, el cambio de color no es virtual sino real. Benton señala que también fue influído por los estudios del color de Josef Albers, y por la obra de Malevich. La influencia de este último es quizá más patente en las nuevas pinturas de Benton, que se exhiben aquí por primera vez, las cuales combinan el uso constructivista del espacio de Male-

vich con las propias tendencias constructivistas de Benton. . . . A pesar de la obvia tridimensionalidad del cuerpo escultórico en sus primeras obras transparentes, Benton las considera casi más pictóricas que escultóricas, porque son vistas esencialmente desde una única perspectiva.

De Jan Butterfield en *Art International*:

En 1978 Benton «descubrió» el acero inoxidable—un fenómeno interesante en sí mismo—puesto que lo había estado utilizando como material de forja para sus obras kinéticas en las que, limpio y labrado, sirvió como material de marco en su arte tecnológico. Ahora bien, al contemplar el material con nuevos ojos, Benton empezó a atacar el acero, cortándolo, estriándolo, puliéndolo y manejándolo de forma tosca y directa, a diferencia de su previo trabajo con bronce realizado con exquisita finura. El resultado son las magníficas nuevas esculturas *Folded Square* o *Alphabet Series* que representan un avance sustancial.

Osadas y fuertes, las nuevas obras poseen un impecable sentido de equilibrio y gravedad. Sus elementos geométricos, lineales y curvilíneos se extienden, se doblan y zigzaguean por sus formas escultóricas, dotándolas de una cualidad delicada, como de dibujo a algunos de sus ángulos, la cual armoniza su plena orquestación. [No. 3-4, noviembre-diciembre 1980/ 126–28]

De Allan Temko en el *San Francisco Sunday Examiner & Chronicle*:

La exposición del Museo de Oakland de «círculos plegados» y «cuadrados plegados» (los cuadrados no son puras abstracciones, sino letras alfabéticas que se encuentran en la geometría) revela a Benton como un soberbio artista del metal, asi como un extraordinario pulidor, esmerilador y pintor de superficies metálicas. . . . No hay nada en esta parte del mundo que sobrepase el brillo labrado de estos objetos. . . . Pero la perfección platónica a ese nivel no es la meta del arte de Benton. El está interesado en la naturaleza misma de las formas, y en las maravillosas sorpresas—tesoros espaciales literalmente inesperados—que él puede extraer de láminas de metal cortadas. [30 de marzo de 1980/36]

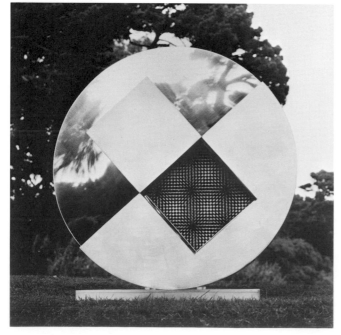

500 Squares, 1973, stainless steel
31 x 31", 79 x 79 cm

Communiqué du Mueée d'Oakland:

«Chaque artiste fixe à son travail des limites qu'il ne doit pas dépasser,» dit Benton, «voici les miennes. Je dois découper à l'intérieur du Musée d'Oakland de «cercles repliés» et et je rencontre toujours un arc ou un bord. J'aime avoir à vaincre ces difficultés. Je les trouve stimulantes. . . . Il serait trop facile de ne pas me fixer de limites et de me contenter d'assembler des morceaux de métal, mais ce n'est pas ce qui m'intéresse. . . .»

Peter Selz, *Fletcher Benton* (La Jolla, Musée d'Art Contemporain de La Jolla, 1972):

Ses objets mouvants appartiennent à un domaine intermédiaire entre la peinture et la sculpture, s'il est vrai que ces classifications traditionnelles signifient quelque chose quand on parle d'un art qui a une dimension temporelle. Qu'il travaille avec des disques qui tournent sur eux-mêmes pour créer des figures géométriques changeantes (comme dans ses premières oeuvres), ou avec des motifs donnant l'illusion de la moire, en lesquels il voit l'équivalent visuel de l'effet Doppler pour le son, ou encore avec des couches superposées de couleurs transparentes, Fletcher Benton travaille essentiellement dans la plat, même si le cadre de ses pièces cristallines devient de plus en plus sculptural.

Dans la plupart de ses oeuvres, il emploie des panneaux de plexiglace transparent et teinté qui glissent les uns sur les autres et se recoupent pour produire des mélanges de couleurs sans cesse renouvelés et tout à fait inattendus. Tirant parti d'une technologie sophistiquée dont il accentue la technicité en attirant l'attention sur l'éclat des éléments d'acier inoxydables, Fletcher Benton fait fusionner couleur et mouvement et crée un spectacle unique et enchanteur.

Diane Ghiraro Burke, *Fletcher Benton, Selected Works 1964–74* (Santa Clara: deSaisset Art Gallery and Museum, 1974):

Benton pourrait certainement être considéré comme le coloriste du Mouvement Cinétique. Ses premières oeuvres en couleur . . . ressemblent d'une manière frappante aux oeuvres des coloristes Morris Louis, Gene Davis et Kenneth Noland, à cette différence près—et elle est d'importance—que dans les oeuvres de Benton les changements de couleur ne sont pas virtuels mais réels. Benton dit lui-même qu'il a aussi été influencé par les études de couleurs de Josef Albers, et par l'oeuvre de Malevich. L'influence de ce dernier est peut-être plus sensible dans les nouvelles peintures de Benton, exposées ici pour la première fois et qui combinent l'exploitation constructiviste de l'espace de Malevich avec les propres tendances constructivistes de Benton. . . . En depit du fait que la masse de la sculpture, dans les premières oeuvres transparentes, est très visiblement en trois dimensions, Benton considère celles-ci plus comme des oeuvres de peinture que comme des sculptures parce qu'elles ne se regardent que d'une seule perspective.

Jan Butterfield dans *Art International*:

En 1978, Benton «découvrit» l'acier inoxydable—phénomène intéressant en soi si l'on considère qu'il l'employait déjà au moulage de ses oeuvres cinétiques dans lesquelles, parce qu'il est net et usiné, il servait au cadrage de ses oeuvres technologiques. En 1978, regardant ce matériau d'un oeil nouveau, Benton se mit à le travailler, le coupant, le creusant et le satinant. Son approche fut rude et directe au lieu d'être délicate, comme elle l'avait été pour le bronze. Le résultat fut les sculptures appelées *Folded Square* ou *Alphabet Series* qui représentent une première importante.

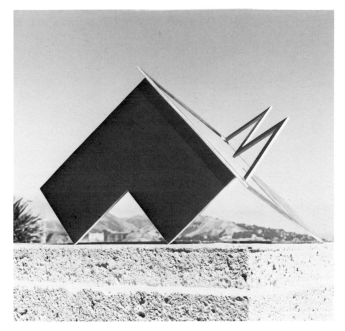

Audacieuses, puissantes ces nouvelles oeuvres ont un sens impeccable de l'équilibre et de la pesanteur. Leurs éléments géométriques, linéaires et curvilignes tour à tour se déploient et se replient en zig-zag autour de leurs formes sculpturales et prêtent une fragilité qui tient du dessin à certains de leurs angles, orchestrant ainsi harmonieusement l'ensemble. [No. 3-4, novembre-décembre 1980/126–28]

Allan Temko dans le *San Francisco Sunday Examiner & Chronicle*:

L'exposition du cadre que je me suis donné, en tenir compte— «carrés repliés» (les carrés ne sont pas de pures abstractions, mais des lettres de l'alphabet trouvées dans la géométrie) révèle en Benton un artiste doué pour le travail du métal, aussi bien qu'un polisseur, un rectifieur et un peintre des surfaces métalliques. . . . L'éclat des surfaces usinées de ces objets n'a pas son égal dans cette partie du monde. . . . Toutefois, l'art de Benton n'est pas à la recherche de la perfection platonicienne. Ce qui l'intéresse, ce sont les formes elles-mêmes et les délicieuses surprises—véritables trésors inattendus, nés des volumes—qu'il est capable d'extraire de feuilles de métal découpées. [30 mars 1980/36]

Folded Square, Alphabet M, 1978, painted aluminum
20 x 20, 51 x 51 cm

Von der Nachrichtenpresse The Oakland Museum:
«Jeder Künstler arbeitet innerhalb gewisser Grenzen,» sagt
Benton, «und diese sind meine. Ich muß in Formen schneiden,
mit ihnen arbeiten—und ein Bogen ist immer da oder eine
gradlinige Kante. Ich finde jene Herausforderungen aufregend.
. . . Es wäre für mich einfach, keine Grenzen zu haben und
einfach Metallstücke zusammenzustecken, aber das ist nicht
etwas, woran ich interessiert bin. . . .»

**Aus Peter Selz, *Fletcher Benton* (La Jolla: La Jolla
Museum of Contemporary Art, 1972):**
Seine beweglichen Gegenstände sind irgendwo in jenem
Grenzland zwischen Malerei und Bildhauerei geblieben, falls in
der Tat diese traditionellen Klassifizierungen in einer Kunst,
welche Zeiten durchfließt, viel Bedeutung haben. Ob er mit
Scheiben arbeitet, die sich drehen, um wechselnde geometrische Entwürfe zu schaffen (wie in seinen frühen Stücken),
oder mit Flammenmustern, die er als visuelles Equivalent zum
Doppler-Effekt ansieht, oder mit durchsichtigen Folien arbeitet,
bleibt Fletcher Benton im wesentlichen auf der Ebene, wenn
auch der Rahmen seiner kristallinen Stücke ständig skulptur-
hafter geworden ist.

   In vielen seiner Werke benutzt er durchsichtige Plexiglas-
Farbplatten, die aneinander vorbeigleiten und sich überlappen
und dabei ständig wechselnde und gänzlich unerwartete
Farbmischungen produzieren. Indem er hochentwickelte Technologie benutzt und tatsächlich die technischen Aspekte in der
Erscheinung seiner glänzenden rostfreien Stahlstücke hervorhebt, verschmilzt Fletcher Benton Farbe und Bewegung in
einzigartige Fenster von Freude und Vergügen.

**Aus Diane Ghiraro Burke, *Fletcher Benton, Selected
Works 1964-74* (Santa Clara: deSaisset Art Gallery
and Museum, 1974):**
In der Tat kann Benton als der Farbkünstler der Kinetischen
Bewegung angesehen werden. Seine frühen Farbwerke . . .
sind den Arbeiten der Farbkünstler Morris Louis, Gene Davis
und Kenneth Noland auffallend ähnlich, nur mit dem wesentlichen Unterschied, daß in Bentons Werken die Farbänderung
nicht eigentlich, sondern tatsächlich ist. Benton deutet an, daß
er auch von den Farbstudien von Josef Albers und von dem
Werk Malevichs beeinflußt wurde. Der Einfluß des letzteren ist
vielleicht am deutlichsten in Bentons neuen Gemälden, die hier
zum erstenmal gezeigt werden und die Malevichs konstruktivistischen Gebrauch des Raumes mit Bentons eigenen konstruktivistischen Neigungen verbinden. . . . Trotz der offensichtlichen Dreidimensionalität des Skulpturkörpers in den
frühen transparenten Werken, hält Benton sie eher für ein
Gemälde als eine Skulptur, weil sie im wesentlichen nur aus
einer Perspektive betrachtet werden.

Von Jan Butterfield in *Art International*:
1978 «entdeckte» Benton rostfreien Stahl—ein interessantes
Phänomen in sich selbst, da er ihn schon andauernd als
Gußstück für seine kinetischen Arbeiten benutzt hatte, wo er
rein und bearbeitet als Rahmen für seine technologischen
Kunst diente. Nun, indem er das Material mit neuen Augen be-
trachtete, begann Benton den Stahl in Angriff zu nehmen, zu
schneiden, auszuhöhlen und zu polieren, damit rauh und direkt umzugehen, nicht mit Glacéhandschuhen, wie er es vorher mit der Bronze getan hatte. Das Ergebnis sind die *Folded
Square* oder die *Alphabet Series* Skulpturen, die einen großen
Durchbruch darstellen.

   Kühn, stark haben die neuen Werke einen unfehlbaren
Sinn für Gleichgewicht und Schwerkraft. Ihre geometrischen,

linearen und krummlinigen Elemente reichen aus, falten sich in
und legen sich im Zick-Zack um ihre skulpturhaften Formen,
verleihen einigen ihrer Winkel eine zarte, zeichnungsähnliche
Eigenschaft, welche die Harmonie für deren volle Orchestrie-
rung zu Verfügung stellt. [No. 3-4, November-Dezember
1980/126-128]

**Von Allan Temko im *San Francisco Sunday Examiner
& Chronicle*:**
Die Oakland Museum Ausstellung der «gefalteten Kreise» und
«gefalteten Vierecke» (die Vierecke sind keine bloßen Abstrak-
tionen, sondern alphabetische Buchstaben aus der Geometrie)
stellen Benton als einen hervorragenden Metallschmied wie
auch einen ausgezeichneten Polierer, Schleifer und Maler me-
tallener Oberflächen heraus. . . . Nichts in diesem Teil der
Welt übertrifft den bearbeiteten Glanz dieser Objekte. . . . Aber
platonische Vollendung dieser Größenordnung ist nicht die
Absicht von Bentons Kunst. Er ist interessiert an der Natur der
Formen ihrer selbst wegen und an den entzückenden Über-
raschungen—buchstäblich unerwartete räumliche Schätze—,
die er den zerschnittenen Metallbögen entziehen kann.
[30. März 1980/36]

Folded Circle, Two Squares, 1982, Cor-ten steel
96 x 96", 244 x 244 cm

Born: Duval County, Florida, 1946
Resides: Venice, California

Guy Dill

Guy Dill

From William Packer in *Art and Artists*:
Packer: Along with the weight of the material you use, there seems to be a very conscious pre-occupation with holding elements in tension, one against another, either suspending or springing them against each other.
Dill: Well, energy is important. Because things rest upon one another, there is real energy in play—which is why I wasn't satisfied with painting. It didn't seem a real situation. Painting is real on another plane. The intrinsic energy that is going on in these pieces is important . . . perhaps. [No. 8, November 1972/38–43]

From press release, Ivory/Kimpton Gallery, San Francisco:
Dill's sculpture is taut and dramatic because of his multi-leveled use of juxtaposition: the rough edge of marble against the geometric right angle variatons of wood, and rounds of fabricated steel or iron. In earlier work, he played the weight of wood timbers against angled planes of glass, creating tension more from the placement of materials, rather than from the kinds used.

Spatially, Dill's work has evolved from occupying a three-dimensional area, and now tends to line up on a singular plane. There is a graphic quality, an incised edge drawn with the shapes. In his new Milwood series, the snaggy lines of marble form a skyline or silhouette. The linear, almost pictorial feel to Dill's recent work hints at his beginnings as a painter, as does his color play—warm tones of wood or marble contrasting with the greys and blacks of steel and iron. [May 1980]

From Peter Plagens in *Artforum*:
If it counts for much anymore, GUY DILL is the most consistent sculptor around: inventive, craftsmanlike, elegant, and reasonably witty. . . . They're sculptures, all right, in the old sense: permanent (although disassemblable), slick (the pillars are subtly rough smooth, colored uncolored, the metal walls deftly corroded), big within room limits, precious (the glass looks so *costly*), and architectonic. [No. 8, April 1974/83–84]

From Edit deAk in *Art in America*:
Dill's most evident theme is calculated stress and tension between three materials: cast concrete, sheet metal and plate glass. The pieces are variations on or conglomerates of frontal, freestanding forms composed usually of two vertical cement slabs flanking rectangular sheets of glass and/or metal. The component between the two cement pillars is either aligned to connect them or is rotated around a central axis to make an open, diagonal configuration. He uses the materials in a way which often contradicts their "normal" properties. Glass appears burdened with the weight of heavy metal, and slim columns seem to support entire post-and-lintel configurations, whose balance seems dependent on a dangerously small floor area. . . . His sculptures' almost indecent beauty is generated largely from aspects which can't be structurally justified, such as slight nonfunctional embellishments of shape or the soft, faded colors which were mixed into the concrete. Applying "cosmetics" to a basically purist style indicates a new kind of esthetic decision—albeit a peculiarly nonaggressive, easygoing one. [No. 2, March 1974/106]

From Melinda Wortz in *Artnews*:
The presentation—a number of flat (as opposed to volumetric) shapes affixed together, rather than carved from a single

monolith—is consciously derived from Constructivism. The long, horizontal flow of shapes across the floor alludes to abstract landscape as well as purist, nonobjective form.

Landscape allusions seem more explicit in a third large floor piece carved from white Grecian marble, presented in two horizontal sections, one behind the other, resting on a marble base. The anterior piece consists of two sections of angular, geometric, smoothly finished marble, while the posterior grouping of three is uneven at the top. Leaving the edges of the upper ridge unfinished, the artist reveals the process of working with marble before it is smoothly polished. In the context of white marble the reference to process recalls Michelangelo, while the obvious sectionalism of the piece also allies it with the more recent Constructivist tradition. [No. 8, October 1978/39–40]

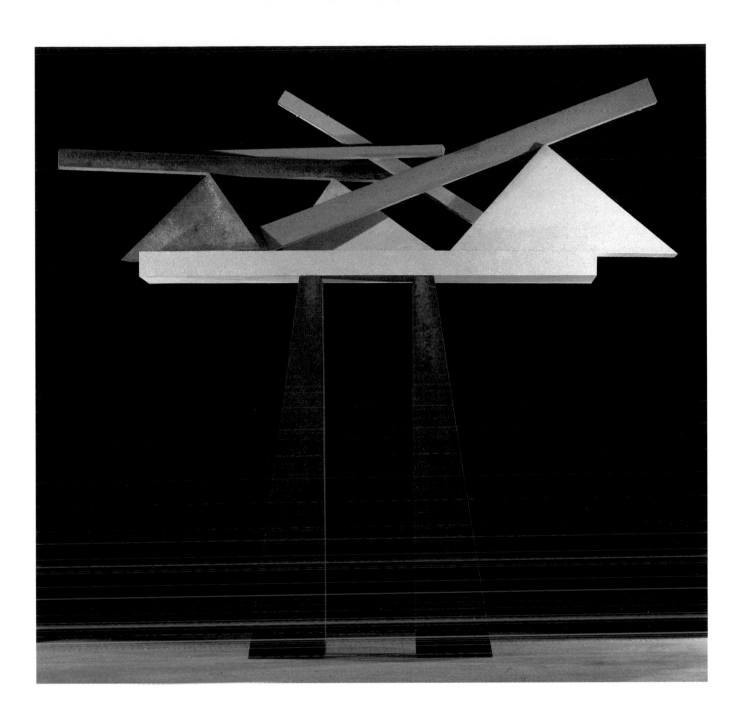

Siduri, 1983
Cast reinforced pigmented concrete
132 × 114 × 48″
335 × 290 × 122 cm
Lent by the artist and Flow Ace Gallery

De William Packer en *Arte y Artistas*:

Packer: Junto al peso del material que Vd. utiliza, parece tener una preocupación muy consciente por mantener los elementos en tensión, en oposición unos con otros, ya suspendiéndolos ya enfrentándolos.

Dill: Bueno, la energía es importante. Debido a que las cosas descansan unas sobre otras, hay una energía real en acción—que es precisamente la razón por la que no estaba satisfecho con la pintura. No parecía una situación real. La pintura es real a otro nivel. La energía intrínseca que se manifiesta en estas piezas es importante . . . tal vez. [No. 8, noviembre de 1972/38–43]

Del boletín de prensa de la Galería Ivory/Kimpton, San Francisco:

La escultura de Dill es tensa y dramática debido al variado uso de la yuxtaposición: el áspero borde del mármol contra las variaciones geométricas en ángulo recto de la madera y círculos de hierro o de acero prefabricado. En sus obras anteriores, jugó con el peso de trozos de madera contra planos angulados de vidrio, creando una tensión que proviene más de la colocación de los materiales que del tipo de materiales empleados.

En el plano espacial, la obra de Dill ha evolucionado de ocupar un área tridimensional a la tendencia a alinearse en un solo plano. Hay una cualidad gráfica, un borde incisivo dibujado con las formas. En su nueva serie Milwood, las líneas irregulares de mármol forman un horizonte o silueta. El sentido lineal, cuasi-pictórico de la obra reciente de Dill apunta a sus comienzos como pintor, como también su juego cromático—cálidos tonos de madera o mármol que contrastan con los grises y negros del hierro y del acero. [Mayo de 1980]

De Peter Plagens en *Artforum*:

Por si tiene relevancia, GUY DILL es el escultor más consistente en la actualidad: inventivo, artesanal, elegante y razonablemente ingenioso. . . . Son, desde luego, esculturas en el sentido tradicional: permanentes (aunque desmontables), pulidas (los pilares son sutilmente áspero-lisos, coloroincoloros, y las paredes metálicas hábilmente oxidadas), grandes pero dentro de los límites de una sala, preciosas (el vidrio parece tan *caro*), y arquitectónicas. [No. 8, abril de 1974/83–84]

De Edit deAk en *Arte en América*:

El tema más evidente de Dill es la presión y tensión precalcladas entre tres materiales: cemento armado, lámina de metal y vidrio cilindrado. Las piezas son variaciones o conglomerados de formas frontales y libres, compuestas normalmente de dos losas verticales de cemento, que flanquean a láminas rectangulares de vidrio y/o metal. El componente entre las dos columnas de cemento está elineado para servir de conexión o gira alrededor de un eje central para lograr una configuración abierta y diagonal. El artista usa los materiales de tal forma que a menudo contradice sus propiedades «normales». El vidrio aparece sobrecargado con el peso del metal, y las delgadas columnas parecen servir de apoyo a configuraciones enteras de poste y dintel, cuyo equilibrio parece depender de un área del suelo peligrosamente pequeña. . . . La belleza casi indecente de sus esculturas se genera principalmente a partir de aspectos que no pueden ser justificados estructuralmente, tales como los adornos ligeramente afuncionales de la figura o los colores suaves y difuminados que fueron mezclados con el cemento. La aplicación de la «cosmética» a un estilo básicamente purista, indica un nuevo tipo de decisión estética—si bien una peculiarmente pacífica, y relajada. [No. 2, marzo de 1974/106]

De Melinda Wortz en *Artnews*:

La presentación deriva conscientemente del constructivismo—un cierto numero de formas planas (en oposición a las volumétricas) conjuntadas, más que talladas a partir de un solo monolito. El largo flujo horizontal de formas a lo ancho del suelo alude tanto a un paisaje abstracto como a una forma purista, no objetiva.

Las alusiones al paisaje parecen más explícitas en una enorme pieza tercera de suelo, tallada a partir de mármol blanco griego, y presentada en dos secciones horizontales, una detrás de otra, apoyadas sobre una base de mármol. La pieza anterior consiste en dos secciones de mármol angular, geométrico, finamente acabado, mientras que el grupo posterior de las tres es desigual en la parte de arriba. Al dejar inacabados los bordes de las aristas superiores, el artista nos revela el proceso de trabajo con mármol antes de su fino pulimiento. En el contexto del mármol blanco la referencia al proceso recuerda a Miguel Angel, mientras que el obvio seccionalismo de la pieza también la incorpora a la tradición constructivista más reciente. [No. 8, octubre de 1978/39–40]

Pit Bull Bitch, 1970, douglas fir
108 x 216 x 72", 274 x 549 x 183 cm
Collection: Newport Harbor Art Museum, Newport Beach, California

William Packer dans *Art and Artists*:
Packer: Vous semblez être très soucieux non seulement du poids du matériau que vous utilisez mais encore de maintenir une tension entre les éléments soit en les suspendant, soit en les faisant jouer les uns contre les autres.
Dill: C'est que l'énergie est importante. Parce que les éléments reposent les uns sur les autres, l'énergie est un facteur qui entre en jeu—ce qui explique pourquoi la peinture ne me satisfaisait pas. Elle était trop éloignée de la réalité. La peinture est réelle sur un autre plan. C'est l'énergie intrinsèque de ces oeuvres qui est importante . . . peut-être. [No. 8, novembre 1972/38-43]

Communiqué à la presse, Ivory/Kimpton Gallery, San Francisco:
La sculpture de Dill est tendue et dramatique parce qu'il juxtapose à plusieurs niveaux: le rebord rugueux du marbre contre les variations géométriques à angle droit du bois et les rondeurs fabriquées de l'acier ou du fer. Dans une oeuvre plus ancienne, il faisait jouer le poids de poutres de bois contre des surfaces de verre anguleuses, faisant naître la tension plus de la position des matériaux que de leur nature.

Dans l'espace, le travail de Dill qui était tri-dimensionnel a évolué et tend maintenant à s'aligner sur une seule surface. Dans les formes, on trouve une qualité graphique, elles sont dessinées avec une bordure incise. Dans sa nouvelle série Milwood, les lignes épineuses du marbre forment une sorte de ligne d'horizon ou de silhouette. Ce qu'il y a de linéaire, presque de pictural dans les dernières oeuvres de Dill donne à penser qu'il est peut-être en train de se tourner vers la peinture—impression renforcée par sa façon de jouer avec les couleurs qui aime à placer en contraste les tons chauds du bois ou du marbre avec les gris et les noirs de l'acier et du fer. [Mai 1980]

Peter Plagens dans *Artforum*:
Cela vaut-il encore la peine de le dire, GUY DILL est le sculpteur le plus conséquent à l'heure actuelle: inventif, artiste dans son métier, élégant et avec juste ce qu'il faut d'humour. . . . Ce sont certainement des sculptures, au vieux sens du terme: permanentes (bien qu'on puisse les désassembler), habiles (les piliers sont subtilement rugueux et lisses, colorés et incolores, les parois de métal habilement corrodées), hautes mais aux dimensions d'une salle, précieuses (le verre a l'air si *coûteux*) et architectoniques. [No. 8, avril 1974/83-84]

Edit deAk dans *Art in America*:
Le thème le plus évident de Dill est la résistance et la tension calculées entre trois matériauz: le béton coulé, la tôle d'acier et la plaque de verre. Les pièces sont des variations sur, ou des conglomérats de formes frontales, dressées libres d'appui, composées, en général, de deux plaques de ciment verticales flanquant des plaques rectangulaires de verre ou de métal. L'élément placé entre les deux piliers de ciment est tantôt aligné pour les faire se rejoindre, tantôt en rotation autour d'un axe central, de façon à former une configuration diagonale. Dill emploie les matériaux d'une façon qui est souvent en contradiction avec leurs propriétés normales. Le verre semble alourdi du poids du métal et de minces colonnes semblent soutenir dans leur totalité des ensembles de poteaux et de linteaux, dont l'équilibre paraît dépendre au sol d'une surface dangereusement réduite. . . . La beauté presque indécente de ses sculptures tient pour une large part à des détails qui ne peuvent pas se justifier structuralement, tels que les légers embellissements non-fonctionnels de la forme ou les couleurs douces et fanées mélangées au béton. Appliquer des touches

«cosmétiques» à un style qui est essentiellement puriste révèle une décision esthétique d'une nouvelle sorte—quoique c'en soit une de particulièrement non-agressive et accommodante. [No. 2, mars 1974/106]

Melinda Wortz dans *Artnews*:
La présentation—un certain nombre de formes plates (il ne s'agit pas ici de volumes) aussujetties ensemble, plutôt que découpées dans un seul bloc, dérive sciemment du Constructivisme. La longue coulée horizontale de formes qui en traversent la surface évoque un paysage abstrait en même temps qu'une forme puriste, non-figurative.

Les allusions à un paysage semblent encore plus explicites dans une troisième oeuvre de grandes dimensions, placée au sol, taillée dans du marbre blanc de Grèce et présentée en deux sections horizontales, placées l'une derrière l'autre et reposant sur un socle de marbre. La pièce antérieure consiste en deux sections de marbre angulaire, géométrique, très bien polies, tandis que la pièce postérieure est formée de trois sections de parties supérieures inégales. En laissant inachevés les rebords de la partie supérieure, l'artiste révèle à quel travail le marbre doit être soumis avant d'offrir une surface lisse. Dans le contexte du marbre blanc, la référence au travail du marbre rappelle Michel-Ange, tandis que le découpage de la pièce en sections la rattache à la tradition plus récente du Constructivisme. [No. 8, octobre 1978/39-40]

Mary, 1971, steel and glass
72 x 120 x 72", 183 x 305 x 183 cm

Von William Packer in *Art and Artists*:

Packer: Zusammen mit dem Gewicht des Materials, das Sie benutzen, scheint ein sehr bewußtes Beschäftigtsein damit zu bestehen, die Teile in Spannung zu halten, eins gegen das andere, sie entweder aufzuhängen oder auf einander losspringen zu lassen.

Dill: Nun, Energie ist wichtig. Weil Dinge aufeinander ruhen, ist richtige Energie im Spiel—deshalb war ich mit Malerei nicht zufrieden. Es schien keine wirkliche Begebenheit zu zein. Malerei wird auf einer anderen Ebene wirklich. Energie in sich, di in diesen Stücken vor sich geht, ist wichtig . . . vielleicht. [No. 8, November 1972/38–43]

Von der Nachrichtenpresse der Ivory/Kimpton Gallery San Francisco:

Dills Skulptur ist straff und dramatisch wegen seines vielschichtigen Gebrauchs von Nebeneinanderstellung: Die unebene Marmorkante gegen die geometrischen, rechtwinkeliger Holzvariationen und runden Gegenstände aus bearbeitetem Stahl oder Eisen. In früheren Werken spielte er das Gewicht von Holzstämmen gegen angewinkelte Glasflächen aus und schuf dadurch Spannung, mehr von der Platzierung des Materials als von den benutzten Sorten.

Räumlich gesehen hat sich Dills Werk von der Einnahme eines dreidimensionalen Raumes herausentwickelt und strebt nach einer Aufreihung auf einer einzelnen Ebene. Es gibt eine graphische Qualität, eine eingeschnittene Kante mit den Formen gezeichnet. In seiner neuen Milwood Serie bilden die knorrigen Linien des Marmors eine Skyline oder eine Silhuette. Das lineare, fast bildhafte Gefühl, das Dills jüngstes Werk hat, weist auf seine Anfänge als Maler hin. Genauso wie sein Farbspiel—warme Marmor- und Holztöne kontrastieren mit den Grau- und Schwarztönen von Stahl und Eisen. [Mai 1980]

Von Peter Plagens in *Artforum*:

Wenn es überhaupt noch zählt, ist Guy Dill der beständigste Bildhauer im Umkreis: erfinderisch, handwerklich, elegant und einfallsreich. . . . Es sind wirklich Skulpturen im alten Sinne: dauerhaft (wenn auch zerlegbar), glänzend (die Säulen sind fein rauh glatt, farbig ungefärbt, die Metallwände sind geschickt korrodiert), groß innerhalb der Grenzen des Raumes, kostbar (das Glas sieht so kostbar aus) und architektonisch. [No. 8, April 1974/83–84]

Von Edit deAk in *Art in America*:

Dills offensichtlichstes Thema ist berechnete Spannung und Belastung zwischen drei Materialien: Gußbeton, Blech und Glasscheiben. Die Stücke sind Variationen auf oder Konglomerate von frontalen, freistehenden Formen, die gewöhnlich aus zwei vertikalen Zementblöcken zusammengestellt sind, die rechteckige Glas- und/oder Metallplatten flankieren. Der Bestandteil zwischen den zwei Betonsäulen ist entweder ausgerichtet, sie zu verbinden, oder wird um eine zentrale Achse gedreht, um eine offene, diagonale Konfiguration zu schaffen. Er benützt die Materialien in einer Weise, die ihren «normalen» Eigenheiten oft widerspricht. Glas erscheint unter dem Gewicht von schwerem Metall zu stehen, und dünne Säulen scheinen ganze Pfeiler- und Sturzanordnungen zu stützen, deren Gleichgewicht scheinbar von einer gefährlich kleinen Bodenfläche abhängt. . . . Die fast ungehörige Schönheit seiner Skulpturen wird zum größten Teil von Aspekten erzeugt, die strukturhaft nicht gerechtfertigt werden können, wie z.B. leicht nichtfunktionale Ausschmückungen der Form oder die sanften, verblaßten Farben, die dem Beton beigemischt wurden. Das Anwenden von «Kosmetik» auf einen grundsätzlich reinen Stil deutet eine neue Art ästhetischer Entscheidung an, wenn auch eine eigenartigerweise nicht aggressive, gemächliche. [No. 2, März 1974/106]

Von Melinda Wortz in *Artnews*:

Die Darstellung—eine Anzahl flacher (im Gegensatz zu volumetrischen) Formen suzammengefügt und nicht aus einem einzelnen Monolith gemeißelt, ist bewußt vom Kostruktivismus abgeleitet. Der lange horizontale Formenfluß längs über dem Boden spielt auf abstrakte Landschaft ebenso wie auf puristische, nicht objektive Formen an.

Landschaftsanspielungen scheinen expliziter in einem dritten großen Bodenstück, das aus weißem griechischem Marmor gemeißelt ist und in zwei horizontalen Sektionen erscheint, eine hinter der anderen, auf einem Marmorsockel ruhend. Das vordere Stück besteht aus zwei Teilen winkeligen, geometrischen, hochpolierten Marmors, während die hintere Gruppierung von dreien oben uneben ist. Indem er die Kanten der oberen Schwelle unbearbeitet läßt, offenbart der Künstler die Arbeitsweise mit Marmor bevor er ihn aufpoliert. Im Kontext von weißem Marmor erinnert der Bezug zum Vorgang an Michelangelo, während der offensichtliche Partikularismus des Stückes es auch mit der jüngeren konstruktivistischen Tradition verbindet. [No. 8, Oktober 1978/39–40]

Untitled, 1972, wood and rope
144 x 144 x 216", 366 x 549 x 366 cm
Collection: The Museum of Contemporary Art, Los Angeles, California

Born: Los Angeles, California, 1944
Resides: Los Angeles, California

Jud Fine

Jud Fine

From *Dokumenta 5* (Kassel, West Germany: Dokumenta 5, 1972):
The soul is fairly terse. The surface lushness flowers manifest—it is not irrelevant here to speak of President James K. Polk. A sense of history, far from anathema, is essential to the completion of these objects. [P. 181]

From Paul Stitelman in *Arts*:
Fine's particular interest . . . is the notion of process, i.e., the procedures of producing the work, which the spectator immediately perceives. . . . Process by itself is meaningless; it is only its mingling with Fine's sensibility that turns it into an aesthetic expression. . . . In retaining this intuitive perspective Fine has not abandoned the cognitive, conceptual experience, in fact, there is, in the final analysis, no real conflict between the two. . . . One issue that has also engaged Frank Stella's attention is the point of how close a painting can go toward being an object before it becomes sculpture, and, conversely, how close can a sculpture come to being painting. In *Defile* Fine uniquely uses a square metal plate which is attached to the wall almost as if it were a canvas-like support. . . . In another work, *Evident Redundancy*, rust is used as a drawing element. . . .

. . . the work is executed not in canvas and paint or in a conventional drawing media but in metal and rust. . . . Fine's art is one of ambiguity; it is neither sculpture nor painting in the strictest sense; it holds fast to a traditional painterly sensibility yet uses issues delineated by contemporary art to express that sensibility. This ambiguity, however, is a richness, not a detriment. Fine's ambiguity is not one of confusion, but of contrast—astonishingly, he has welded these contrasts into an organic whole. [No. 1, September 1974/40–42]

From Carter Ratcliff in *Artforum*:
Fine etched a statement about the meaning of the piece on the upper surface of the table. This statement is obscure, even eccentric. It supports, in an oblique way, the conclusion that the artist has intentionally joined a symbol of a unified, non-Western culture to a late Minimalist form—the table. The point of this becomes clear when it is remembered that Minimalism attempted to "offer a maximum resistance to perceptual separation." In other words, Minimalism was a variety of esthetic primitivism, an attempt to bring new unity and clarity to perception. Fine bolsters one of the most recent Western efforts to purify perceptual experience with a reference to the presumed purities of a non-Western culture. [No. 3, November 1975/60]

From Constance Mallinson in *Artweek*:
Fine's poles are informational maps, wrapped and decorated in metal coils, brightly colored string and cord, knotted ropes, colored tapes, chicken wire and sections of canvas painted with images relating to the drawings and typed with personal notes on the making of the pieces. Fine has incised, painted on bright enamel bands, punctured, doweled, nailed, gilded and tagged the poles, which may be made of natural materials or of copper, steel or fiber glass. Flip-flopping between readymade (natural) and manmade, they are a self-generative combination of pattern, color and ornament. Japanese bows and flutes, fishing rods, carved Indian totems, antennas, primitive weaponry and Brancusi's *Endless Columns* come to mind. [No. 21, 2 June 1979/3]

From Joan Hugo in *Artweek*:
For the past couple of years Fine has chosen to work in a range whose ideational resonance is transcultural. That is, he has deliberately chosen obscure but conceptually rich cultural constructs—such as preliterate navigational schemes, east-Asian grass-bundle rituals and northern European stone circle sites—as synonyms for the progression of creative thought. His area of interest, derived from and referential to archaeology and anthropology, has been the translation from observationally deduced codes to visual systems. His premise is that the relationship of hand and brain is a paradigm for all subsequent technologies. [No. 40, 28 November 1981/1]

Horizontal Pillar #5, 1983
Steel, wood, galvanized steel,
copper, rubber, wire, string
36 × 960 × 9″
91 × 2438 × 23 cm
Lent by Margo Leavin Gallery

De Dokumenta 5 (Kassel, Alemania Occidental: Dokumenta 5, 1972):

El alma es primorosamente tersa. La exuberancia de la superficie hace florecer un manifiesto—no es irrelevante hablar en este caso del Presidente James K. Polk. Es esencial un sentido de la historia, lejos del anatema, para completar estos objetos [pág. 181]

De Paul Stitelman en *Arts*:

El interés particular de Fine . . . es la noción de proceso, esto es, los procedimientos para producir la obra, que son percibidos inmediatamente por el espectador. . . . El proceso por sí mismo carece de significancia; sólo su fusión con la sensibilidad de Fine lo convierte en expresión estética. . . . Al retener esta perspectiva intuitiva, Fine no ha abandonado la experiencia cognitiva, conceptual; de hecho, no hay conflicto real entre las dos en un análisis último. . . . Un tema que ha llamado la atención de Frank Stella es cuánto puede acercarse una pintura a la esencia de un objeto antes de hacerse escultura, e inversamente, cuánto puede aproximarse la escultura a la pintura. En *Defile*, Fine utiliza peculiarmente una lámina cuadrada de metal pegada a la pared como si fuera un marco de lona. . . . En otra obra, *Evident Redundancy*, el óxido se emplea como elemento de dibujo. . . .

. . . la obra no es ejecutada con lona y pintura o con un material convencional de dibujo sino con metal y artificio. . . . El arte de Fine es ambiguo; no es ni escultura ni pintura en su sentido más estricto; se adhiere más bien a una sensibilidad pictórica tradicional, sin embargo utiliza temas aportados por el arte contemporáneo para expresar esa sensibilidad. Esta ambigüedad, no obstante, es enriquecedora y no empobrecedora. La ambigüedad de Fine no sugiere confusión, sino contraste—sorprendentemente, ha soldado estos contrastes en un conjunto orgánico. [No. 1, septiembre de 1974/40–42]

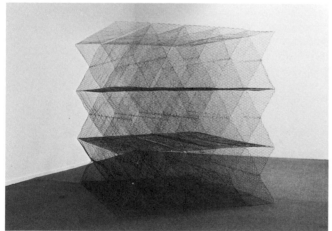

De Carter Ratcliff en *Artforum*:

Fine realizó al aguafuerte un grabado sobre el significado de la pieza que está en la superficie superior de la mesa. Esta manifestación es oscura, e incluso excéntrica. De una forma oblicua apoya la conclusión de que el artista ha unido intencionalmente el símbolo de una cultura unificada no occidental a una forma minimalista tardía—la mesa. Esto se hace evidente al evocar que el minimalismo intentaba «ofrecer una resistencia máxima a la separación perceptual.» En otras palabras, el minimalismo fué una variedad de primitivismo estético, un intento de aportar una unidad y claridad nuevas a la percepción. Fine representa uno de los esfuerzos occidentales más recientes de purificar la experiencia perceptual con referencia a la alegada pureza de una cultura no occidental. [No. 3, noviembre de 1975/60]

Untitled, 1970, chicken wire
72 x 72 x 72", 183 x 183 x 183 cm

De Constance Mallinson en *Artweek*:

Las pértigas de Fine son mapas informativos, envueltos y decorados con rollos de metal, cuerda y cable brillantemente coloreados, cuerdas con nudos, cintas coloreadas, alambradas y secciones de lona pintadas con imágenes relacionadas con los dibujos y notas personales grabadas sobre la confección de las piezas. Fine ha tallado, ha pintado en cintas de charol, perforado, enclavijado, clavado, dorado y etiquetado las pértigas, que pueden construirse con materiales naturales o con cobre, acero o fibra de vidrio. Oscilando entre lo hecho naturalmente y lo hecho manualmente, constituyen una combinación auto-generativa de modelos, color y adornos. Nos evocan arcos y flautas japoneses, cañas de pescar, tótems indios en bajorrelieve, antenas, armas primitivas y por fin las *Interminables Columnas* de Brancusi. [No. 21, 2 de junio de 1979/3]

De Joan Hugo en *Artweek*:

Durante los últimos dos años Fine ha decidido trabajar con una gama cuya resonancia ideacional es transcultural. Esto es, él ha elegido deliberadamente constructos culturales obscuros pero ricos conceptualmente—tales como esquemas de navegación preliterarios, rituales herbarios del Asia Oriental y monumentos megalíticos de piedra norte-europeos—como sinónimos del avance del pensamiento creativo. Su área de interés, derivada y referente a la arqueología y la antropología ha sido la traducción de códigos deducidos observacionalmente a sistemas visuales. Su premisa postula que la relación entre la mano y la mente es un paradigma de todas las tecnologías subsiguientes. [No. 40, 28 de noviembre de 1981/1]

Paru dans *Dokumenta 5* (Cassel, République Fédérale d'Allemagne: Dokumenta 5, 1972):
L'âme qui s'exprime ici le fait avec concision. La luxuriance des fleurs à la surface, manifeste—il n'est pas hors de propos de parler ici du Président James K. Polk. Le sens de l'histoire, loin de l'anathème, est essentiel à l'achèvement de ces objets. [p. 181]

Paul Stitelman dans *Arts*:

Ce qui intéresse particulièrement Fine . . . c'est la notion de création, c'est à dire la façon dont travaille l'artiste à l'oeuvre que le spectateur perçoit immédiatement. . . . Ce processus de création, en soi, n'a pas de signification; c'est seulement lorsque Fine y mêle sa sensibilité qu'elle devient expression esthétique. . . . En fixant cette perspective intuitive, Fine n'a pas abandonné l'expérience cognitive conceptuelle, de fait, en dernière analyse, il n'y a pas de réel conflit entre les deux. . . . L'attention de Frank Stella a aussi été attirée par un autre point: celui de savoir jusqu'où un tableau peut tendre à se faire objet avant de devenir une sculpture et vice-versa. Dans *Defile*, Fine utilise uniquement une plaque de métal carré qui est attachée au mur, presque comme s'il s'agissait du support d'une toile. . . .

Dans une autre oeuvre, *Evident Redundancy* (Redondance évidente), Fine emploie de la rouille pour réaliser son dessin . . . il exécute son oeuvre non pas sur une toile et avec de la peinture ou par quelqu'autre méthode conventionnelle, mais sur métal et avec de la rouille. . . . L'art de Fine est ambigu; il n'appartient ni à la sculpture, ni à la peinture au sens le plus strict de ces termes; il est fidèle à la sensibilité traditionelle de la peinture mais il utilise des moyens définis par l'art contemporain pour exprimer cette sensibilité. Cette ambiguïté, quoiqu'il en soit, est une richesse, non pas un manque. L'ambiguïté de Fine n'est pas sortie de la confusion mais du jeu des contrastes—d'une manière étonnante, Fine a soudé ces contrastes en un tout organisé. [No. 1, septembre 1974

Carter Ratcliff dans *Artforum*:

Fine a gravé une déclaration expliquant la signification de l'oeuvre sur la surface supérieure de la table. Cette déclaration est obscure, voire même excentrique. Elle soutient, de manière oblique, la conclusion que l'artiste a joint intentionellement le symbole d'une culture non-occidentale unifiée à une récente forme Minimaliste—la table. Il est plus facile de comprendre ce que cela signifie lorsqu'on se souvient que le Minimalisme essaya d' «offrir une résistance maxima à la séparation perceptuelle». En d'autres termes, le Minimalisme était une variété de primitivisme esthétique, un effort pour mettre une unité et une clarté nouvelles dans la perception. Fine appuie l'un des efforts les plus récents de l'Occident pour purifier l'expérience perceptuelle en se référant aux puretés présumées de la culture non-occidentale. [No. 3, novembre 1975/60]

Constance Mallinson dans *Artweek*:

Les poteaux de Fine sont enveloppés et décorés de spirales de métal, de cordelette et de corde brillamment colorée, de corde nouée, de rubans colorés, de barbelés et de sections de toiles peintes d'images en rapport avec les dessins et sur lesquelles sont tapées des remarques personnelles sur l'élaboration des pièces. Fine a incisé, peint sur bandes d'émail de couleur vive, troué, chevillé, cloué, doré et étiqueté les poteaux, qui sont faits aussi bien de matériaux naturels que de cuivre, d'acier ou de fibre de verre. Sautant du naturel à l'artificiel, ils forment une combinaison génératrice elle-même de motifs, de couleurs et de décors. On pense à des arcs et à des flûtes du

Japon, à des cannes à pêche, à des totems indiens sculptés, à des antennes, à des armes primitives et aux *Colonnes sans fin* de Brancusi. [No. 21, 2 juin 1979/3]

Joan Hugo dans *Artweek*:

Depuis deux ans, Fine a choisi de travailler dans un domaine dont les concepts ont une résonance transculturelle. C'est à dire qu'il a délibérément choisi des constructions culturelles obscures mais riches de concepts—tels que certains plans de navigation datant d'avant l'invention de l'écriture, certains rituels dits «de la botte d'herbe» de l'Extrême-Orient ou les sites des temples mégalithiques de l'Europe du Nord—comme étant synonymes de la progression de la pensée créatrice. Le domaine qui l'intéresse, dérivé de et se référant à l'archéologie et l'anthropologie, a été la transposition en systèmes visuels de codes déduits par l'observation. Son postulat est que le rapport entre la main et le cerveau est le paradigme de toutes les technologies subséquentes. [No. 40, 20 novembre 1981/1]

Watts Last Decision, 1972, bamboo, string, fiberglass, gold leaf, latex, wire 120" high, 305 cm

Aus *Dokumenta 5* (Kassel, West Germany: Dokumenta 5, 1972):

Die Seele ist ziemlich kurz und bündig. Die Oberflächen-Üppigkeit-Blumen offenbaren—es ist hier nicht irrelevant von Präsident James K. Polk zu sprechen. Eine Ahnung von Geschichte, weit von der Verbannung, ist wesentlich bei der Vollendung dieser Gegenstände. [p. 181]

Von Paul Stitelman in *Arts*:

Fines besonderes Interesse . . . ist die Ahnung vom Vorgang, d.h., die Prozedur bei der Herstellung der Arbeit, die der Betrachter sofort wahrnimmt. . . . Vorgang in sich selbst ist bedeutungslos; es ist nur dieser Vermischung mit Fines Feinfühligkeit, was ihm einen ästhetischen Ausdruck verleiht. . . . Beim Beibehalten dieser intuitiven Perspektive hat sich Fine nicht von der kognitiven/konzeptuellen Erfahrung gelöst, tatsächlich entsteht zwischen beiden in letzter Untersuchung kein wirklicher Konflikt. . . . Eine Sache, die auch Frank Stellas Aufmerksamkeit erregt hat, ist der Punkt, wie nah ein Gemälde an einen Gegenstand herangehen kann, bevor es eine Skulptur wird, und umgekehrt, wie sehr eine Skulptur sich einem Gemälde nähern kann. In *Defile* benutzt Fine in einzigartiger Weise eine quadratische Metallplatte, die an der Wand befestigt ist, fast als wäre sie ein leinwandähnlicher Aufhänger. . . . In einem anderen Werk, *Evident Redundancy*, wird Rost als Zeichenmaterial benutzt. . . .

Das Werk wird nicht mit Leinwand und Farbe oder mit einem herkömmlichen Zeichenmaterial ausgeführt, sondern mit Metall und Kniff. . . . Fines Kunst ist doppelsinniger Natur; im strengsten Sinne ist sie weder Skulptur noch Malerei; sie hält fest an einer traditionellen malerhaften Feinfühligkeit, und doch benützt sie Ideen, die von der zeitgenössischen Kunst umrissen wurden, diese Feinfühligkeit auszudrücken. Diese Doppeldeutigkeit jedoch stellt einen Reichtum dar und keinen Abbruch. Fines Doppeldeutigkeit ist nichy die eines Durcheinanders, sondern die eines Kontrastes—erstaunlicherweise hat er diese Kontraste in ein organisches Ganzes geschweißt. [No. 1, September 1974/40–42]

Von Carter Ratcliff in *Artforum*:

Fine ätzte eine Feststellung über die Bedeutung des Stückes auf die obere Fläche des Tisches. Diese Feststellung ist undeutlich, ja sogar ekzentrisch. Sie unterstützt in indirekter Weise die Schlußfolgerung, daß der Künstler mit Absicht ein Symbol einer einheitlichen, nicht-westlichen Kultur mit einer späten Minimalistenform—dem Tisch—verbindet. Dieser Punkt wird klar, wenn man sich daran erinnert, daß der Minimalismus versucht hat, «einen maximalen Widerstand gegen wahrnehmbare Trennung aufzubringen.» Mit anderen Worten war der Minimalismus eine Vielfalt ästhetischen Primitivismusses, ein Versuch, der Wahrnehmung neue Einheit und Klarheit zu geben. Fine fördert eine der jüngsten westlichen Bemühungen, die Wahrnehmungserfahrung unter Bezug auf die vorausgesetzten Gediegenheiten einer nicht-westlichen Kultur zu reinigen. [No. 3, November 1975/60]

Von Constance Mallinson in *Artweek*:

Fines Stangen sind informationsreiche Landkarten, umwickelt und verziert mit Metallwindungen, hellgefärbten Fäden und Kordeln, verknoteten Seilen, farbigen Bändern, Maschendraht und Teilen von Leinwand, die mit Abbildern bemalt sind, welche sich auf die Zeichnungen beziehen und mit getippten persönlichen Notizen zur Anfertigung des Stückes versehen sind. Fine hat graviert, auf helle Emaille-Bänder gemalt, gelocht, mit Dübeln befestigt, genagelt, vergoldet und die Stangen genietet, die aus natürlichen Materialien oder aus

Kupfer, Stahl oder Fiberglas gemacht sein können. Hin- und hergehend zwischen dem Fertigen (Natürlichen) und Künstlichen ist eine aus sich selbst hervorgehende Kombination an Mustern, Farbe und Ornament. Japanische Bögen und Flöten, Angelruten, geschnitzte Indianer Totems, Antennen, primitive Waffen und Brancusis *Endless Columns* kommen einem in den Sinn. [No. 21, 2. Juni 1979/3]

Von Joan Hugo in *Artweek*:

In den letzten paar Jahren hat Fine es vorgezogen, in einem Gebiet zu arbeiten, dessen vorstellunghafte Resonanz transkulturell ist. Das heißt, er hat absichtlich obskure, aber konzeptuell reiche kulturelle Gebilde gewählt—wie Navigations-Schemata, ostasiatische Grasbüschel-Rituale und Nordeuropäische Steinkreis-Plätze—als Synonyme für das Fortschreiten kreativen Denkens. Sein Interessengebiet, abzuleiten von und in Verbindung mit Archäologie und Anthropologie, war eine Übertragung der aus Beobachtung abgeleiteter Kodes auf ein visuelles System. Seine Prämisse ist, daß die Beziehung von Hand und Verstand ein Paradigma für alle nachfolgenden Technologien ist. [No. 40, 28. November 1981/1]

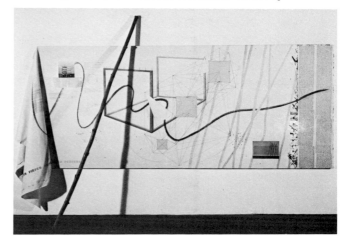

Untitled, 1974, acrylic, paper, photo, ink, pencil, xerox
Canvas 60 x 192" on a 60 x 144" stretcher
Canvas 152 x 488 cm on a 152 x 366 cm stretcher
Bamboo pole 108", 274 cm

Born: Seattle, Washington, 1936
Resides: Berkeley, California

Tom Holland

Tom Holland

From Tom Holland as told to Jan Butterfield:
I love the stuff of painting: the weight, the stickiness, and most of all the color. I build things to paint on. I build them for the wall, and I build freestanding things as well. I consider them all to be paintings. There is no verbal content in what I do. I take the titles out of the phonebook. To paint a construction out of inert materials and have it take on a life of its own, through color and the other qualities, is magic for me. [February 1984]

From Fidel Danieli in *Art International*:
Up to two years ago Tom Holland was producing paintings and constructions which were undoubtedly among the ugliest, funkiest, most hysterically individual works to be seen in Los Angeles. . . . These newest works are constructed of lengths of commercial creamy or frosted fiberglass sheeting material which is bolted or riveted together and covered with freely flowing enamel paint. The building of the picture planes of assembled sections through panels often woven together, or hanging flapping loose and secured only at the top, and the use of ribbons which twist across the surfaces all indicate a sculptor's sense of relief dimension. . . . Whereas three years ago I would have ignored this artist as a provincial eccentric I now suggest he is a major younger talent to be seriously considered. [Vol. XIV/I, January 1970/86]

From Jerome Tarshis in *Artforum*:
Holland emphasizes the layered nature of his work by the rivets and the dozen coats of paint, and also by cutting lines through several layers of paint, sometimes through a whole layer of fiberglas. In each painting one of the figure layers passes under the ground layer, through a slot. Each piece is a world of color in itself; the group of colors being explored in each one is so peculiar to itself, and so autonomous, that any one painting would suffice to make Holland's point. Many artists create a body of work that is exciting as a series or an aggregation; Holland creates increasingly rich individual paintings. [No. 11, October 1972/90]

From Fred Martin in *Art International*:
Most of the work also partakes of his rough and ready approach to physical construction, from canvas, one by two's and staples in the earlier work to the rivets and fibreglas sheets of the later things. The change between the two groups of works, then, is not so much a switch from oil/canvas to epoxy/fibreglas as a switch from wild and powerful iconography to a work without overt reference, a work seeming to be more about visual order and much less about bizarre personal fantasy. For this reviewer, you pay your money and you take your choice. If you like to watch strange bag ladies getting it from freight trains, or Burney Falls as the crotch of the spring of the waters of life with grape decorations for immortality, the middle sixties things at Richmond are for you: but if you like a dark golden rain at night with a red and a black ribbon wriggling together all disguised as mainstream formal concern for process and structure, the new stuff is for you. [No. 34, March-April 1976/81]

From Charles Schere in the *Oakland Tribune*:
The gesture in this work is not intuitive, though the result of the painting gesture may be relatively uncontrolled. Holland's work has always balanced geometry and lyricism, has always looked for the painterly implications of no longer plane surfaces. . . . This new work is disconcerting at first: the palette is very bright and bold, occasionally even playing with "psychedelic" fuschias and reds, and even the dark tones— deep blues, forest greens, blacks—have a surface gloss and a deep intensity which threatens to tire the eye. But 20 minutes' viewing reveals enough substance, form and depth to match that immediate effect. The show is very strong indeed, a reminder that sustained activity (Holland's been at it for nearly 20 years) and a strong individual vision can even reconcile Constructivist geometry and fabrication with free-association, organically developed abstract imagery. [18 March 1980]

Norton, 1983
Acrylic urethane on aluminum
144 × 60 × 60"
366 × 152 × 152 cm
Lent by James Corcoran Gallery

De Tom Holland en conversación con Jan Butterfield:

Me encanta la cuestión de la pintura: el peso, la pegajosidad, y sobre todo el color. Construyo cosas para pintarlas. Las hago para colgarlas en la pared y realizo cosas auto-estables también. A todas las considero pinturas. No hay contenido verbal en lo que hago. Los títulos los saco del listín telefónico. Para mí es mágico pintar una composición de materiales inertes para que tome vida por sí misma, por medio del color y de las otras cualidades. [Febrero de 1984]

De Fidel Danieli en *Art International*:

Hasta hace dos años, Tom Holland estaba produciendo pinturas y composiciones que se encuentran indudablemente entre las más feas, más estrambóticas y las más histéricamente individualistas que se puedan ver en Los Angeles. . . . Estas obras recientes están construídas con tiras de material comercial laminado de fibra de vidrio cremado o escarchado que están atadas y remachadas y cubiertas con pintura de charol que fluye libremente. La realización de los planos pictóricos con secciones ensambladas por medio de paneles a menudo entretejidos, o que cuelgan sueltos y fijados sólo en su parte superior, y el uso de cintas que se retuercen a través de las superficies, todo ello indica el sentido de dimensión de relieve de un escultor. . . . Mientras que hace tres años hubiera ignorado a este artista por ser un provinciano excéntrico ahora sugiero que es uno de los mayores talentos jóvenes a ser tomado en cuenta seriamente. [vol. XIV/I, enero de 1970/86]

De Jerome Tarshis en *Artforum*:

Holland enfatiza la naturaleza de capas de su obra por medio de los remaches y las docenas de capas de pintura, y también por cortar líneas a través de varias capas de pintura, a veces a través de una capa completa de fibra de vidrio. En cada pintura una de las capas de la figura pasa por debajo de la capa de fondo, a través de una ranura. Cada pieza es en sí misma un mundo de color; la serie de colores con los que se experimenta en cada una es tan peculiar y tan autónoma que cualquiera de las pinturas bastaría para reflejar la intención de

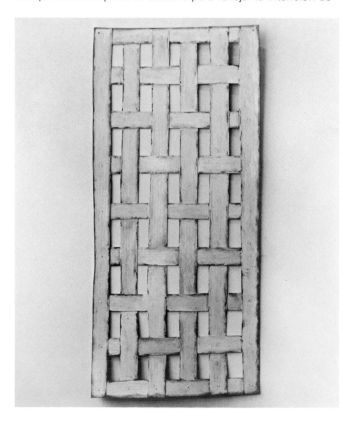

Malibu Series #27, 1968, epoxy and fiberglass
(no size given)

Holland. Muchos artistas crean un cuerpo de trabajo que es emocionante ya sea como una serie o un agregado; Holland crea pinturas individuales cada vez más enriquecidas. [No. 11, octubre de 1972/90]

De Fred Martin en *Art International*:

La mayoría de su obra también comparte su aproximación directa a las composiciones físicas, que va desde la lona, de uno por dos, y tejido en su obra temprana a los remaches y láminas de fibra de vidrio en su obra posterior. El cambio entre los dos grupos de obras no es tanto un cambio de óleo/lona a epoxia/fibra de vidrio cuanto un cambio de la iconografía salvaje y poderosa a una obra sin referencia explícita, una obra que parece centrarse mucho más en el orden visual y mucho menos en la fantasía personal grotesca. Para este crítico, cada uno que pague su dinero y elija. Si Vd. desea admirar señoras con vestidos de noche en trenes de carga o las cataratas de Burney como la fuente de las aguas de la vida con uvas de adorno para la posteridad, para Vd. son las cosas de los años sesenta de Richmond: pero si por el contrario le gusta la lluvia dorada y oscura de la noche con cintas rojinegras serpenteando juntas disfrazadas como el interés formal convencional por el proceso y la estructura, entonces este material nuevo es para Vd. [No. 34, marzo-abril de 1976/81]

De Charles Schere en el *Oakland Tribune*:

El gesto de esta obra no es intuitivo, aunque el resultado del gesto pictórico puede estar relativamente incontrolado. La obra de Holland siempre ha tenido una geometría y lirismo equilibrados, siempre ha buscado las implicaciones pictóricas de superficies que ya no son planas. . . . Esta nueva obra es desconcertante al principio: la paleta es muy brillante y osada, a veces incluso jugando con fucsias y rojos «psicodélicos», e incluso con tonos oscuros—azules profundos, verdes forestales, negros—que tienen un brillo de superficie y una intensidad profunda que amenazan con cansar la vista. Pero después de 20 minutos de apreciación se revelan la sustancia, forma y profundidad suficientes para igualar ese efecto inmediato. El espectáculo es en efecto muy fuerte, un recuerdo que la actividad continuada (Holland ha trabajado en ello por casi 20 años) y una fuerte visión individual pueden reconciliar incluso la geometría y composición constructivistas con la libre asociación de la imágen abstracta orgánicamente desarrollada. [18 de marzo de 1980]

Tom Holland interviewé par Jan Butterfield:
J'aime le côté matériel de la peinture: ce qu'elle a de pesant, de collant et, par-dessus tout, la couleur. Je construis des objets pour pouvoir les peindre. Je construis des objets à accrocher au mur, et d'autres à placer debout. Je les considère tous comme des peintures. Ce que je fais, je ne peux pas le verbaliser. Pour lui donner un nom, je lui fabrique des titres en découpant l'annuaire du téléphone. Peindre un objet construit à partir de matériaux inertes et le voir s'animer d'une vie propre, grâce à la couleur et à ses autres qualités, pour moi, c'est de la magie. [Février 1984]

Fidel Danieli dans *Art International*:
Jusqu'à il y a deux ans, Tom Holland faisait des peintures et des constructions qui étaient, à n'en pas douter, parmi les oeuvres les plus laides, les plus bizarres et les plus follement individuelles de Los Angeles. . . . Les dernières oeuvres sont construites de morceaux de plaques de fibre de verre de couleur crémeuse ou cristallisée qui sont boulonnées ou rivetées ensemble et couvertes de peinture laquée, appliquée par ruissellement. La construction des plans du tableau qui sont formés de sections assemblées par des panneaux souvent tissés ensemble ou qui sont suspendus, attachés seulement par le haut et laissés libres sur les côtés, l'emploi de rubans tressés sur la surface, tout cela révèle un sens du relief et des dimensions propres à un sculpteur. . . . Alors qu'il y a trois ans, j'aurais ignoré cet artiste, le prenant pour un provincial excentrique, je suggère maintenant qu'il est un jeune talent majeur que l'on doit prendre au sérieux. [Vol. XIV/I, janvier 1970/85]

Jerome Tarshis dans *Artforum*:
Holland met en relief la nature stratifiée de son travail en employant des rivets et une douzaine de couches de peinture et en y taillant des lignes, coupant parfois à travers toute l'épaisseur d'une plaque de fibre de verre. Dans chaque peinture, l'une des couches de la figure passe sous la couche au sol, par une tente. Chaque pièce est, en elle-même, un monde de couleur; les associations de couleurs explorées dans chacune sont si spéciales, si autonomes que n'importe laquelle de ces peintures suffirait à faire ressortir ce que Holland cherche à faire. Nombreux sont les artistes qui créent un ensemble d'oeuvres intéressantes en tant que partie d'une série ou d'un tout, Holland crée, de plus en plus, des peintures individuellement riches. [No. 11, octobre 1972/90]

Fred Martin dans *Art International*:
La plus grande partie de l'oeuvre est exécutée comme il [Holland] exécute tout ce qui est construction, c'est à dire frustement, à partir de toile et de planches d'un pouce par deux pouces assujetties par des agraphes dans les premières oeuvres et à partir de plaques de fibre de verre dans les oeuvres récentes. En sorte que la différence entre les deux groupes d'oeuvres ne tient pas tant au fait que Holland est passé de l'huile et de la toile à la résine et à la fibre de verre, qu'à un glissement, d'une iconographie farouche et puissante, à un travail sans références manifestes, à un type de travail plus visuel, remplaçant l'expression de bizarres fantaisies personnelles. De l'avis de ce critique, c'est à l'amateur d'art de décider. Si vous aimez regarder d'étranges femmes-chauve-souris écrasées par des trains de marchandises, ou les cascades de Burney Falls devenues fontaines de jouvence et décorées de grappes de raisin en guise de symboles d'immortalité, alors les oeuvres exécutées à Richmond, au milieu des années soixante, sont pour vous; mais si vous préférez une sombre pluie dorée, la nuit, parcourue d'un ruban noir et

rouge, le tout exprimant une préoccupation essentielle pour le processus de création et pour la structure, alors les oeuvres récentes sont pour vous. [No. 34, mars-avril 1976/81]

Charles Schere dans le *Oakland Tribune*:
La touche dans cette oeuvre n'est pas intuitive, bien que le résultat puisse en être relativement spontané. L'oeuvre de Holland a toujours été en équilibre entre la géométrie et le lyrisme, a toujours cherché, du point de vue du peintre, ce que cela signifie de ne plus travailler sur des surfaces plates. . . . Cette nouvelle oeuvre est déconcertante, à première vue: la palette en est très vive et audacieuse, jouant même, à l'occasion, avec des tons «psychédéliques» fuchsia et rouges. Les couleurs sombres elles-mêmes—les bleus foncés, les verts-forêt, les noirs—ont un brillant de surface et une intensité de profondeur qui menacent de fatiguer l'oeil. Mais après avoir contemplé la pièce pendant vingt minutes, on perçoit que la substance, la forme et la profondeur sont en proportion de cet effet. Le spectacle est vraiment très puissant et nous rappelle qu'une activité ininterrompue (Holland travaille depuis près de 20 ans) et une puissante vision personnelle peuvent réconcilier jusqu'à la géométrie et la fabrication Constructivistes avec l'imagerie abstraite. [18 mars 1980]

Berkeley Series #111, 1970, epoxy on fiberglass
48 x 36", 122 x 91 cm

Von Tom Holland wie es Jan Butterfield erzählt wurde:
Ich liebe alles, was mit Malerei zu tun hat: das Gewicht, die Klebrigkeit und vor allem die Farbe. Ich baue Dinge, um sie zu bemalen. Ich baue sie für die Wand, und ich baue ebenso freistehende Dinge. Ich betrachte sie alle als Gemälde. Es gibt keinen verbalen Sinn, in dem, was ich tue. Ich nehme die Überschriften aus dem Telefonbuch. Eine Konstruktion aus starrem Material zu malen und es ein eigenes Leben entwickeln zu lassen, durch Farbe und andere Eigenschaften, ist magisch für mich. [Februar 1984]

Von Fidel Danieli in _Art International_:
Bis vor zwei Jahren hat Tom Holland Gemälde und Gebilde hergestellt, die zweifellos zu den häßlichsten, funkigsten und hysterischsten Einzelwerken gehören, die man in Los Angeles sehen kann. . . . Diese neuesten Werke sind aus Längen von handelsüblichem milchigen oder bereiften Fiberglas-Überzugsmaterial konstruiert, das mit Bolzen befestigt oder zusammengenietet und mit freifließender Emaille bedeckt ist. Der Bau der Bildflächen aus zusammengefügten Teilen durch oft zusammengewebte Flächen, oder lose hängend und nur an der Decke gesichert, und der Gebrauch von Bändern, welche sich über die Oberflächen drehen, all das zeigt den Sinn eines Bildhauers für Reliefdimension. . . . Wenn ich noch vor drei Jahren diesen Künstler als provinziellen Ekzentriker übersehen haben würde, bin ich nun der Meinung, daß er ein größeres junges Talent ist, das ernst genommen werden sollte. [Vol. XIV/I, Januar 1970/86]

Von Jerome Tarshis in _Artforum_:
Holland betont die geschichtete Anordnung seiner Arbeit durch die Nieten und dutzende von Farbauflagen und auch dadurch, daß er Linien durch mehrere Farbauflagen ritzt, manchmal durch eine ganze Fiberglasschicht. In jedem einzelnen Gemälde führt eine der Figurenschichten durch einen Schlitz unter die Grundschicht. Jedes Stück ist eine Farbenwelt in sich; die Farbgruppierung, die in jeder einzelnen erforscht wird, ist in sich selbst so eigenartig und so autonom, daß jedes einzelne Gemälde Hollands Punkt nachkommen würde. Viele Künstler schaffen ein Gesamtwerk, das als eine Serie oder eine Ansammlung aufregend ist; Holland schafft zunehmend reiche individuelle Gemälde. [No. 11, Oktober 1972/90]

Von Fred Martin in _Art International_:
Die meisten seiner Arbeiten nehmen an seiner groben Annäherung physischer Konstruktion teil, angefangen mit den 1 inch × 2 inch Brettern und Heftklammern in dem früheren Werk

bis zu den Nieten und den Fiberglasbögen der späteren Dinge. Der Wechsel zwischen den zwei Gruppen von Arbeiten ist dann nicht so sehr ein Austausch von Öl/Leinwand zu Epoxy/Fiberglas als ein Umschalten von wilder und kraftvoller Ikonographie zu einem Werk ohne offenen Bezug, ein Werk, das nicht von einer visuellen Ordnung zu handeln scheint und viel weniger von bizarrer, persönlicher Einbildung. Für diesen Rezensenten gilt: «you pay your money and you take your choice. If you like to watch strange bag ladies getting it from freight trains, or Burney Falls as the crotch of the spring of the waters of life with grape decorations for immortality, the middle sixties things at Richmond are for you»: aber wenn man einen tiefgoldenen nächtlichen Regen mit einem roten und schwarzen Band zusammengekringelt mag, alles verkleidet als Hauptrichtung für formales Interesse an Vorgang und Struktur, dann ist das Neue für einen. [No. 34, März-April 1976/81]

Von Charles Schere in der _Oakland Tribune_:
Die Gestik in diesem Werk ist nicht intuitiv, auch wenn das Ergebnis der Gemäldegestik verhältnismäßig unkontrolliert sein mag. Hollands Werk hat immer die Geometrie und den Lyrismus ausgewogen, hat immer nach den malerhaften Implikationen gesucht, wo Oberflächen nicht länger Flächen sind. . . . Dieses neue Werk ist auf den ersten Blick verwirrend: Die Palette ist sehr hell und kühn, gelegentlich sogar mit «psychedelischen» Lila- und Rottönen, und sogar die drunklen Töne—tiefes Blau, Waldgrün und Schwarztöne—haben einen Oberflächenglanz und eine tiefe Intensität, die das Auge zu ermüden droht. Aber ein zwanzigminütiges Betrachten setzt genug Substanz, Form und Tiefe frei, die unmittelbare Wirkung gleichzumachen. Die Ausstellung ist in der Tat sehr eindrucksvoll, eine Mahnung, daß aufrechterhaltene Tätigkeit (Holland ist seit fast 20 Jahren dabei) und eine starke individuelle Vision sogar konstruktivisitische Geometrie und Arbeiten mit frei-assoziierender, organisch entwickelter abstrakter Bildhaftigkeit vereinbaren kann. [18. März 1980]

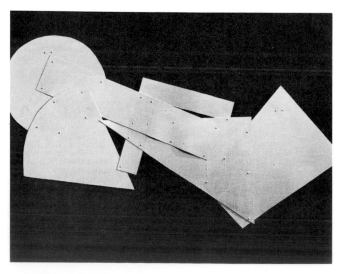

Light Flight, 1975, epoxy on fiberglass
43.5 x 103." 109 x 261 cm

Robert Hudson

Born: Salt Lake City, Utah, 1938
Resides: Cotati, California

Robert Hudson

From John Marlowe with Robert Hudson in _Currant_:
Marlowe: Does someone have to understand your personal life to understand your assemblages?
Hudson: No, not at all . . . I make things that are good to look at over and over. . . . You build up the knowledge that doesn't make sense to anyone and you gradually get it into this kind of shape that communicates. That's what art does . . . . I mean all art, writing, films, music . . . it's the soul of the people.
Marlowe: Do you develop your drawings the same as your assemblages?
Hudson: Yah, like this one. I poured some blue paint out of a cup onto the paper, and then, like reading a road map, I followed it as it went along. I don't sketch before I start. . . . It develops from what's inside my head. There's just a little blue left, that small part I've outlined there. And there's a part that sort of came into being a Hopi mask. It all develops. [April/May 1975/33]

From Peter Schjeldahl, _East and West and Robert Hudson_ (Philadelphia: Moore College of Art, 1978):
Robert Hudson . . . by himself might appear practically archetypal of the Bay Area artist. Hudson's work in sculpture, construction, ceramics, collage, painting, drawing and whatnot mediums is certainly various enough, and there's no gainsaying the "eccentricity" of his images. However, Hudson is also extremely sophisticated in his eclecticism, with a kind of sophistication that tends to elude New York tastes precisely because it includes and exceeds them.

From David Bourdon in _The Village Voice_:
. . . Robert Hudson, only 27, [is] considered one of the pivotal figures in the New San Francisco Sculpture. . . . Hudson's polychrome steel sculptures are eclectic combinations of California's bop surrealism, neo-Dada, pop art, assemblage, junk sculpture, and op art. Almost nothing is left out, yet nothing is superfluous after having been processed by Hudson's antic imagination. His conceptual and technical facility is reckless but controlled. With meandering pipes and geometric planes angled precariously into space, the sculptures resemble irresponsible machine tools decorated by one of California's most tangerine-flake hot rodders. [21 October 1965]

From Gabriel Laderman in _Artforum_:
Robert Hudson . . . continues to work in the direction that has brought him national recognition in the last two years. His ability to positively confound the viewer by making heavy three-dimensional volumes appear virtually flat, and, conversely, flat planes appear three dimensional is strongly apparent in the eight works displayed at the San Francisco Art Institute Gallery. . . . As a student at the San Francisco Art Institute Hudson's work was held in very high esteem by virtually every professional metal sculptor who ever saw it. The older artists were amazed at his virtuosity in manipulating large sections of heavy metal plate and bar stock into complex forms. Hudson was, as a student, and remains a very ambitious and prolific artist. In a very brief span of years he mastered the prevailing problems of metal sculpture with such breadth, daring and consummate skill that one wondered what he could possibly do next. . . . Such clarity of thought is rare enough in an artist twenty-three or four years old and rarer still is the ability to grasp the situation and act upon it in so forthright a manner. The why of his present work becomes clearer when one realizes that his ambition is not just to make excellent pieces in a manner at least partially resolved by others, but to make great pieces in an area no one dreamed existed. [November 1967/45]

From Jan Butterfield in _Robert Hudson_ (New York: Allan Frumkin Gallery, 1976):
Robert Hudson is an innocent and a naive with a highly developed sensitivity to primitive imagery; he also has an intuitive, sophisticated sense of color and balance. . . . Hudson's recent works are an amalgamation of abstract and representational images; primitive magic objects such as feathers, rawhide, string, beads, sticks, rocks, carved twigs and branches which co-mingle with exquisitely painted arcs, circles, volumes and triangles. He acknowledges a visual debt to Kandinsky which is strongly evidenced in the new paintings and drawings. . . . "About those pieces . . . I think there was just a sort of spirit creature coming out. I turned on to a few things in particular—mostly color. For example, I'd do one special thing—that worked, and then I would make pieces especially for that particular color—because I knew what that color would do."

The unique involvement with trompe l'oeil painting on these early pieces was perhaps the most extraordinary thing about them. "It just came from painting," Hudson relates. "It started with painting the sculptural pieces. I liked making something thin out of a fat edge for example. I liked making it be two things at the same time." These works were remarkable not only because of the sheer bravura of the painting itself, but because of its innovation. No one in 1964–66 was working in that curious nether land between painting and metal sculpture in the sense that Hudson was.

These early works were marvelously sleight-of-hand. In them hard appeared viscous; solid appeared hollow; flat elements with trompe l'oeil painting became stairs. Many of these early works were "slotted"—Hudson's term for opening up the space in order to belie, deny or confuse the viewer's perception of volume. Juxtaposition became the byword. He combined round pipes with cubes, real or depicted squared edges with those which appeared to be molten or viscous (albeit frozen in time) and overpainted all of them with exquisite care. "The thing I liked about those sculptures was making flat things go round with paint—just being able to have that object be what it is and then also be just a whisper and a dance and a whole bunch of things. I don't know if there is any particular thing about them that has to do with life—but it is about magic."

Figure of Speech, 1984 (in progress)
Steel
170 × 104 × 62″
432 × 264 × 157 cm
Lent by the artist

De John Marlowe con Robert Hudson en *Currant*:

Marlowe:¿Es necesario comprender su vida personal para entender sus composiciones?

Hudson: No, en absoluto . . . Hago cosas buenas para ser apreciadas una y otra vez. . . . Se reúne el conocimiento que no tiene sentido para ninguna otra persona y gradualmente se introduce en este tipo de formas comunicativas. Eso es lo que hace el arte. . . . Es decir, cualquier tipo de arte, la literatura, el cine, la música . . . es el alma de la gente.

Marlowe: ¿Desarrolla Vd. sus dibujos de la misma forma que sus composiciones?

Hudson: Pues sí, como ésta. He vertido un poco de pintura azul de una taza sobre un papel, y luego, de la misma forma que se lee un mapa de carreteras la he seguido a medida que se deslizaba. Yo no bosquejo antes de comenzar. . . . Todo se desarrolla dentro de mi mente. Sólo queda un poco de pintura azul, esa pequeña porción que he esbozado allí. Y hay una parte que medio cobró vida como una máscara de los Hopi. Todo funciona. [Abril/mayo de 1975/33]

De Peter Schjeldahl, *El Occidente y el oriente y Robert Hudson* (Filadelfia: Moore College of Art, 1978):

Robert Hudson . . . puede parecer por sí solo prácticamente como un arquetipo del artista de la zona de la Bahía de San Francisco. La obra de Hudson en escultura, construcción, cerámica, collage, pintura, dibujo y otros medios es ciertamente muy variada, y está de sobra hablar de la «excentricidad» de sus imágenes. No obstante, Hudson es extremadamente sofisticado en su eclecticismo, con un tipo de sofisticación que tiende a eludir el gusto neoyorquino precisamente porque lo incluye y lo excede.

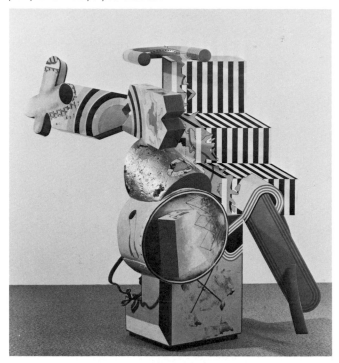

De Gabriel Laderman en *Artforum*:

Robert Hudson . . . continúa trabajando en la dirección que le dió reconocimiento nacional en los últimos dos años. Su habilidad para confundir totalmente al espectador al hacer aparecer volúmenes tri-dimensionales como virtualmente planos, y a la inversa, planos que parecen tri-dimensionales está a la vista en sus ocho obras en la Galería del Instituto de Arte de San Francisco. . . . Como estudiante en el Instituto de Arte de San Francisco la obra de Hudson gozó de mucha estima

Double Time, 1963, painted steel and aluminum
58.75 x 50 x 35", 150 x 127 x 89 cm

entre todos los escultores en metal profesionales que la vieron. Los artistas más viejos quedaron impresionados de su virtuismo en manipular grandes secciones de pesadas láminas de metal y barras de hierro para convertirlas en formas complejas. Hudson fué como estudiante, y lo sigue siendo, un artista muy ambicioso y prolífico. En un lapso de años muy corto ha dominado los problemas predominantes de la escultura en metal con tanta profundidad, osadía y habilidad consumada que uno podría preguntarse qué es lo que podría realizar en su próxima ventura. . . . Tal claridad de ideas se encuentra rara vez en un artista de veintitrés o veinticuatro años y es más extraña todavía su habilidad de captar una situación y actuar de una manera tan directa. El porqué de la presente obra se aclara cuando uno se da cuenta de que su ambición no es simplemente realizar piezas excelentes en un modo al menos parcialmente resuelto por otros, sino crear piezas en un área que nadie soñó existía. [Noviembre de 1967/45]

De Jan Butterfield en *Robert Hudson* (Nueva York: Galería Allan Frumkin, 1976):

Robert Hudson es un ser inocente e ingenuo con una sensibilidad altamente desarrollada hacia las imágenes primitivas; también tiene un sentido intuitivo y sofisticado del color y del equilibrio. . . . Las obras recientes de Hudson son una amalgamación de imágenes abstractas y representacionales; objetos mágicos primitivos tales como plumas, cuero sin curtir, cuerda, cuentas, palos, rocas, ramitas talladas y ramas que se entremezclan con arcos exquisitamente pintados, círculos, volúmenes y triángulos. El reconoce su deuda visual a Kandinsky lo cual es muy patente en sus nuevas pinturas y dibujos. . . . «En cuanto a esas piezas . . . creo que de ellas salía una especie de criatura. Me dediqué a unas cuantas cosas en particular—principalmente al color. Por ejemplo, haría una cosa especial—que funcionaba, y luego haría piezas especiales para ese color particular—porque sabía el efecto que ese color produciría.»

El singular empleo de pintura al trompe l'oeil en esas piezas tempranas era lo más extraordinario de ellas. «Me vino de pintar,» cuenta Hudson. «Comenzó con la pintura de piezas escultóricas. Me gustaba hacer algo fino de una arista gruesa por ejemplo. Me gustaba hacer que fueran dos cosas al mismo tiempo.» Estas obras eran notables no sólo por el puro arrojo de la pintura misma, sino también por su faceta innovadora. Nadie entre 1964-66 estaba trabajando en esa curiosa área intermedia entre la pintura y la escultura de la forma como lo hacía Hudson.

Estas obras tempranas fueron una maravillosa treta de prestidigitación. En ellas lo duro parecía viscoso; lo sólido se mostraba hueco y los elementos planos realizados con pintura al trompe l'oeil se hacían escalonados. Muchas de estas obras primerizas eran «acanaladas»—denominación de Hudson de la apertura del espacio con objeto de falsear, negar o confundir la percepción del volumen en el espectador. La yuxtaposición se convirtió en un proverbio. Combinaba tubos redondos con cubos, aristas cuadradas reales o imaginadas aquéllas que parecían derretidas o viscosas (si bien inmóviles en el tiempo) y las sobrepintó todas ellas con exquisito cuidado. «Lo que me gustaba de esas esculturas era hacer que las cosas planas parecieran redondas por medio de la pintura—el ser capaz de dejar al objeto ser lo que es y luego también ser al mismo tiempo un murmullo y una danza y muchas cosas más. Yo no sé si hay algo particular en ellas que tenga que ver con la vida—pero se trata de algo mágico.»

Interview avec Robert Hudson par John Marlowe, paru dans *Currant*:

Marlowe: Est-ce qu'on doit comprendre votre vie personnelle pour comprendre vos assemblages?

Hudson: Non, pas du tout. . . . Je fais des choses que l'on prend plaisir à voir et à revoir. . . . On accumule un savoir qui n'a pas de sens pour les autres et on le fait passer dans ces formes qui établissent la communication. L'art, c'est ça . . . tous les arts, l'écriture, les films, la musique . . . l'art, c'est l'âme des gens.

Marlowe: Est-ce que vous vous y prenez pour dessiner comme vous vous y prenez pour faire vos assemblages?

Hudson: Ma foi, prenez celui-ci. J'ai versé de la peinture bleue sur le papier avec une tasse et ensuite, comme s'il s'était agi d'une carte routière, je l'ai suivie. Je ne fais pas de sketch préliminaire. . . . L'oeuvre se développe à partir de ce que j'ai en tête. Il reste juste un peu de peinture bleue, ce petit coin que j'ai tracé, ici. Ailleurs, c'est devenu quelque chose qui ressemble à un masque Hopi. Ça se fait de soi-même. [Avril-mai 1975/33]

Peter Schjeldahl, *East and West and Robert Hudson* (Philadelphie: Moore College of Art, 1978):

Robert Hudson . . . peut, à lui tout seul, être considéré comme l'archétype de l'artiste de la Baie [de San Francisco]. Son oeuvre, tant en sculpture, qu'en construction, en céramique, collage, peinture, dessin et Dieu sait quel autre medium offre, à n'en pas douter, assez de variété, et il ne sert à rien de mentionner l'eccentricité de ses images. Cependant, Hudson est aussi d'un éclectisme extrêmement sophistiqué, de cette sophistication qui a tendance à éluder les goûts de New York, précisément parce qu'elle les englobe et les surpasse en même temps.

Dans *Artforum*:

Robert Hudson . . . continue à travailler dans la direction qui lui a valu d'être mondialement reconnu au cours des deux dernières années. Le don qu'il a de confondre le spectateur en faisant apparaître plates de lourdes machines tri-dimensionnelles et, inversement, de donner une apparence de volume à des surfaces plates est une fois de plus très visible dans les huit oeuvres qu'il expose au San Francisco Art Institute Gallery. . . . En tant qu'étudiant du San Francisco Art Institute, le travail de Hudson a été tenu en haute estime par pratiquement tous les sculpteurs sur métal qui le virent. Ses aînés étaient stupéfiés par la virtuosité avec laquelle il manipulait de larges sections de lourdes plaques ou de barres de métal et parvenait à leur donner des formes très complexes. Quand il était étudiant, Hudson était un artiste très ambitieux et très prolifique, il l'est toujours. En quelques brèves années, il a su maîtriser l'art de résoudre les problèmes les plus importants de la sculpture sur métal avec tant de souffle, d'audace et d'habileté consommée que l'on se demande jusqu'où il va aller. . . . Il est rare de trouver chez un artiste de vingt-trois ou vingt-quatre ans, une pensée aussi claire et il est plus rare encore d'y trouver la capacité de saisir la situation et d'agir en conséquence d'une manière si directe. Les raisons qui le poussent à travailler s'éclairent quand on réalise que son ambition n'est pas seulement de produire d'excellentes pièces en triomphant de difficultés qui avaient été, au moins partiellement, résolues par d'autres, mais de créer de grandes oeuvres là ou personne ne pensait que ce fût possible. [Novembre 1967/45]

Jan Butterfield dans *Robert Hudson* (New York: Allan Frumkin Gallery, 1976):

Robert Hudson est un innocent et un naïf avec une sensibilité à l'imagerie primitive très développée; il possède aussi un sens intuitif et sophistiqué de la couleur et de l'équilibre. . . . Les oeuvres récentes de Hudson sont un amalgame d'images abstraites et figuratives; des objets magiques primitifs tels que plumes, peaux non tannées, cordes, perles, batons, rocs, brindilles et branches sculptées pêle-mêle avec des arcs, des cercles, des volumes et des triangles peints de façon exquise. Il reconnaît avoir une dette visuelle envers Kandinsky, ce qui est clairement apparent dans ses nouvelles peintures et dans ses nouveaux dessins. . . . «A propos de ces pièces . . . je pense qu'il s'en dégageait une sorte de créature, comme un esprit. Je me suis tourné vers deux ou trois choses en particulier—surtout vers la couleur. J'essayais quelque chose—ça réussissait, alors je composais des pièces spécialement pour cette couleur-là—parce que je savais l'effet qu'elle produirait.»

Ce qu'il y avait peut-être de plus remarquable dans ces premières oeuvres était leur préoccupation avec la peinture en trompe-l'oeil. «Cela a commencé en peignant,» explique Hudson, «en peignant les pièces sculpturales. J'aimais faire quelque chose de fin à partir d'un large rebord, par exemple.» Ces oeuvres étaient remarquables non seulement à cause de la pure bravura de la pièce elle-même, mais aussi parce qu'elles représentaient d'innovation. Personne, en 1964–66 ne travaillait dans ce domaine inconnu entre la peinture et la sculpture en métal comme le faisait Hudson.

Ces premières oeuvres étaient de véritables tours de passe-passe. Le dur y apparaissait visqueux, le solide y apparaissait creux, des éléments plats, peints en trompe-l'oeil, devenaient un escalier. Nombre de ces éléments étaient «avec des fentes»—expression employée par Hudson pour élargir l'espace de façon à tromper, contredire ou confondre la perception que le spectateur avait du volume. «Juxtaposition» devint le mot-clef. Il combinait des tuyaux ronds avec des cubes, des rebords réels ou peints, de forme carrée, avec d'autres qui semblaient être fondus ou visqueux (mais gelés dans le temps) et sur tout cela, il peignait en en rajoutant, avec un soin infini. «Ce qui me plaisait dans ces sculptures était, en peignant, de donner à un objet plat l'apparence d'un objet arrondi—de garder un objet tel quel ou de le transformer en murmure, en pas de danse, en toutes sortes de choses. Je ne sais pas si, en eux, quelque chose avait du rapport avec la vie—mais ils en avaient certainement avec la magie.»

Running Through the Woods, 1975, mixed media with stuffed deer 76.5 x 49 x 49", 193 x 124 x 124 cm

Von John Marlowe mit Robert Hudson in *Currant*:

Marlowe: Muß man Ihr Leben verstehen, um Ihre Montagen zu verstehen:

Hudson: Nein, ganz und gar nicht. . . . Ich stelle Dinge, die sich gut anschauen lassen, immer wieder her. . . . Man schaffte sich die Kenntnis, die für niemanden einen Sinn ergibt, und allmählich bringt man sie in eine solche Form, die mitteilt. Das ist es, was Kunst tut. . . . Ich meine alle Kunst, Schriftstellerei, Filmkunst, Musik. . . . Es ist die Seele des Volkes.

Marlowe: Entwickeln Sie Ihre Zeichnungen so wie Ihre Montagen?

Hudson: Ja, wie diese. Ich goß etwas blaue Farbe aus einem Becher auf das Papier, und dann, wie eine Straßenkarte, verfolgte ich sie, wie sie zerfloß. Ich skizziere nicht bevor ich anfange. . . . Es entwickelt sich aus dem, was in meinem Kopf ist. Da ist nur ein bißchen blau übrig, dieser kleine Teil, den ich dort abgehoben habe. Und da ist ein Teil, der zufällig zu einer Hopi Maske geworden ist. Alles entwickelt sich. [April/Mai 1975/33]

Aus Peter Schjeldahl, *East and West and Robert Hudson* (Philadelphia: Moore College of Art, 1978):

Robert Hudson . . . könnte für sich alleine praktisch archetypisch für den Bay-Gegend-Künstler erscheinen. Hudsons Arbeit in Bildhauerei, Konstruktion, Keramik, Kollage, Malerei, Zeichnen und was sonst noch an Medien, ist sicherlich vielfältig genug, und die «Ekzentrizität» seiner Bilder ist nicht wegzuleugnen. Jedoch ist Hudson auch überaus intellektuell in seinem Eklektrizismus, mit einer Art von Sophistik, die danach neigt, den New Yorker Geschmäckern auszuweichen, eben weil sie sie einschließt und überschreitet.

Von Gabriel Laderman in *Artforum*:

Robert Hudson . . . arbeitet weiter in der Richtung, die ihm in den letzten beiden Jahren nationale Anerkennung gebracht hat. Seine Fähigkeit, den Betrachter positiv zu bestürzen, indem er großes Dreidimensionales fast eben erscheinen, und umgekehrt, ebene Flächen dreidimensional erscheinen läßt, wird sehr in den acht Werken deutlich, die in der San Francisco Art Gallery ausgestellt sind. . . . Als er Student am San Francisco Art Institute war, wurde Hudsons Werk von praktisch jedem berufsmäßigen Metallbildhauer, der es je gesehen hat, hoch eingeschätzt. Die älteren Künstler waren von seiner Virtuosität, große Stücke schwerer Metallplatten und Rohmaterial in komplexe Formen zu manipulieren, erstaunt. Hudson war als Student und heute immer noch ein sehr ehrgeiziger und produktiver Künstler. In einer sehr kurzen Spanne von Jahren meisterte er die vorherrschenden Probleme der Metallbildhauerei mit solcher Breite, Wagemut und vollendetem Geschick, daß man sich wunderte, was er denn als nächstes tun würde. . . . Solche Gedankenklarheit ist selten genug in einem Künstler von 23 oder 24 Jahren, und noch seltener ist die Fähigkeit, die Situation zu erfassen und danach in so direkter Weise zu handeln. Das Warum seiner gegenwärtigen Arbeit wird klarer, wenn man sich bewußt wird, daß sein Ehrgeiz ist, nicht nur ausgezeichnete Stücke in einer Weise zu machen, die wenigstens teilweise von anderen bestimmt ist, sondern auch großartige Stücke in einem Gebiet zu machen, dessen Existenz sich niemand erträumen ließ. [November 1967/45]

Aus Jan Butterfield in *Robert Hudson* (New York: Allan Frumkin Gallery, 1967):

Robert Hudson ist eine Unschuld und ein Naiver mit stark entwickelter Feinfühligkeit zur primitiven bildlichen Sprache; er hat auch einen intuitiven, hochentwickelten Sinn für Farbe und Gleichgewicht. . . . Hudsons jüngste Werke sind ein Amalgam abstrakter und repräsentativer Bilder; Objekte primitiver Magik wie Federn, Riemen, Bindfäden, Perlen, Stöcke, Steine, geschnitzte Ästchen und Zweige, die sich mit äußerst fein bemahlten Bögen, Kreisen, Behältern und Dreiecken vermischen. Er gibt zu, daß er Kandinsky Visuelles Schuldet, was stark in den neuen Gemälden und Zeichnungen zum Ausdruck kommt. . . . «Was diese Stücke angeht . . . Ich glaube, eine Art Geistkreatur kam aus ihnen heraus. Einigen Dingen öffnete ich mich besonders—meistens Farbe. Zum Beispiel würde ich etwas Besonderes machen—das funktionierte, und dann würde ich Stücke besonders für jene spezifische Farbe machen—denn ich wußte, was diese Farbe ergeben würde».

Das einzigartige Einhergehen von trompe l'oeil Malerei mit diesen frühen Stücken war vielleicht das Außergewöhnlichste an ihnen. «Es ergab sich aus dem Malen», erwähnt Hudson. «Es begann mit dem Bemalen der bildhauerischen Stücke. Zum Beispiel wollte ich etwas Dünnes aus einer dicken Kante machen. Ich wollte es zu zwei Dingen zur gleichen Zeit machen.» Diese Werke waren nicht nur bemerkenswert wegen der wahren Bravour des Gemäldes selbst, sondern wegen seiner Innovation. Niemand in den Jahren 1964–66 arbeitete in diesem eigenartigen Niemandsland zwischen Malerei und Metallbildhauerei im Sinn wie Hudson.

Diese frühen Werke waren wunderbare Kunstgriffe. In ihnen erschien Hartes zäh; Solides hohl; flache Elemente mit trompe l'oeil Malerei wurden Treppen. Viele dieser frühen Werke waren «gekerbt»—Hudsons Begriff für Öffnung des Raumes zum Zwecke, der Wahrnehmung des Raumes von seiten des Betrachters nicht zu entsprechen, sie in Abrede zu stellen oder in Unordnung zu bringen. Gegenüberstellung wurde zum Schlagwort. Er kombinierte runde Röhren mit Würfeln, wirkliche oder angedeutete Kanten mit jenen, die flüssig oder zäh erschienen (wenn auch erstarrt in der Zeit) und übermalte alle von ihnen mit feiner Sorgfalt. «Was ich an diesen Skulpture mochte, waren flache Dinge, die durch die Farbe rund wurden—nur in der Lage zu sein, den Gegenstand sein zu lassen, was er ist und darüber hinaus auch nur ein Flüstern, ein Tanz und eine ganze Menge von Dingen. Ich weiß nicht, ob es irgendetwas Besonderes an ihnen gibt, das mit dem Leben zu tun hat—aber es hat mit Magik zu tun».

Tlingit, 1981, aluminum and paint
180 x 96 x 48", 457 x 244 x 122 cm

Born: Sanger, California, 1930
Resides: Benicia, California

Manuel Neri

Manuel Neri

From Jan Butterfield in *Images & Issues*:
Neri: I have to explain that the figure is just a vehicle for all of those other ideas—all of that painting that I used to do before on canvas—all those ideas came into the figure. What's taking place on the surface of the structure when I move the material around or hack into it is no different from pushing paint around. The color on the surface is a natural extension of the way I have always worked. Color can either destroy a surface or it can accent or draw attention to a certain area or spot or form. Thank God the camera came along at the turn of the century and freed us from a lot of literalness. In spite of the camera, we are still tied to that millstone hanging around our necks that has "reality" printed on it. "Reality in Art." It is true that "art is what the artist says it is," but art's much bigger than that. The reality in the art is the artist. That personality. You can't separate the person from his work, even if the person and the work don't seem to jibe. [Spring 1981/38–43]

From Thomas Albright in the *San Francisco Chronicle*:
It has long been my impression that Neri is one of the most powerful sculptors alive; yet the force, the drama, the brooding, compelling mystery that one feels when seeing his work all together in the former Benicia church which he uses as a studio. . . . Like the paintings of de Kooning, Neri's sculptures seem to exist primarily as embodiments of energies and processes—an impulsive, spontaneous gesture here, a more considered refinement or recomplication there—locked in a tense, seemingly temporary, equilibrium. They are "works in progress," or perhaps in decay, but arrested together and gathered here in a collective expression of great power, pathos and grandeur. [30 September 1976]

From George Neubert, *Manuel Neri, Sculptor* (Oakland: The Oakland Museum, 1976):
Generally, these chalk-white figures are faceless and fragmented, invoking rather than mimicking natural human gestures and stances. Their bodies are usually female, although the description of sex and personality relies upon the sensuousness of the material and sculpted forms rather than upon specific references to anatomy.

The figure has provided Neri with a vehicle for personal expression and seems to exist as an embodiment of energies and processes sealing its feelings and emotions. The temporal quality of the medium and Neri's spontaneous method of exploration, rethinking and reworking emphasize the artist's conception of matter and spirit. He has discovered that this union of spirit and matter can be best demonstrated by returning to its most primitive conditions. . . .

From Thomas Albright in *Artnews*:
By the early 1960s, Neri's use of electric, violent surface color reached a peak; the sense of genre yielded to more self-contained forms. By contrast, his figures . . . tend to reduce color to spectral whites or ashen grays; the forms are more attenuated and fragile-looking than those of his earlier figures, a sense of frozen movement is emphasized rather than the formal relations of planes, which now tend to be less chiseled and rounded, more gnarled and globby, bearing fewer traces of cutting and sanding tools, more of the hand itself. In spirit, these new pieces suggest a parallel to the early paintings of Nathan Oliveira, with their bleak pathos and tragic beauty—and, of course, lurking in the wings, the sculpture of Giacometti. [1 January 1977/90]

From Jan Butterfield in *Images & Issues*:
The tradition of the figure as image and metaphor is one of the most pervasive themes in western sculpture. If we trace a line through the history of classical, figurative sculpture—from Egypt and archaic Greece through Michelangelo and Rodin—Manuel Neri is clearly an inheritor. Historically, his figures straddle time; they have more in common with their predecessors than with their contemporaries, yet their relationship to Abstract Expressionism is an important source of their impact and power. Neri's figures continue Bay Area figurative attitudes in sculptural rather than two-dimensional concerns; in fact, it is to the paintings of California's Elmer Bischoff, Nathan Oliveira, and (later) Joan Brown that one must look for peer group influence. [Spring 1981/38]

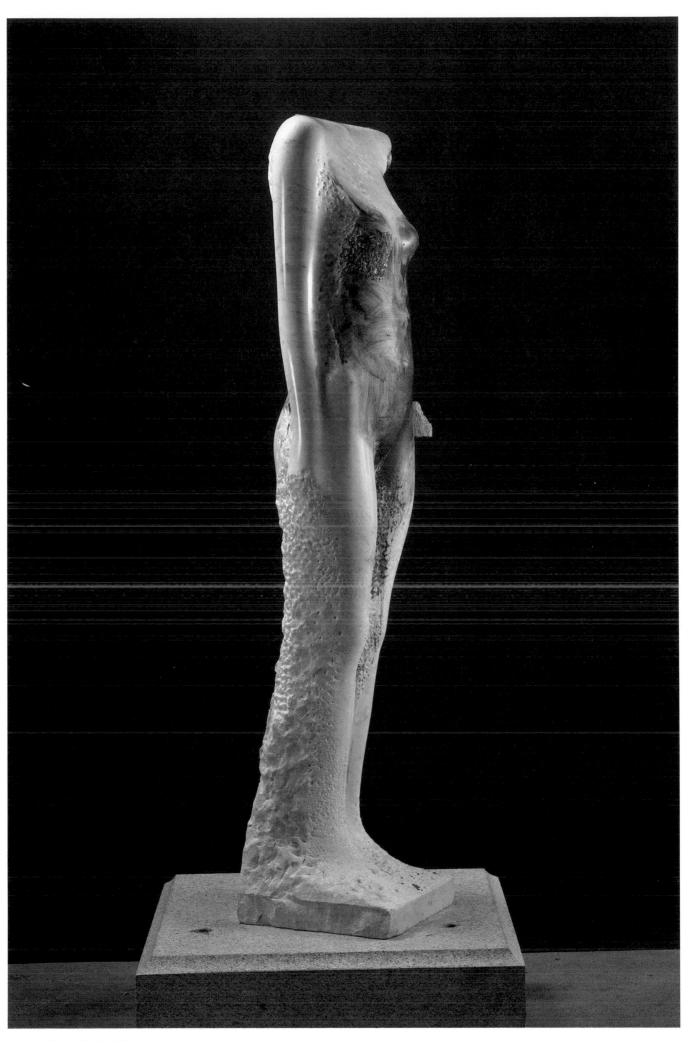

Carriona Figure No. 2, 1981
Marble with oil-based pigment
58 x 16 x 12"
147 x 41 x 30 cm
From a private collection

De Jan Butterfield en *Imágenes & Temas*:
Neri: Debo explicar que la figura es precisamente un vehículo
para todas las demás ideas—todas aquella pintura que solía
hacer antes en lona—todas esas ideas se incorporaron a la
figura. Lo que está ocurriendo en la superficie de la estructura
cuando manipulo el material o lo recorto no es diferente de
dar unas pinceladas. El color de la superficie es una extensión
natural de mi forma de trabajar habitual. El color puede des-
truir una superficie o puede acentuar o llamar la atención
hacia una cierta área o lugar o forma. Gracias a Dios que la
cámara fotográfica apareció a principios de siglo y nos liberó a
todos de la excesiva literalidad. A pesar de la cámara, todavía
estamos atados a esa piedra de molino que cuelga de
nuestros cuellos y que tiene la «realidad» grabada en ella.
«Realidad en el arte.» Es verdad que «el arte es lo que el artista
dice que es,» pero el arte es mucho más que eso. La realidad
en el arte es el artista. Es su personalidad. No se puede separar al hombre de su obra, incluso si la persona y la obra no
parecen coincidir. [Primavera de 1981/38–43]

De Thomas Albright en el *San Francisco Chronicle*:
Desde hace mucho tiempo he tenido la impresión de que Neri
es uno de los escultores más poderosos que todavía viven; sin
embargo, la fuerza, el drama, la meditación y el misterio en-
volvente que uno siente cuando contempla su obra en su conjunto en la antigua iglesia de Benicia que él utiliza como su
estudio. . . . Como las pinturas de de Kooning, las esculturas
de Neri parecen existir fundamentalmente como encarna-
ciones de energías y procesos—un gesto impulsivo y espontáneo aquí, un refinamiento o complicación más estudiados
allá—encerrados en un equilibrio tenso y aparentemente
transitorio. Son «obras en progreso,» o quizás en decadencia,
pero siempre capturadas y reunidas aquí en una expresión
colectiva de gran poder, patetismo y grandeza. [30 de
septiembre de 1976]

**De George Neubert, *Manual Neri, escultor* (Oakland:
El Museo de Oakland, 1976):**
Generalmente estas figuras de tiza blanca no tienen faz y están
fragmentadas, invocando, más que imitando, los gestos y las
posturas humanas naturales. Sus cuerpos son generalmente
femeninos, aunque la descripción del sexo y la personalidad
se basa en la sensualidad del material y de las formas exculpi-
das más que en referencias específicas a la anatomía.

La figura ha suministrado a Neri el vehículo de expresión
personal y parece existir como una encarnación de energías
y procesos que sellan sus sentimientos y emociones. La cualidad temporal del medio y el método espontáneo de explora-
ción, reconsideración y retoque de Neri, enfatizan la concep-
ción de la materia y el espíritu en el artista. Ha descubierto que
esta unión de espíritu y materia puede ser mejor demostrada
mediante el retorno a sus condiciones más primitivas. . . .

De Thomas Albright en *Artnews*:
Hacia principios de los años sesenta, el uso del color electri-
zante y violento en las superficies alcanzó su punto álgido en
Neri; el sentido de género dió paso a formas más autosufi-
cientes. En contraste, sus figuras . . . tienden a reducir el
color a blancos espectrales o a grises ceniza; las formas son
más tenues y parecen más frágiles que las de sus primeras
figuras; se acentúa un sentido de movimiento suspendido más
que las relaciones formales de los planos, que ahora tienden a
ser menos cinceladas y redondas, más rugosas e irregulares,
dejando menos huellas del uso de herramientas cortantes y de
lija, más de su propia mano. El espíritu de estas nuevas piezas
sugiere un paralelismo con las pinturas primerizas de Nathan

Oliveira, con su seco patetismo y su trágica belleza—y, por
supuesto, la escultura de Giacometti acechando en las alas.
[1 de enero de 1977/90]

De Jan Butterfield en *Imágenes & Temas*:
La tradición de la figura como imágen y metáfora es uno de
los temas más persistentes de la escultura occidental. Si trazá-
ramos una línea a través de la historia de la escultura clásica y
figurativa—desde Egipto y la Grecia antigua hasta Miguel
Angel y Rodin—Manuel Neri es claramente un directo sucesor.
Históricamente, sus figuras están a caballo en el tiempo;
tienen más rasgos en común con sus predecesores que con
sus contemporáneos, sin embargo su relación con el expresionismo abstracto es una importante fuente de su impacto y
poder. Las figuras de Neri representan una continuidad de la
tradición figurativa del Area de la Bahía de San Francisco hacia
preocupaciones escultóricas más que bidimensionales; de
hecho, hay que buscar la influencia de grupo en las pinturas
de Elmer Bischoff, Nathan Oliveira y (más tarde) Joan Brown,
todos ellos de California. [Primavera de 1981/38]

Seated Girl, 1959, plaster, wood, enamel
44 x 29.5 x 27.5″, 112 x 76 x 71 cm

Jan Butterfield, paru dans *Images & Issues*:
Neri: Je dois expliquer que la figure n'est qu'un véhicule pour toutes les autres idées—ce qu'avant je peignais sur une toile—toutes ces idées-là sont passées dans la figure. Ce qui se produit à la surface de la structure quand je ré-arrange le matériau ou quand je l'entame n'est pas différent de ce qui se passe quand j'étends la couleur. Quant à la couleur, elle est une extension de la manière dont j'ai toujours travaillé. La couleur peut détruire une surface ou elle peut accentuer ou attirer l'attention sur un certain point, ou sur une certaine forme. Grâces à Dieu, on a inventé l'appareil-photo au début du siècle et cela nous a délivrés pour une large part de la litéralité, mais en dépit de la photographie, nous continuons à porter, pendue à notre cou, cette meule qui porte gravé le mot «réalité», «la réalité en art». Il est vrai que «l'art est ce que l'artiste dit qu'il est», mais l'art est beaucoup plus que cela. La réalité dans l'art, c'est l'artiste, sa personnalité. Il est impossible de séparer la personne de son oeuvre, même si la personne et l'oeuvre ne semblent pas aller ensemble. [Printemps 1981/38–43]

Thomas Albright dans le *San Francisco Chronicle*:
Je suis d'avis depuis très longtemps que Neri est l'un des plus puissants sculpteurs en vie aujourd'hui; cependant la force, le drame, l'humeur sombre, le mystère irrésistible que l'on devine en voyant son oeuvre dans son ensemble dans l'ancienne église, à Benicia, qu'il a transformée en atelier. . . . Comme les tableaux de de Kooning, les sculptures de Neri semblent exister surtout comme des représentations d'énergies—une touche impulsive, spontanée ici, un détail plus pensé ou plus compliqué là—prisonnières d'un équilibre tendu, précaire en apparence. Ce sont des oeuvres «en devenir», ou peut-être en train de se défaire, mais suspendues et rassemblées là dans une expression collective de grande puissance, de pathos et de grandeur. [30 septembre 1976]

George Neubert, *Manuel Neri, Sculpteur* (Oakland: The Oakland Museum, 1976):
Généralement, ces figures d'un blanc de craie sont sans visage et fragmentées, suggérant plutôt qu'imitant les gestes et les postures naturelles du corps humain. Leurs corps sont d'habitude des corps de femme, bien que l'allusion au sexe et à la personnalité soit obtenue plutôt grâce à la sensualité qui se dégage du matériau et des formes sculptées que par des références spécifiques à l'anatomie.

La figure a fourni à Neri un véhicule d'expression personnelle et semble exister en tant qu'elle incarne des énergies qui en scellent les sentiments et les émotions. La qualité temporelle du medium et la méthode spontanée qu'a Neri d'explorer, de repenser et de retravailler mettent en valeur la conception que se fait l'artiste de la matière et de l'esprit. Il a découvert que la meilleure façon de décrire l'union de l'esprit et de la matière est de retourner à ses conditions les plus primitives. . . .

Thomas Albright dans *Artnews*:
Au début des années soixante, l'emploi par Neri de violentes couleurs électriques pour ses surfaces atteignit son apogée; son sens du genre le céda à des formes plus indépendantes. Par contraste, ses figures . . . tendent à réduire la couleur à un blanc spectral ou à des gris-cendre; les formes sont plus atténuées et d'apparence plus fragile que celles des figures premières, un sens de mouvement suspendu s'en dégage plutôt que celui de rapports de plans qui tendent maintenant à être moins ciselés et arrondis, plus rugueux et globuleux, portant moins la marque des outils à couper et à poncer et davantage celle de la main elle-même. Pour ce qui en est de l'esprit dans lequel elles ont été exécutées, ces sculptures

nouvelles font penser aux premières peintures de Nathan Oliveira dont elles ont la tristesse, le pathétique et la beauté tragique—et, bien sûr, à la sculpture de Giacometti. [1 er janvier 1977/90]

Jan Butterfield dans *Images & Issues*:
La tradition de la figure comme image et métaphore est l'un des thèmes les plus répandus de la culture occidentale. Si l'on remonte le fil de l'histoire de la sculpture classique figurative—de l'Egypte et de la Grèce archaïque à Michel-Ange et Rodin—Manuel Neri en est clairement l'héritier. Historiquement, ses figures chevauchent le temps; elles ont plus en commun avec les oeuvres de ses prédécesseurs qu'avec celles de ses contemporains, cependant, leur parenté avec l'Expressionisme abstrait est une source importante de leur impact et de leur puissance. Les figures de Neri perpétuent les attitudes figuratives de la Baie [de San Francisco] en sculpture plutôt qu'en peinture; de fait, c'est aux oeuvres des peintres californiens Elmer Bischoff, Nathan Oliveira et (plus tard) Joan Brown qu'il est redevable. [Printemps 1981/38]

Posturing Series No. 5, 1978, plaster, string, wood, wire, steel armature, styrofoam core
30 x 14 x 11.5", 76 x 36 x 30 cm

Von Jan Butterfield in *Images & Issues*:
Neri: Ich muß erklären, daß die Figur nur ein Gefährt für all diese anderen Ideen ist—das ganze Malen, das ich vorher auf der Leinwand zu tun pflegte—all diese Ideen kamen in die Figuren hinein, was sich auf der Oberfläche der Struktur abspielt, wenn ich das Material herumbewege oder in es hineinhacke ist nicht anders, als Farbe hin und her zu schieben. Die Farbe auf der Oberfläche ist eine natürliche Ausdehnung der Art und Weise, wie ich immer gearbeitet habe. Farbe kann entweder eine Oberfläche zerstören, oder sie kann betonen oder kann Aufmerksamkeit auf eine gewisse Fläche oder Stelle oder Form lenken. Gott sei Dank kam die Kamera um die Jahrhundertwende und hat uns von einer Menge Buchstäblichkeit befreit. Trotz der Kamera sind wir immer noch an den Mühlstein um unseren Hals gebunden, der «Wirklichkeit» darauf gedruckt hat. «Wirklichkeit in Kunst». Es ist wahr, daß «Kunst ist, was der Künstler sagt, sie ist», aber Kunst ist viel größer als das. Die Wirklichkeit in der Kunst ist der Künstler. Jene Persönlichkeit. Man kann die Person nicht von seinem Werk trennen wenn auch die Person und das Werk nicht übereinzustimmen scheinen. [Frühjahr 1981/38–43]

Von Thomas Albright im *San Francisco Chronicle*:
Ich hatte schon seit langem den Eindruck, daß Neri einer der kraftvollsten lebenden Bildhauer ist; und doch die Kraft, das Drama, das Brütende, zwingende Geheimnis, das man fühlt, wenn man sein ganzes Werk in der ehemaligen Benicia Kirche sieht, die er als Studio benutzt. . . . Wie die Gemälde von de Kooning, scheinen Neris Skulpturen in erster Linie als Verkörperung von Energien und Vorgängen zu existieren—eine impulsive spontane Geste hier, eine überlegte Verfeinerung oder Wiederverwicklung dort—in ein angespanntes, scheinbar zeitweiliges Gleichgewicht geschlossen. Sie sind «Werke im Fortschritt» oder vielleicht im Verfall, aber zusammen aufgehalten und gesammelt in einem kollektiven Ausdruck von großer Kraft, Pathos und Herrlichkeit. [30. September 1976]

Aus George Neuberg, *Manuel Neri, Sculptor* (Oakland: The Oakland Museum, 1976):
Im allgemeinen sind diese kalkweißen Figuren ohne Gesicht fragmentiert und rufen eher natürliche menschliche Gesten und stellungen hervor als sie zu imitieren. Ihre Körper sind gewöhnlich weiblich, allerdings ist die Beschreibung von Geschlecht und Persönlichkeit durch die Empfindlichkeit des Materials und der gehauenen Formen bedingt und nicht durch einen spezifischen Bezug zur Anatomie.

Die Figur hat Neri mit einem Gefährt für persönlichen Ausdruck versehen und scheint als eine Verkörperung von Energien und Vorgängen zu existieren, die ihre Gefühle und Gemütsbewegungen versiegelt. Die zeitliche Eigenschaft des Stoffes und Neris spontane Methode der Untersuchung, des Nocheinmaldenkens und -arbeitens betonen das Verständnis des Künstlers von Stoff und Geist. Er hat entdeckt, daß diese Verbindung von Stoff und Geist am besten dadurch darzustellen ist, indem man zu seinen primitivsten Zuständen zurückkehrt. . . .

Von Thomas Albright in *Artnews*:
Anfang der 60er Jahre erreichte Neris Gebrauch von elektrischer, heftiger Oberflächenfarbe einen Höhepunkt; das Gefühl für Gattung gab in sich selbst geschlossenen Formen Raum. Als Kontrast neigen seine Figuren dazu, Farben zu spektralem Weiß oder Aschgrau zu reduzieren; die Formen sind gedämpfter und gebrechlicher aussehend als jene seiner früheren Figuren, betont ist mehr ein Sinn für erstarrte Bewegung als die formalen Beziehungen von Flächen, welche jetzt weniger gemeißelt und gerundet, mehr knorrig und klumpig zu sein scheinen, und weniger Spuren von Schneid- und Schleifwerkzeugen tragen, mehr von der Hand selbst. Im Geiste schlagen diese neuen Stücke eine Parallele zu den frühen Gemälden von Nathan Oliveira vor, mit ihrem blassen Pathos und tragischer Schönheit—und natürlich in den Kulissen lauernd, die Bildhauerei von Giacometti. [1. January 1977/90]

Von Jan Butterfield in *Images & Issues*:
Die Tradition der Figur als Bild und Metapher ist eins der durchdringendsten Themen in westlicher Bildhauerei. Wenn wir eine Linie durch die Geschichte klassischer, figurativer Bildhauerei ziehen—von Ägypten und dem antiken Griechenland bis Michelangelo und Rodin—Manuel Neri ist offensichtlich ein Erbe. Historisch gesehen dehnen sich seine Figuren über die Zeit aus; sie haben mehr mit ihren Vorläufern gemeinsam als mit ihren Zeitgenossen, und doch ist ihre Beziehung zum Abstrakten Expressionismus eine wichtige Quelle ihrer Wirkung und Macht. Neris Figuren setzen die figurativen Einstellungen der Bay Gegend zu bildhauerischen und nicht zweidimensionalen Interessen fort; tatsächlich muß man zu den Gemälden Kaliforniens Elmer Bischoff, Nathan Oliveira und später Joan Brown schauen, um den Einfluß einer ebenbürtigen Gruppe zu entdecken. [Frühjahr 1981/38]

Blue Blond, 1979, plaster with dry pigment and water, steel armature, styrofoam core
34 x 18 x 25", 86 x 46 x 114 cm

Born: Oakland, California, 1934
Resides: Oakland, California

Sam Richardson

Sam Richardson

From Jan Butterfield in *Sam Richardson* (New York: Martha Jackson Gallery, 1976):
The new "Sierra Snow" series resulted from a "superbly lucky accident," which occurred on a commercial plane trip across the country: "the plane flew out of pattern because of a storm, and we came in off the Rockies over a particular section between California and the Sierras. I had driven over that part of the country before and had seen the buttes just kind of rising out of nowhere. I always liked the feeling of it, but felt I couldn't do too much with it. Suddenly this time, when we got to the top of the Sierras, they were covered with deep drifts of snow. It was very powerful, and it really hit me—the whole sense of it, and I knew I had to somehow deal with the magic. I don't suppose it would ever happen in quite that same way again"

From Orrel E. Thompson, *Sam Richardson* (Akron: Akron Art Museum, 1972):
as [sic] one confronts these environments, one becomes increasingly aware of their reference to a gigantic earth core—a cross-section lifted from the earth's crust, transplanted and isolated in a neutral visual space. It is partially this abstraction from site that forces the viewer to perceive his forms in a non-literal manner. we must call upon our memory of sensations built of past experiences to truly comprehend the innate beauty and meaning of his works.

From *The Museum of California* (The Oakland Museum):
Richardson's earliest work was as a landscape painter. He saw his early landscapes as being "somewhere between Diebenkorn and Bischoff, and there wasn't room to move there."

Having had an interest since childhood in model airplanes and automobiles, Richardson became caught up in the new plastic materials and paints of the 1960's, and his three-dimensional landscapes "were a natural outgrowth of all that new technology." [No. 8, February 1978/12]

From Joanne Dickson in *Visual Dialog*:
Sam Richardson loves the land. Snow capped mountains, ocean, rolling hills and wooded thickets are all part of his terrestrial gestalt. The desert is the theme underlying the current series of . . . work seen recently at the Hansen-Fuller Gallery. Masterfully skirting sentimentality, Richardson addresses himself to both literal and metaphorical issues.

Supple chamois suggests the color, texture and lateral sweep of the desert land. The leather is pale, delicately luminous. Surfaces are differentiated by the scars and striations inherent in the leather. Subtle manipulations, such as water staining, or traces of chalk create a further dimension. Occasionally, vestiges of pigment are introduced. The subdued tones are so atomized that one is never quite sure whether or not color is there at all.

These tiny landscape fragments are joined to slender wooden obelisks or float gently against the wall. Miniaturized objects interrupt the isolated stretches of land. These mysterious images are evidence of man's transient presence. In a literal sense they are drawn from archeology. . . . Richardson's references may have roots in antiquity but the work is far more densely contemporary in its realized form. The "Desert Images" series crystalize universal feelings regarding duration, space and loneliness. [No. 3, Spring 1979/27]

From Jan Butterfield in *Sam Richardson* (Chicago: Klein Gallery, 1982):
What one notices first is the color—exquisite, intense and glowing. There are virtually no parallels for this work. Few overpaint on sculpture, and no one in recent memory has treated seemingly abstract surfaces with the delicate, painterly sensibility so much in evidence here. What impacts next is the sense of movement, of activity, coupled with some undefined sense of purpose. The sculptures are clear and strong and it is impossible to shake their archaeological overtones. These works belong to history, and have hooked into it a long way back. This linkage gives them strength and meaning, for they are the inheritors of hundreds upon hundreds of years of making. . . . It is because of the enigma, the pondering, that this work has such strength. We *cannot* "know" and yet we *sense*: something has happened here—there is a purpose behind these structures that we can almost recall. Did our civilization worship at such an altar eons ago? Was this structure originally part of a ceremony now lost to us? Is there a meaning in the color? These ancient echoes stir the psyche and tap into the collective unconscious. We long to know that which we have been terrestrially a part of.

Split and Tied, 1984
Steel, bronze, acrylic urethane enamel
132 × 60 × 72"
335 × 152 × 183 cm
Lent by the artist

De Jan Butterfield en *Sam Richardson* (Nueva York: Galería Martha Jackson, 1976):

La nueva serie «Nieve de la sierra» fue el resultado de un «accidente increíblemente afortunado,» que ocurrió en un vuelo comercial cruzando el país: «el avión se salió de su rumbo debido a una tormenta y aparecimos en una determinada zona entre California y las Sierras pasando las Montañas Rocosas. Había conducido antes por esa parte del país y había visto las colinas que parece que salen de la nada. Siempre me había gustado esa sensación pero sentía que no podía aprovecharla. Esta vez, de repente, cuando sobrevolamos las cimas de las Sierras, estaban cubiertas con densas capas de nieve. Era una visión poderosa y me impresionó—en toda su dimensión, y entonces supe que tenía que enfrentarme a su magia. Supongo que esto no volverá a ocurrir de la misma forma.

De Orrel E. Thompson en *Sam Richardson* (Akron: Museo de Arte de Akron, 1977):

A medida que uno se enfrenta a estos entornos, uno se da cuenta cada vez más de su referencia a un núcleo terrestre gigantesco—una sección transversal que se eleva de la corteza terrestre, transplantada y aislada a un espacio visual neutral. Es en parte esta abstracción de lugar lo que obliga al espectador a percibir sus formas de una manera no literal. Debemos recurrir a nuestros recuerdos de sensaciones formados con experiencias pasadas para comprender cabalmente la belleza innata y el significado de sus obras.

De *El Museo de California* (El Museo de Oakland):

La obra temprana de Richardson se centraba en los cuadros de paisajes. El vislumbraba estos primeros paisajes como si estuvieran «en algún lugar entre Diebenkorn y Bischoff, y no hubiera espacio para deambular por allí.»

Richardson, quien siempre había tenido interés desde su niñez por aviones y automóviles de diseño, quedó prendado de los nuevos materiales y pinturas plásticos de los años 60, y sus paisajes tri-dimensionales «eran una extensión natural de toda aquella nueva tecnología.» [No. 8, febrero de 1978/12]

De Joanne Dickson en *Diálogo Visual*:

Sam Richardson ama la tierra. La montañas cubiertas de nieve, el océano, las colinas escarpadas y los bosques, son todos parte de su Gestalt terrestre. El desierto que subyace a su serie actual de . . . obras expuestas recientemente en la Galería Hansen-Fuller. Bordeando magistralmente el sentimentalismo, Richardson se compromete con temas literales y metafóricos.

La gamuza elástica sugiere el color, la textura y la extensión lateral del paisaje desértico. El cuero es pálido, delicadamente luminoso. Las superficies están diferenciadas por medio de las cicatrices y estrías inherentes al cuero. Las sutiles manipulaciones, tales como el descoloramiento con agua, o trazos de tiza crean una dimensión adicional. De vez en cuando se introducen también vestigios de pigmentos Los atenuados tonos han sido atomizados de tal manera que uno nunca puede tener la seguridad de si el color está o no presente.

Estos diminutos fragmentos de paisaje están unidos a delgados obeliscos de madera o flotan gentilmente contra la pared. Las extensiones aisladas de tierra son interrumpidas por objetos miniaturizados. Estas misteriosas imágenes son evidencia de la presencia transitoria del hombre. En un sentido literal están sacadas de la arqueología. . . . Es posible que las referencias de Richardson estén enraizadas en la antigüedad, pero su obra es mucho más densamente contemporánea en su ejecución. Las «Imágenes desérticas» constituyen una serie

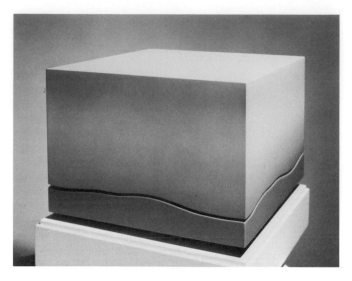

que cristaliza los sentimientos universales hacie el tiempo, el espacio y la soledad. [No. 3, primavera de 1979/27]

De Jan Butterfield en *Sam Richardson* (Chicago: Galería Klein, 1982):

Lo primero que salta a la vista es el color—exquisito, intenso y luminoso. Su trabajo no tiene paralelos. Pocos pintan sobre esculturas, y nadie que podamos recordar ha tratado, al parecer, las superficies abstractas con la delicada sensibilidad pictórica que se manifiesta aquí. Lo próximo que nos impresiona es el sentido de movimiento, de actividad junto con un vago sentido de propósito. Las esculturas son claras y fuertes, y es imposible desprenderse de sus alusiones a la arqueología. Estas obras pertenecen a la historia, y se han incorporado a ella desde hace mucho tiempo. Este enlace les dota de poder y significado, puesto que son las sucesoras de cientos y cientos de años de creatividad. . . . Es a causa de este enigma, de esta meditación, que su trabajo posee tal fuerza. *No podemos* «saber» y sin embargo lo *presentimos*: algo ha ocurrido aquí—detrás de estas estructuras hay un propósito que casi podemos recordar. ¿Es que nuestra civilización adoraba tal altar hace miles de años? ¿Era esta estructura parte de un ritual ya perdido? ¿Tiene el color un significado ancestral? Estos ecos antiguos conmueven la psique y penetran en el subconsciente colectivo. Ansiamos conocer aquello que constituye nuestro pasado terrestre.

It's Dawn Over that Guy's Sand Dunes (2 pieces, closed), 1968
fiberglass, plywood, lacquer
9 x 13 x 13", 23 x 33 x 33 cm

Jan Butterfield dans *Sam Richardson* (New York: Martha Jackson Gallery, 1976):

La nouvelle série intitulée «Sierra Snow» fut le résultat d'un «accident fort heureux», qui eut lieu à bord d'un avion commercial au cours d'un vol transcontinental: «L'avion fut dérouté à cause du mauvais temps et nous émergeâmes des Rocheuses au-dessus des Sierras de la Californie. J'avais traversé en voiture cette partie du pays et j'avais vu comment les sommets semblent, tout à coup, sortir de terre. Le spectacle m'avait frappé mais je ne pensais pas pouvoir l'utiliser. Cette fois, lorsque l'avion survola les sommets des Sierras, nous les découvrîmes sous une épaisse couche de neige. Mon impression fut très forte, cela tenait de la magie et je compris que j'allais devoir en faire quelque chose. Je doute que pareille expérience se reproduise.»

Orrel E. Thompson, *Sam Richardson* (Akron: Akron Art Museum, 1972):

En regardant ces paysages, l'on devient de plus en plus conscient qu'ils font allusion à un gigantesque noyau terrestre—à une coupe de la croûte terrestre, transplantée et isolée dans un espace visuel neutre. C'est en partie ce site abstrait qui force le spectateur à en percevoir les formes d'une manière non littérale. Nous devons chercher dans nos souvenirs d'expériences passées pour vraiment comprendre la beauté et la signification de ses oeuvres.

Paru dans *The Museum of California* (The Oakland Museum):

A ses débuts, Richardson était paysagiste. Il situait ses premières oeuvres «entre Diebenkorn et Bischoff. J'étais coincé,» dit-il.

Depuis son enfance, Richardson s'intéressait à la construction de modèles d'avion et d'automobiles; dans les années soixante, il fut séduit par les nouveaux matériaux en plastique et par les nouvelles peintures, et ses paysages en trois dimensions «furent issus de cette technologie nouvelle.» [No. 8, février 1970/12]

Joanne Dickson dans *Visual Dialog*:

Sam Richardson aime la terre. Les montagnes couvertes de neige, l'océan, les collines qui ondulent et les bois touffus, tout cela fait partie de sa *gestalt* terrestre. La série d'oeuvres à laquelle il travaille maintenant et qui vient d'être exposée à la galerie Hansen-Fuller, a pour thème le désert. Superbement habile à éviter la sentimentalité, Richardson s'intéresse à des questions à la fois littérales et métaphoriques.

Un chamois souple suggère la couleur, la texture et l'étendue du désert. Le cuir est pâle, délicatement lumineux. Les surfaces sont différenciées par les balafres et les striures inhérentes au cuir. Un traitement subtil, tel que des taches d'eau ou des traces de craie créent une dimension supplémentaire. De temps en temps, il introduit un soupçon de pigment. Les tons assourdis sont si atomisés que l'on ne peut jamais dire avec certitude s'il a employé de la couleur ou non.

Ces petits fragments de paysages sont joints par de minces obélisques de bois ou flottent avec légèreté contre le mur. Des objets en miniature interrompent la monotonie des bandes de terre isolées. Ces images mystérieuses sont comme des preuves attestant la présence éphémère de l'homme. Au sens littéral, elles ont pour source l'archéologie . . . mais, même si les références de Richardson ont leurs racines dans l'antiquité, l'oeuvre, dans sa forme, est tout à fait contemporaine. La série des «Images du désert» cristallise les sentiments universels que l'on éprouve envers la durée, l'espace et la solitude. [No. 3, printemps 1979/27]

Jan Butterfield dans *Sam Richardson* (Chicago: Klein Gallery, 1982):

Ce qui se remarque tout d'abord est la couleur—exquise, intense et lumineuse. Cette oeuvre n'a pas sa pareille. Il y a très peu d'artistes qui peignent leurs sculptures et, récemment, personne n'a traité de surfaces en apparence abstraites avec une sensibilité de peintre telle que celle que nous découvrons ici. Ce qui frappe ensuite est une impression de mouvement, d'activité, associée à intention qu'il est difficile de définir. Les sculptures sont nettes et puissantes et il est impossible de ne pas remarquer ce qu'elles doivent à l'archéologie. Ces oeuvres appartiennent à l'histoire, dans laquelle elles sont ancrées très loin. C'est cette parenté qui leur donne force et signification, car elles sont héritières de centaines d'années de devenir . . . c'est ce qu'il y a en elles d'énigme et de réflexion qui leur donne leur force. On *ne peut pas* «savoir» ce qu'elles représentent mais on *devine* que quelque chose s'est produit là—ces structures ont un but que nous pouvons presque identifier. Notre civilisation a-t-elle adoré au pied de ces autels, il y a des millénaires? Cette structure faisait-elle partie, autrefois, d'une cérémonie dont nous avons oublié les rites? Faut-il donner un sens rituel à la couleur? Ces échos du passé ébranlent notre psychisme et vont puiser dans l'inconscient collectif. Nous avons la nostalgie de retrouver ce dont nous avons fait partie terrestrement.

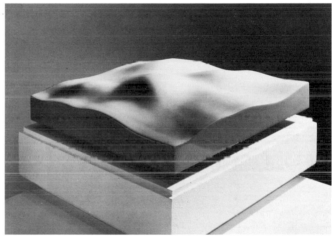

It's Dawn Over that Guy's Sand Dunes (2 pieces, open), 1968
fiberglass, plywood, lacquer
9 x 13 x 13", 23 x 33 x 33 cm

Von Jan Butterfield in *Sam Richardson* (New York: Martha Jackson Gallery, 1976):
Die neue «Sierra Snow» Reihe entstand aus einem «überaus glückhabenden Unfall», der sich auf einer normalen Flugreise durch das Land ereignete: «Das Flugzeug kam wegen eines Sturms von Kurs ab, und wir gerieten jenseits der Rockies in ein bestimmtes Gebiet zwischen Kalifornien und der Sierras. Ich bin vorher schon durch diesen Teil des Landes gefahren und habe die steilen Berge, die irgendwo aus dem nichts auftauchen, gesehen. Ich habe immer das Gefühl davon gemocht, aber merkte, daß ich nicht allzu viel damit anfangen konnte. Dieses Mal plötzlich, als wir auf der Spitze der Sierras ankamen, waren sie mit tiefen Schneewehen bedeckt. Es war sehr beeindruckend, und es hat mich sehr getroffen—das ganze Aufnehmen, und ich wußte, daß ich mich irgendwie mit dem Zauber beschäftigen mußte. Ich nehme nicht an, daß es jemals wieder in genau der gleichen Weise vorkommen wird.»

Von Orrel E. Thompson in *Sam Richardson* (Akron: Akron Art Museum, 1972):
Ist man mit diesen Umgebungen konfrontiert, wird einem zunehmend ihr Bezug zu einem gigantischen Erdkern bewußt—ein Querschnitt, der von der Erdkruste abgehoben ist, transplantiert und isoliert in einem neutralen visuellen Raum. Es ist teils diese Abstraktion von der Lage, die den Betrachter zwingt, seine Formen in einer nicht buchstäblichen Weise wahrzunehmen. Wir müssen auf unsere Erinnerung an Sensationen, die auf Erfahrungen in der Vergangenheit aufgebaut sind, zurückgreifen, um die angeborene Schönheit und Bedeutung seiner Stücke voll zu verstehen.

Aus *The Museum of California* (The Oakland Museum):
Richardsons frühestes Werk entstand als Landschaftsmaler. Er Diebenkorn und Bischoff, und es gab keinen Platz, dorthin zu ziehen».
Richardson, der seit seiner Kindheit ein Interesse an Modellbauflugzeugen und -autos hatte, wurde von den neuen Kunststoffmaterialien und Farben der 60er Jahre ergriffen, und seine dreidimensionalen Landschaften, «waren ein natürlicher Auswuchs all dieser neuen Technologie». [No. 8, Februar 1978/12]

Von Joanne Dickson in *Visual Dialog*:
Sam Richardson liebt das Land. Schneebedeckte Berge, das Meer, hügelige Landschaften und hölzerne Dickichte sind alle Teil seiner irdischen Gestalt. Die Wüste ist das Thema, das der derzeitigen Reihe von . . . Stücken, die kürzlich in der Hansen-Fuller Gallery gesehen werden konnte, zugrunde liegt. Richardson, der sich meisterhaft am Rande der Sentimentalität befindet, wendet sich selbst sowohl den buchstäblichen als auch den metaphorischen Fragen zu.
Geschmeidiges Polierleder suggeriert die Farbe, die Maserung und die seitliche Ausdehnung der Wüstenlandschaft. Das Leder ist blaß, fein leuchtend. Die Oberflächen sind durch Narben und Furchen innerhalb des Leders unterschiedlich gehalten. Kleine Kunstgriffe wie Wasserflecke oder Kreidestriche bilden eine weitere Dimension. Gelegentlich werden Überreste von Farbe mit eingebracht. Die gedämpften Farbtöne sind so zerstäubt, daß man nie ganz sicher ist, ob Farbe überhaupt vorhanden ist.
Diese winzigen Landschaftsfragmente werden mit schmalen hölzernen Obelisken verbunden oder gleiten sanft gegen die Wand. Verkleinerte Objekte unterbrechen die einsamen Landstriche. Diese mysteriösen Bilder sind Zeugnis des vergänglichen Daseins des Menschen. Im buchstäblichen Sinn sind sie der Archäologie entnommen. . . . Richardsons Bezüge könnten Wurzeln im Altertum haben, aber das Kunstwerk ist in seiner realisierten Form wesentlich zeitgenössischer. Die «Desert Images» Reihe kristallisiert allgemeine Gefühle, die die Dauer, den Raum und die Einsamkeit angehen. [No. 3, Frühjahr 1979/27]

Von Jan Butterfield in *Sam Richardson* (Chicago: Klein Gallery, 1982):
Was einem zuerst auffällt, ist die Farbe—fein, intensiv und glühend. Dem Wesen nach gibt es keine Parallelen zu diesem Kunstwerk. Einige übertreiben das Malen auf Skulpturen, und niemand in jüngster Erinnerung hat scheinbar abstrakte Oberflächen mit der zarten, malerhaften Feinfühligkeit, deren Beweis es hier genug gibt, bearbeitet. Was als nächstes einschlägt, ist der Sinn für Bewegung, für Tätigkeit, was mit einem undefinierbaren Sinn für wirkung verbunden ist. Die Skulpturen sind klar und stark, und es ist unmöglich, ihre archäologischen Obertöne abzuschütteln. Diese Kunstwerke gehören der Geschichte an und haben sich einen langen Weg zurück an ihre Fersen geheftet. Diese Verbindung gibt ihnen Kraft und Bedeutung, denn sie sind Erben jahrhundertjahrelangen Schaffens. . . . Wegen der Rätselhaftigkeit, dem Grübeln, gewinnt das Kunstwerk so an Ausdruckskraft. Wir *können nicht* «wissen» und doch *fühlen* wir: irgendetwas hat sich hier ereignet—da ist eine Absicht hinter diesen Strukturen, die wir fast erahnen können. Hat unsere Zivilisation vor Ewigkeiten an solch einem Altar Andacht verrichtet? War dieses Bauwerk ehemals Teil einer uns verlorengegangenen Feierlichkeit? Liegt in der Farbe eine Bedeutung? Diese antiken Echoes wühlen die Psyche auf und zapfen das kollektive Unterbewußtsein an. Wir sehnen uns danach, das zu wissen, wovon wir irdisch ein Teil sind.

Wedge Lifter, 1983, wood, paper, acrylic, string
7 x 15 x 15", 18 x 38 x 38 cm

Born: Omaha, Nebraska, 1935
Resides: Los Angeles, California

Michael Todd

Michael Todd

From Michael Todd cited in Thomas H. Garver, *Michael Todd: Recent Sculpture* (La Jolla: The Salk Institute, 1969-70):
Walk a line, run a plane, trip a curve, curve a tube, bridge a gap, curb a plane, roll a circle, dribble a cube. [P. 11]

From Thomas H. Garver, *Michael Todd: Recent Sculpture* (La Jolla: The Salk Institute, 1969-70):
Michael Todd's sculptures are lines, edges, and spaces, junctions and disjunctions, compositions by assembly and distribution. Working in New York in the mid-sixties Todd's sculptural response to his environment was that of a draftsman and assembler, reflecting his painterly background; and the forms he used tended to be spikey, linear and narrow. . . . He has been and remains a formalist, "less concerned," he says, "with imagery than with compositional attitude of the sculpture—to its position in space and its relationship to the ground. . . ." Thus Todd's most recent work turns again to his pictorial sensibilities. His sculptures become a variation upon the plane on which they rest and are, in effect, almost painterly in their effect, the more traditional sculptural considerations of containment of spaces being replaced by color spots, edges and lines. These sculptures act out their subversions, however, for they trap one's motion across them, impeding movement across their field, and acknowledging their physicality with quiet, yet insistent authority. [PP. 5, 6]

From Charles Kessler in *Journal/The Los Angeles Institute of Contemporary Art*:
Kessler: In Southern California there aren't many sculptors working in metal—resin has been the most popular medium.
Todd: Well, for me, metal, although very hard and stubborn, is ultimately the most flexible medium in sculpture. I can get so much more variety of form than anything that is cast or fabricated. I can get structural support I couldn't get out of clay, as much as I like the feeling and texture of clay. I can work larger, with greater openness in space and form, than with any other medium.
   I am somewhat unique on the West Coast, since my work is about form, abstract form as opposed to color, light and finish the way Los Angeles sculpture is.
Kessler: Do you think you relate better to West Coast painters, than to the sculptors?
Todd: I can't find any specific relationship, although I certainly like the work of Sam Francis, Ed Moses, Richard Yokomi, Ron Davis, Diebenkorn, and a lot of California painters. Also, I would like to leave the option of painting open for myself.
Kessler: Do you think you might move into painting?
Todd: Since I returned to California, I have been painting in spare moments between sculpture and teaching. And in the future I hope to get into it further. My painting, as little of it as there is, has helped liberate my sculpture. There is a definite dialog. Eventually, perhaps the painting will have more to say than the sculpture. I don't know—it remains to be seen.
Kessler: Do you think painting might influence you to make colored sculpture?
Todd: No. Only in terms of the fluidity of line and plane does it influence the sculpture. It can't influence the sculpture in terms of color. [No. 10, March-April 1976/18, 19]

From Wade Saunders in *Art in America*:
In the ten years he has made sculpture on the West Coast, Michael Todd has exchanged a jaunty, axial geometry for an open calligraphic format, and has introduced mangled material and foundry spill into his vocabulary of plates and pipes. He developed his earlier work in the round; the recent pieces are more frontal. He has retained his insistent references to the gestural marking exemplified in Zen painting. [No. 66, November-December 1978/159]

From Carrie Rickey in *Artforum*:
Todd is obviously after associations with the Japanese art of flower arrangement. What's in a name? Well, Todd's sculptures are astonishingly delicate and arranged like . . . flowers. The components are bulky pieces of steel detritus, and consequently it's no mean achievement that the junk is arranged with such grace. Some of the sculptures are monumental— one is ten feet high—but they seem weightless. Almost the work of a draughtsman rather than a sculptor, these works are arranged rather than constructed. Outside the laws of gravity, they seem to float rather than stand. . . . What makes Todd's sculptures so remarkable is that for large-scale steel work they are never priapic and heavy, but have an aerated, open quality that's exhilarating in work of its size and material. Todd transforms the menacing and rusty scraps of steel into elegantly lacquered confluences. The dynamic between the draughtsman's line and the sculptor's mass makes this work exciting. [No. 17, March 1979/71, 72]

Nataraja I, 1982
Steel
216 × 192 × 96″
549 × 488 × 244 cm
Lent by the artist

De Michael Todd citado en Thomas H. Garver,
Michael Todd: escultura reciente **(La Jolla:**
El Instituto Salk, 1969-70):
Andar una línea, manejar un avión, salirse de una curva,
doblegar un tubo, llenar un vacío, controlar un plano, esbozar
un círculo, esquivar un cubo. [pág. 11]

De Thomas H. Garver, *Michael Todd: escultura*
reciente **(La Jolla: El Instituto Salk, 1969-70):**
Las esculturas de Michael Todd son líneas, aristas, espacios,
uniones y disyunciones, son composiciones de ensamblaje y
distribución. En su trabajo en Nueva York a mediados de los
sesenta la respuesta escultórica de Todd a su entorno fue la
de un diseñador y montador, lo que refleja su formación como
pintor; las formas que usó tendían a ser radiales, lineales y
estrechas. . . . Fue y sigue siendo un formalista, «menos preo-
cupado,» asegura, «con las imágenes que con la actitud de
composición en su escultura—con su posición en el espacio y
a sus relaciones con el suelo. . . .» Así pues la obra más reciente de Todd vuelve de nuevo a su sensibilidad picórica. Sus
esculturas se tornan una variación sobre el plano en el que se
apoyan y son, en efecto, casi pictóricas en el efecto que pro-
ducen, y las consideraciones escultóricas más tradicionales en
cuanto a contención de espacios son reemplazadas por
manchas de color, aristas y líneas. Estas esculturas expresan
sus subversiones puesto que atrapan el movimiento entre
ellas, impidiendo que éste atraviese su campo y reconociendo
su naturaleza física con autoridad calmada pero insistente.
[págs. 5, 6]

De Charles Kessler en *Journal/El Instituto de Arte*
*Contemporáneo de Los Angeles***:**
Kessler: En California del Sur no hay muchos escultores que
trabajen con el metal—la resina ha sido el medio más popular.
Todd: Bueno, para mí el metal, aunque duro y obstinado, es
en definitiva el material más flexible para la escultura. Yo
puedo obtener una variedad de forma mayor que lo que se
forja o se fabrica. Puedo lograr un apoyo estructural que no
podría conseguir con la arcilla, por mucho que me guste el
tacto y la textura de la arcilla. Puedo trabajar a mayor escala,
con mayores aperturas de espacio y forma, más que con
cualquier otro medio.

De alguna forma soy único en la Costa Oeste, puesto que
mi obra está preocupada por la forma, la forma abstracta en
oposición al color, la luz y el acabado que privan en la escultura de Los Angeles.
Kessler: ¿Cree Vd. que se identifica mejor con los pintores de
la Costa Oeste que con los escultores?
Todd: No puedo encontrar una relación especiífca, aunque
ciertamente me gusta la obra de Sam Francis, Ed Moses,
Richard Yokomi, Ron Davis, Diebenkorn y muchos otros pintores californianos. Asimismo, me gustaría tener siempre
abierta la opción de pintar.
Kessler: ¿Cree Vd. que podría cambiarse a la pintura?
Todd: Desde que he vuelto a California he estado pintando en
momentos de ocio entre mi trabajo escultórico y la enseñanza.
Y en el futuro espero dedicarme más a ella. Mi pintura, por
escasa que sea, me ha ayudado a liberar mi escultura. Hay
definitivamente un diálogo entre ellas. Más tarde quizá con la
pintura pueda expresar más que con la escultura. No lo sé—
queda por ver.
Kessler: ¿Cree Vd. que la pintura puede llevarle a realizar escultura en color?
Todd: No. Sólo influye en mi escultura en referencia a la flui-
dez de la línea y del plano. No puede influir a mi escultura en
cuanto al color. [No. 10, marzo/abril de 1976/18, 19]

De Wade Saunders en *Arte en América***:**
En los diez años de escultor en la Costa Oeste Michael Todd
ha cambiado una geometría vistosa y axial por un formato
abiertamente caligráfico, y ha introducido material deformado
y el vertido de fundición a su vocabulario de planchas y tubos.
Sus primeras obras se desarrollaron en lo esférico; las piezas
más recientes son más frontales. Pero ha mantenido sus
insistentes referencias a los rasgos gestuales ejemplificados en
las pinturas Zen. [No. 66, noviembre-diciembre de 1978/
159]

De Carrie Rickey en *Artforum***:**
Todd persigue obviamente el tipo de asociaciones del arte
japonés de la disposición floral. ¿Qué hay en un nombre?
Bueno, las esculturas de Todd son sorprendentemente delica-
das y están dispuestas como . . . flores. Los componentes
son piezas masivas de detrito de acero, y por consiguiente no
es logro pequeño que el escombro esté dispuesto con tal
gracia. Algunas de las esculturas son monumentales—una de
ellas mide diez pies de alto—pero parecen no tener peso.
Estas obras más dispuestas que compuestas, reflejan la obra
de un diseñador más que la de un escultor. Eludiendo las leyes
de la gravedad, parecen flotar más que erguirse. . . . Lo que
hace notable a las esculturas de Todd es que, para ser obras
de acero a gran escala, nunca se hacen priápicas y pesadas,
sino que más bien poseen una cualidad abierta y oreada, que
es regocijante en obras de este tamaño y material. Todd trans-
forma las amenazadoras y oxidadas virutas de acero en con-
fluencias elegantemente barnizadas. El dinamismo entre la
línea del diseñador y la masa del escultor le da a la obra una
emoción especial. [No. 17, marzo de 1979/71, 72]

Encinitas, 1968, Cor-ten steel
84 x 144 x 96", 213 x 366 x 244 cm

Michael Todd cité dans Thomas H. Garver, *Michael Todd: Sculpture récente* (La Jolla: The Salk Institute, 1969-70):

Il tire une ligne, développe une surface, saute une courbe, courbe un tube, remplit un espace, ferme un cercle, dribble un cube. [p. 11]

Thomas H. Garver, *Michael Todd: Sculpture récente* (La Jolla: The Salk Institute, 1969-70):

Les sculptures de Michael Todd sont lignes, rebords et espaces, jonctions et disjonctions, compositions par assemblage et distribution. Alors qu'il travaillait à New York, au milieu des années soixante, la réponse de Todd, en tant que sculpteur, à son environnement fut celle d'un dessinateur industriel et d'un monteur, attitude qui réfléchissait sa formation de peintre; et les formes qu'il employait tendaient à être pointues, linéaires et étroites. . . . Il a été et demeure un amoureux de la forme, «moins attaché» dit-il, «à l'imagerie qu'à la composition des pièces, à leur position dans l'espace et à leur rapport avec le sol. . . .» Ainsi le travail le plus récent de Todd marque-t-il un retour à sa sensibilité de peintre. Ses sculptures deviennent des variations sur la surface sur laquelle elles reposent et sont, effectivement, d'un effet presque pictural, les considérations de volumes, traditionnelles dans la sculpture, le cédant aux taches de couleur, aux rebords et aux lignes. Toutefois, ces sculptures expriment leurs subversions, car elles emprisonnent le mouvement, en empêchent la progression à travers leur champ et accusent leur physicalité avec une autorité tranquille mais forte. [pp. 5, 6]

Charles Kessler dans *Journal/The Los Angeles Institute of Contemporary Art*:

Kessler: En Californie du Sud, il n'y a pas beaucoup de sculpteurs qui travaillent le métal—la résine est beaucoup plus populaire.

Todd: En ce qui me concerne, le métal, bien qu'il soit dur et qu'il résiste, est finalement le matériau qui se prête le mieux à la sculpture. Je peux en tirer beaucoup plus de formes que de n'importe quoi d'autre de moulé ou de fabriqué. Je peux en obtenir un support structural que ne me donnerait pas l'argile, bien que j'aime la texture de l'argile. Je peux faire plus grand, avec plus d'ouverture d'espace et de forme que je ne le pourrais avec quoi que ce soit d'autre.

Mon travail est unique, sur la Côte Ouest, en ce sens qu'il y est question de la forme, de la forme abstraite et non pas de la couleur, de la lumière et du fini comme dans les autres sculptures créées à Los Angeles.

Kessler: Vous découvrez-vous plus d'affinités avec les peintres de la Côte Ouest qu'avec ses sculpteurs?

Todd: Je ne trouve pas de rapports spécifiques entre ces derniers et moi, bien que j'aime ce que font Sam Francis, Ed Moses, Richard Yokomi, Ron Davis, Diebenkorn et beaucoup d'autres peintres californiens. J'aimerais bien aussi me réserver l'option de peindre si l'envie m'en prenait.

Kessler: Pensez-vous passer un jour de la sculpture à la peinture?

Todd: Depuis que je suis revenu en Californie, j'ai fait de la peinture pendant mes loisirs, quand je ne suis pas occupé à sculpter ou à enseigner. Dans l'avenir, j'espère y consacrer davantage de temps. Ma peinture, le peu qu'il y a, m'a aidéà me libérer en sculpture. Il y a un dialogue certain entre les deux. Peut-être la peinture finira-t-elle par avoir plus à dire que la sculpture. Je n'en sais rien—on verra.

Kessler: Pensez-vous que la peinture puisse vous inspirer des sculptures colorées?

Todd: Non, elle ne peut influencer la sculpture qu'en termes

de fluidité de ligne et de surface, pas de couleur. [No. 10, mars-avril 1976/1'8, 19]

Wade Saunders dans *Art in America*:

Depuis dix ans qu'il sculpte sur la Côte Ouest, Michael Todd est passé d'une sorte de géométrie axiale insouciante à un format qui tient de la calligraphie et il a introduit les rognures de métal lacérées et les déchets de fonderie dans son vocabulaire de plaques et de tuyaux. Il créait ses premières oeuvres en ronde-bosse, les dernières se regardent plus de face. Toutefois, il a conservé son goût prononcé pour les indications gestuelles de la peinture Zen. [No. 66, novembre-décembre 1978/159]

Carrie Rickey dans *Artforum*:

Il est évident que Todd cherche des associations avec l'art japonais des arrangements floraux. Je veux dire par là que les sculptures de Todd sont extraordinairement délicates et disposées comme . . . des fleurs. Elles sont formées de gros morceaux de déchets d'acier et, par conséquent, ce n'est pas peu de dire que toute cette ferraille est arrangée avec grâce. Certaines de ces sculptures sont monumentales—l'une d'entre elles mesure dix pieds de haut—mais elles ne semblent pas peser. Paraissant plutôt l'oeuvre d'un dessinateur industriel que celle d'un sculpteur, ces oeuvres sont arrangées au lieu d'être construites. Etrangères aux lois de la gravité, elles donnent l'impression de flotter et non de se tenir debout. . . . Ce qui les rend si remarquables, c'est que pour un travail sur métal de cette taille, elles ne sont jamais ni priapiques ni lourdes, mais au contraire ouvertes, aérées, ce qui est vivifiant si nous en considérons les dimensions et le matériau dont elles se composent. Todd transforme les déchets d'acier rouillé et menaçant en confluences élégamment laquées. C'est la dynamique entre la ligne du dessinateur et la masse du sculpteur qui fait l'intérêt de l'oeuvre. [No. 17, mars 1979/71, 72]

Monet Lily Pad Table, 1969, painted steel
18 x 96 x 54", 46 x 244 x 137 cm

**Von Michael Todd zitiert in Thomas H. Garver,
Michael Todd: Recent Sculpture (La Jolla: The Salk
Institute, 1969-70):**
«Walk a line, run a plane, trip a curve, curve a tube, bridge a
gap, curb a plane, roll a circle, dribble a cube». [p. 11]

**Aus Thomas H. Garver, *Michael Todd: Recent
Sculpture* (La Jolla: The Salk Institute, 1969-70):**
Michael Todds Skulpturen sind Linien, Kanten und Räume,
Verbindungen und Trennungen, Kompositionen durch Mon-
tage und Verteilung. Während Todd Mitte der 60er Jahre in
New York arbeitete, war seine bildhauerische Antwort auf
seine Umgebung die eines Zeichners und Monteurs, die seinen
malerhaften Hintergrund widerspiegelten; die Formen, die er
benutzte, neigten dazu, spitz, gradlinig und eng zu sein. . . .
Er war und bleibt ein Formalist, «weniger» wie er sagt «sich um
Bildhaftigkeit als um kompositorische Haltung der Skulptur zu
kümmern—in ihrer Lage im Raum und ihrem Bezug zum Boden». . . . So wendet sich Todds jüngste Arbeit wieder seinen
bildhaften Feinfühligkeiten zu. Seine Skulpturen werden anders
auf der Fläche, auf der sie ruhen, und sind tatsächlich fast malerhaft in ihrer Wirkung, je häufiger traditionelle bildhauerische
Betrachtungen der Beschaulichkeit der Räume durch Farb-
flecke, Kanten und Linien ersetzt werden. Diese Skulpturen
stellen jedoch ihre Umstürze dar, denn sie fangen den Gang
eines jeden über sich ein, hindern Bewegung über ihr Feld und
erkennen ihre physische Natur mit ruhiger und doch beharrli-
cher Authorität an. [pp. 5, 6]

**Von Charles Kessler in *Journal/The Los Angeles
Institute of Contemporary Art*:**
Kessler: In Südkalifornien gibt es nicht viele Bildhauer, die mit
Metall arbeiten—Harz ist der populärste Stoff.
Todd: Nun für mich ist Metall, wenn auch sehr hart und
strengflüssig, letztlich der vielseitigste Stoff in der Bildhauerei.
Ich kann so viel mehr Arten von Form herausholen, als mit
irgendetwas anderem, das gegossen oder hergestellt ist. Ich
kann strukturelle Stütze bekommen, die mir Ton nicht bietet,
so sehr ich auch das Gefühl und die Beschaffenheit mag. Ich
kann in größeren Maßstäben arbeiten, mit einer größeren
Offenheit an Raum und Form, als mit einem anderen Stoff.

Tulip, 1969, lacquered steel
69 x 148 x 148", 175 x 376 x 376 cm

An der Westküste bin ich etwas einzigartig, da meine
Arbeit sich mehr auf die Form bezieht, abstrakte Form im
Gegensatz zu Farbe, Licht und Vollendung wie es die Los
Angeles Skulptur ist.
Kessler: Glauben Sie, Sie tendieren eher zu den Westkü-
stenmalern als zu den Bildhauern?
Todd: Ich kann keine spezifische Beziehung feststellen, wenn
ich auch sicherlich die Arbeit von Sam Francis, Ed Moses,
Richard Yokomi, Ron Davis, Diebenkorn und einer Reihe kali-
fornischer Maler schätze. Ferner möchte ich mir die Wahl zur
Malerei selbst offenhalten.
Kessler: Glauben Sie, Sie könnten in die Malerei gehen?
Todd: Seitdem ich nach Kalifornien zurückgekehrt bin, habe
ich in spärlichen Momenten zwischen Bildhauerei und Lehrtä-
tigkeit gemalt. In der Zukunft hoffe ich, mich mehr mit ihr zu
beschäftigen. Meine Malerei, so wenig es auch von ihr gibt
trug dazu bein, meine Skulptur zu befreien. Es gibt eine be-
stimmte Korrespondenz. Gelegentlich hat die Malerei vielleicht
mehr zu sagen als die Bildhauerei. Ich weiß nicht—man muß
es sehen.
Kessler: Glauben Sie, daß Malerei Sie beeinflussen könnte,
farbige Skulpturen zu machen?
Todd: Nein. Nur in Begriffen des Flusses von Linie und Fläche
beeinflußt sie die Bildhauerei. Sie kann die Bildhauerei nicht in
Hinsicht auf Farbe beeinflussen. [No. 10, März/April 1976/18, 19]

Von Wade Saunders in *Art in America*:
In den zehn Jahren, in denen er an der Westküste Bildhauerei
betrieben hat, hat Michael Todd eine umschweifende Axial-
geometrie gegen ein offenes kalligraphisches Format ausge-
tauscht und hat zerstückeltes Material und Gießereiüberreste in
sein Vokabular von Platten und Röhren eingeführt. Er entwickelte sein früheres Werk in der Runde; die jüngeren Stücke
sind vordergründiger. Er hat seine beharrlichen Bezüge zu den
gestischen Kennzeichnungen, wie sie in der Zen-Malerei
beispielhaft sind, beibehalten. [No. 66, November-Dezember
1978/159]

Von Carrie Rickey in *Artforum*:
Todd ist offentsichtlich auf Assoziationen mit der japanischen
Kunst des Blumensteckens aus. Was steckt hinter einem Na-
men? Nun, Todds Skulpturen sind erstaunlich delikat und
angeordnet wie . . . Blumen. Die Bauteile sind klobige Stücke
von Stahlschutt, und folglich ist es keine geringe Leistung, daß
der Abfall mit solcher Anmut angeordnet ist. Einige der Skulpturen sind monumental—eine ist 10 Fuß hoch—aber sie
erscheinen schwerelos. Fast das Werk eines Zeichners und
nicht eines Bildhauers, sind diese Werke angeordnet und nicht
gebaut. Jenseits der Gesetze der Schwerkraft scheinen sie
eher zu schweben als zu stehen. . . . Was Todds Skulpturen
so bemerkenswert macht, ist, daß sie als großmaßstäbige
Stahlstücke niemals priapisch und schwer sind, sondern eine
poröse, offene Qualität haben, die in einem Werk seiner Größe
und seines Stoffes aufheiternd ist. Todd verwandelt die be-
drohlichen und rostigen Stahlteile in elegant lackierte Vereini-
gungen. Die Dynamik zwischen der Linie des Zeichners und
der Masse des Bildhauers macht dieses Werk aufregend.
[No. 17, März 1979/71, 72]

Born: Fort Collins, Colorado, 1936
Resides: Venice, California

DeWain Valentine

DeWain Valentine

From John Coplans, *DeWain Valentine: Recent Sculpture* (Pasadena: Pasadena Museum of Art, 1970):

Valentine: In a sense, I feel the larger pieces are much freer— much more open. I'm really interested in a kind of spatial openness within and around the piece. A kind of totally transparent space. I think the change of scale is obviously one of the most important differences. It is not so much that the pieces have become larger, but that the viewer has to perceive them and see in a much different way even though the same piece could be made smaller. Otherwise the viewer can't become involved with the kind of field of transparency that interests me most. I'm really interested in them much more as fields of transparency and as fields of transparent color than sculptural shapes.

Coplans: And light?

Valentine: And light, yes.

Coplans: So therefore they have to have an architectural environment to resonate against.

Valentine: Yes, and I think that ultimately—even though I have mixed feelings about this—my work will operate better in a specific architectural environment, a very specific kind of space that encloses and operates with the piece to unify the viewer's experience of the transparency of the volume around the piece, as well as the transparency and light quality within the piece.

Coplans: As a matter of interest, have you ever thought of making environments—i.e., by controlling the Architectural space more directly than by placing an object in space.

Valentine: Absolutely. And the obvious extension would be to somehow totally enclose the viewer or totally involve him in some kind of environmental situation in which he is confronted by a complete situation—of a total volume of transparency in which he could exist physically. In effect, the problem is to construct one. It would have to be built in a specific place and it would exist for a period of time and continue to exist in this specific place or be destroyed.

From John Lloyd Taylor in *Art International*:

Valentine is an artist who possesses remarkable technical virtuosity—an excellence of craftsmanship equaled only by Larry Bell amongst his West Coast peers, and an elegance perhaps unmatched by sculptors elsewhere. Valentine and Bell have brought to the sensibility of sculptural form and illusion the embodiment of minimalistic precisionism initially set forth by Donald Judd. . . . Valentine has worked with widely varied sculptural forms, moving continuously toward his eventual recent abandonment of sculptural objectness. Yet within every stylistic development arc his pervading concerns for transparency, translucency, and the diffractive qualities of prismatic color suspended volumetrically in space. [No. 7, September 1973/21–24]

From Peter Plagens, *DeWain Valentine Sculpture* (New York: Denise René Gallery, 1973):

For the past half-dozen years, Valentine's work has been among the most important solid-object sculpture on the West Coast, and of those who have stuck with the ageless precept of an irreducible object, among the best sculpture in the country. These judgements should overshadow the important, but secondary fact that Valentine is a premier technician among those artists working in resin. He has managed, in spite of problems with heat, weight, and the danger of impurities, optics as clear and pure as those of his colleagues, while retaining the convincing mass of major sculpture.

But his major achievement has been the development of substantial sculpture during the Sixties, bringing together the presence of physical mass in palpable kinesthetic space and the "advanced" optical/perceptual properties precursing such artists as James Turrell, Michael Asher, later Robert Irwin, and Ron Cooper's newer work. I wrote of a DeWain Valentine piece in 1971: "DeWain Valentine gives the most muscle and spectacle of all the many area artists casting in resin; he does what obviously ought to be done with the material, exploiting its capacities for purity, color, transparency, and mystique. His man-size transparent "purple" disc. . . . is paradoxically thicker *and* lighter at its base. And, in spite of its plastic glamour, the disc is a beautifully honest work: the thickness articulates the circle naturally, and the same concentration is required to stabilize the sculpture on the floor; the color is pretty, but its fade is ingenerate and its hue quite cozy in the glassy solid." [*Artforum*, October 1971]

From Fran Preisman in *Artweek*:

A passion for light and a response to light as a phenomenon have lead DeWain Valentine to capture its transitory aspects. Creating a visual diary of the myriad changes in light from sunrise to sunset, he filters light from the sky and sea through a high density area into a controlled environment. Valentine states that he is still working with transparent colored space, but now he builds it within a given area and therefore incorporates access to daylight into the work. Through a more direct use of light he captures the atmospheric sensations of the sea and sky. These resulting environmental pieces are a logical progression in a ten-year involvement with "light-space-transparency." [No. 26, 26 July 1975/3]

From Jean-Luc Bordeaux in *Art in America*:

In his quest to investigate the physics and the metaphysics of the color spectrum, Valentine has developed, and increasingly varied, a vocabulary of translucent or transparent discs, rings, slabs, wedges and other precise, simple forms in cast polyester resin or acrylic plastic—and, more recently, glass. Since 1966, these have been vehicles for a gamut of solid colors, as well as variegated ones that shift within a limited range of the spectrum. These hues, radiant or mysteriously dim, fuse with his prismatic shapes to demonstrate the sculptor's dual affinities—to formalistic precisionism and to beguiling illusion.

The colors of each work may evoke a variety of moods; changes in viewpoint and in ambient light may heighten their suggestive and seductive power. Valentine's works, particularly his large, perfect, color-saturated circles, can establish themselves as an unmistakable focus of spirituality—something like a mandala, expressing the totality of the psyche. . . . [No. 8, 6 December 1979/102–06]

Sky Gate III, 1984 (maquette)
Laminated glass, bronze
114 × 96 × 24″
290 × 244 × 61 cm
Lent by the artist

De John Coplans, *DeWain Valentine: escultura reciente* (Pasadena: Museo de Arte de Pasadena, 1970):

Valentine: En algun sentido creo que las piezas más grandes son mucho más libres—mucho más abiertas. En realidad estoy interesado en un tipo de apertura espacial dentro de y alrededor de la pieza. Una especie de espacio totalmente transparente. Creo que el cambio de escala es obviamente una de las diferencias más importantes. No es tanto que las piezas se hayan hecho más grandes, sino que el espectador tiene que percibirlas y ver de una forma muy diferente aunque la misma pieza podría hacerse a menor escala. Por otra parte el espectador no puede involucrarse con el tipo de campo de transparencia que a mi me interesa más. En realidad me interesan mucho más como campos de transparencia y como campos de color transparente que como formas esculturales.

Coplans: ¿Y de luz?

Valentine: Y de luz, sí.

Coplans: Entonces ellas tienen que tener un contexto arquitectónico contra el cual se refracta.

Valentine: Sí, y yo creo que en definitiva—aunque tengo reparos sobre ello—mi trabajo va a operar mejor en un contexto arquitectónico específico, un tipo de espacio muy específico que envuelva y opere con la pieza para unificar en el espectador la experiencia de la transparencia del volumen que rodea a la pieza así como la transparencia y la cualidad luminosa dentro de la pieza.

Coplans: Por motivo de interés, ¿ha pensado alguna vez en realizar entornos—es decir, controlando el espacio arquitectónico de forma más directa que la colocación de un objeto en un espacio determinado?

Valentine: Por supuesto. Y la extensión obvia sería envolver por completo al espectador de alguna forma o involucrarlo totalmente en algún tipo de situación contextual en la que se enfrente a una situación total—de un volumen total de transparencia en la que pueda existir físicamente. En efecto, el problema es construir uno. Tendría que realizarse en un lugar específico y existiría durante algún período de tiempo y continuaría existiendo en ese lugar específico o sería destruido.

De John Lloyd Taylor en *Art International*:

Valentine es un artista que posee una virtuosidad técnica notable—una excelencia artesanal equiparable solamente a la de Larry Bell entre sus compinches de la costa oeste, y una elegancia quizá inigualada por ningún otro escultor. Valentine y Bell han·añadido a la sensibilidad de la forma y la ilusión esculturales, la encarnación del preciocismo minimalista iniciado por Donald Judd. . . . Valentine ha trabajado con formas esculturales ampliamente variadas, moviéndose constantemente hacia su eventual abandono reciente del objetivismo escultural. Sin embargo, dentro toda su evolución estilística encontramos su insistente preocupación por la transparencia, translucidez y las cualidades difractorias del color prismático suspendido volumétricamente en el espacio. [No. 7, septiembre de 1973/21-24]

De Peter Plagens, *DeWain Valentine escultura* (Nueva York: Galería Denise René, 1973;(

En los últimos lustros la obra de Valentine se encuentra entre la escultura sólida más importante de la Costa Oeste, y entre la mejor escultura del país considerando a aquéllos que se han adherido al precepto atemporal de la irreductibilidad del objeto. Estos juicios deberían ensombrecer el hecho importante pero secundario de que Valentine es un técnico de primer orden entre aquellos artistas que trabajan con la resina. A pesar de los problemas del trabajo en caliente, peso, el peligro de impurezas, ha conseguido ópticas tan claras y puras

como las de sus colegas pero reteniendo al mismo tiempo la masa convincente de la escultura sobresaliente.

Pero su mayor logro radica en el desarrollo de una escultura sustancial durante los años sesenta, conjuntando la presencia de la masa física en un espacio kinestético palpable y las propiedades ópticas/perceptuales «avanzadas» precediendo en ello a artistas como James Turrell, Michael Asher, el difunto Robert Irwin y la obra más reciente de Ron Cooper. Yo escribí siguiente sobre una pieza de DeWain Valentine en 1971: «DeWain Valentine es el que mayor poder y espectáculo confiere a la resina de entre todos los artistas que con ella trabajan; obviamente hace lo que hay que hacer con el material, explotando su capacidad de pureza, color, transparencia y misticismo. Su disco «púrpura» transparente de tamaño humano. . . . es paradójicamente más grueso y más ligero en su base. Y, a pesar de su exaltación plástica, el disco es una obra maravillosamente honrada: el grosor articula el círculo naturalmente, y se necesita la misma concentración para estabilizar la escultura en el suelo; el color es lindo, pero su palidez es congénita y su matiz es muy ameno en el vidrioso sólida.» [*Artforum*, octubre de 1971]

De Fran Preisman en *Artweek*:

Su pasión por la luz y una respuesta a la luz como fenómeno han llevado a DeWain Valentine a capturar sus aspectos transitorios. El filtro la luz del cielo y del mar a través de un área de alta densidad a un contexto controlado, creando un diario visual de los cambios luminosos innumerables desde la salida a la puesta del sol. Valentine afirma que todavía está trabajando con el espacio transparente de color, pero él lo compone dentro de una cierta área y por ello incorpora el acceso de la obra a la luz del día. Mediante un uso más directo de la luz él captura las sensaciones atmosféricas del mar y del cielo. Estas piezas ambientales resultantes constituyen una progresion lógica en una dedicación a la «luz-espacio-transparencia» que ya dura diez años. [No. 26, 26 de julio de 1975/3]

Installation view, 1971, cast polyester resin

**John Coplans, *DeWain Valentine: Recent Sculpture*
(Pasadena: Pasadena Museum of Art, 1970):**

Valentine: Dans un sens, je crois que les oeuvres de plus
grandes dimensions ont plus de liberté. Ce qui m'intéresse
vraiment, c'est une espèce d'ouverture dans l'espace, à l'intérieur et autour de la pièce. Une sorte d'espace complètement
transparent. A mon avis, le changement d'échelle est évidem-
ment la différence la plus importante. Ce n'est pas tant le fait
que les pièces soient devenues plus grandes, c'est que celui
qui les regarde est obligé de les percevoir et de les regarder
d'une façon très différente, bien que la pièce puisse être réali-
sée à une échelle beaucoup plus petite. Mais si elle l'était,
alors le spectateur ne pourrait pas percevoir le champ de
transparence qui est ce qui m'intéresse le plus. Je vois beaucoup plus des champs de transparence et des champs de couleur transparente que des formes sculpturales.
Coplans: Et la lumière?
Valentine: Ah, oui, la lumière compte.
Coplans: En sorte que vos oeuvres ont besoin d'un environnement architectural contre lequel résonner.
Valentine: Oui, et je pense que finalement—encore que je n'en
sois pas tout à fait sûr—mes oeuvres feront plus d'effet dans
un cadre architectural spécifique, un espace très défini qui les
enserrait et agirait sur elles de façon à unifier l'impression qu'a
le spectateur de la transparence du volume autour de la pièce,
aussi bien que celle qu'il a de la transparence et de la qualité
de la lumière à l'intérieur de la pièce elle-même.
Coplans: Par curiosité, avez-vous jamais pensé à créer un
environnement—c'est à dire à contrôler l'espace architectural
plus directement qu'en plaçant un objet dans un espace?
Valentine: Absolument. Un développement logique serait
d'entourer complètement le spectateur, de le placer dans un
volume total de transparence au sein duquel il pourrait exister
physiquement. Le problème est de construire un tel cadre. Il
faudrait qu'il soit construit à un endroit spécifique où il existe-
rait pour un temps et continuerait d'exister là, ou serait détruit

John Lloyd Taylor, paru dans *Art International*:

Valentine est un artiste qui possède une virtuosité technique remarquable—une sûreté d'exécution qui n'a d'égale que celle
de Larry Bell parmi les artistes de la Côte Ouest et une
élégance qui n'a peut-être pas sa pareille où que ce soit.
Valentine et Bell ont apporté à la sensibilité de la forme sculpturale et de l'illusion la précision «minimaliste» de Donald
Judd. . . . Valentine a travaillé à des formes sculpturales très
variées, progressant sans cesse vers l'abandon des formes
figuratives auquel il vient de parvenir. Cependant, dans chacun
de ses développements stylistiques on retrouve son souci de
la transparence, de la translucidité et les qualités diffractives
de la couleur prismatique suspendue en volumes dans
l'espace. [No. 7, septembre 1973/21–24[

**Peter Plagens, *DeWain Valentine Sculpture* (New
York: Denise René Gallery, 1973):**

Depuis une demi-douzaine d'années, le travail de Valentine représente un type de sculpture parmi les plus importants de la
Côte Ouest, et, pour ceux qui adhèrent toujours au précepte
ancien de la sculpture en tant qu'objet irréductible, son oeuvre
est peut-être la meilleure dans tous les Etats-Unis. Ces jugements devraient éclipser le fait, important mais secondaire,
que Valentine est un technicien de premier ordre parmi les
artistes qui travaillent en employant la résine. Il est parvenu, en
dépit des problèmes causés par la chaleur, le poids et le
danger des impuretés, à créer des objets à l'optique aussi
claire et pure que celle de ses collègues, tout en retenant la
masse imposante de la sculpture de grandes dimensions.

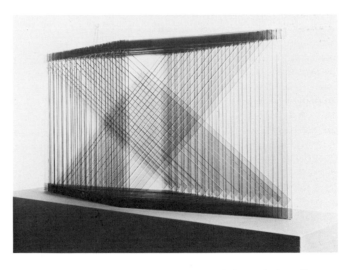

Son plus grand accomplissement a été la création d'une
sculpture substantielle pendant les années soixante, rassemblant une masse physique dans un espace cinétique palpable et
les propriétés optiques et perceptuelles de pointe qui annon-
çaient des artistes tels que James Turrell, Michael Asher, puis
Robert Irwin et le travail le plus récent de Ron Cooper. En
1971, j'écrivais, à propos d'une oeuvre de DeWain Valentine:
«Parmi tous les artistes qui, par ici, travaillent la résine,
DeWain Valentine est celui dont l'oeuvre a le plus de muscle
et de sens du spectacle; il est évident qu'il sait traiter le matériau dont il exploite au maximum les capacités de pureté, de
couleur, de transparence et la mystique. Son disque «pour-
pre». . . . est, paradoxalement plus épais *et* plus léger à sa
base. En dépit de son attrait plastique, le disque est une
oeuvre belle et honnête: c'est l'épaisseur qui articule le cercle
naturellement et la même concentration est nécessaire pour
stabiliser la sculpture sur le plancher; la couleur est jolie, mais
son ton passé est intérieur et sa nuance tout à fait à sa place
dans le solide vitreux.» [*Artforum*, octobre 1971]

Fran Preisman dans *Artweek*:

La passion de DeWain Valentine pour la lumière et sa ré-
action à la lumière en tant que phénomène l'ont amené à en
capturer les aspects transitoires. Créant une sorte de journal
visuel des myriades de changements par lesquels passe la
lumière de l'aube au crépuscule, Valentine filtre la lumière du
ciel et de la mer à travers une zone de haute densité dans un
environnement contrôlé. Selon lui, il n'a pas cessé de travailler
sur espace coloré transparent, mais maintenant il le construit
dans un espace déterminé et incorpore l'accès à la lumière
dans l'oeuvre. D'une manière plus directe, il capture les
sensations atmosphériques de la mer et du ciel. Ces oeuvres
s'inscrivent logiquement dans l'évolution d'un travail qui,
depuis dix ans, s'intéresse à «la lumière, à l'espace et à la
transparence.» [No. 26, 26 juillet 1975/3]

Open Diamond Double Diagonal, gray, 1979, laminated glass
18 x 36 x 8", 46 x 91 x 20 cm

Aus John Coplans, *DeWain Valentine: Recent Sculpture* (Pasadena Museum of Art, 1970):

Valentine: In gewisser Weise habe ich das Gefühl, daß die größeren Stücke freier sind—viel offener. Ich bin wirklich an einer Art von räumlicher Offenheit innerhalb und außerhalb des Stückes interessiert, an einer Art von transparentem Raum. Ich meine, der Wechsel im Maßstab ist offensichtlich einer der wichtigsten Unterschiede. Es ist nicht so sehr, daß die Stücke umfangreicher geworden sind, sondern daß der Betrachter sie in einer ganz anderen Art und Weise wahrnehmen und betrachten muß, obwohl das gleiche Stück kleiner gemacht werden könnte. Sonst kann der Betrachter nicht mit der Art und Weise eines Gesichtsfeldes der Transparenz verwickelt werden, an der ich am meisten interessiert bin. Ich bin wirklich an ihnen mehr als Feldern von Transparenz und Feldern von transparenter Farbe als an bildhaurischen Formen interessiert.

Coplans: Und Licht?

Valentine: Und Licht, ja.

Coplans: Deshalb brauchen sie eine architektonische Umgebung, um widerzuhallen.

Valentine: Ja, und ich denke, wenn auch mit gemischten Gefühlen, daß mein Werk am Ende besser in einer spezifischen architektonischen Umgebung wirken wird, in einer sehr spezifischen Art von Raum, der das Stück einschließt und mit ihm arbeitet, um des Betrachters Erfahrung mit der Transparenz des Rauminhalts um das Stück herum sowie auch mit der Transparenz und Lichtqualität innerhalb des Stückes zu vereinen.

Coplans: Haben Sie jemals interessehalber daran gedacht, Umgebungen zu schaffen—d.h., einen architektonischen Raum eher unmittelbarer zu kontrollieren als einen Gegenstand in einen Raum zu stellen.

Valentine: Durchaus. Die offensichtliche Ausdehnung würde sein, den Betrachter irgendwie völlig einzuschließen oder ihn völlig in irgendeiner Art von Umweltsituation zu involvieren, in der er von einer vollständigen Situation konfrontiert wird—von einem totalen Rauminhalt von Transparenz, in welchem er physisch existieren könnte. Tatsächlich ist das Problem, einen solchen zu konstruieren. Er müßte an einem bestimmten Platz gebaut werden, und er würde für einen Zeitraum existieren und fortfahren, in diesem bestimmten Platz zu existieren oder zerstört zu werden.

Von John Lloyd Taylor in *Art International*:

Valentine ist ein Künstler, der bemerkenswerte technische Virtuosität besitzt—eine Vortrefflichkeit an Handwerkskunst, der unter seinen Westküstengefährten nur die Larry Bells gleichkommt, und eine Eleganz, die vielleicht von Bildhauern anderswo nicht erreicht wird. Valentine und Bell besitzen neben Empfindsamkeit von bildhauerischer Form und Illusion die Verkörperung von minimalistischer Präzision, die ursprünglich von Donald Judd dargelegt wurde. . . . Valentine hat mit sehr unterschiedlichen bildhauerischen Formen gearbeitet und bewegte sich fortwährend auf sein eventualles jüngstes Verlassen bildhauerischer Gegenständlichkeit hin. Jedoch innerhalb jeder stilistischen Entwicklung schlagen seine durchdringenden Mühen um Transparenz, Lichtdurchlässigkeit und die brechenden Eigenschaften prismatischer Farbe, die volumetrisch im Raum schwebt, Brücken. [No. 7, September 1973/21–24]

Von Peter Plagens, *DeWain Valentine Sculpture* (New York: Denise René Gallery, 1973):

Während der letzten sechs Jahre war Valentines Werk mit die wichtigste Feststoff-Bildhauerei an der Westküste und bei denen, die an dem zeitlosen Gebot eines nicht verwandelbaren Gegenstandes festhielten, unter den besten Skulpturen des Landes. Diese Urteile sollten die wichtige, aber sekundäre Tatsache überschatten, daß Valentine der Haupttechniker unter jenen Künstlern ist, die mit Harz arbeiten. Er hat trotz Problemen mit Hitze, Gewicht und der Gefahr der Unreinheiten Optisches fertiggebracht, das so klar und rein ist wie jenes seiner Kollegen, während er die überzeugende Masse größerer Bildhauerei beibehielt.

Aber seine größere Leistung war die Entwicklung wesentlicher Bildhauerei während der sechziger Jahre, als er die Gegenwart von physischer Masse in fühlbarem kinästhetischem Raum und die «fortgeschrittenen» optischen/wahrnehmbaren Eigenschaften verband, die Vorboten solcher Künstler wie James Turrell, Michael Asher, später Robert Irwin und von Coopers neuerem Werk. Ich schrieb 1971 über ein DeWain Valentine Stück: «DeWain Valentine gibt das meiste an Substanz und Großartigkeit von all den vielen regionalen Künstlern, die mit Harzguß arbeiten; er macht, was augenscheinlich mit dem Material getan werden soll, indem er dessen Fähigkeiten für Reinheit, Farbe, Transparenz und Mystik ausschöpft. Seine mannsgroße transparente «purpurne» Scheibe. . . . ist paradoxerweise dicker *und* leichter am Sockel. Trotz ihres Plastikzaubers ist die Scheibe eine durch und durch saubere Arbeit: die Dicke bringt den Kreis natürlich hervor, und dieselbe Konzentration wird benötigt, der Skulptur auf dem Boden einen festen Halt zu geben; die Farbe ist hübsch, aber ihr Verblassen ist unfruchtbar, und ihr Ton ganz behaglich in dem glasigen Dauerhaften.» [*Artforum*, Oktober 1971]

Von Frank Preisman in *Artweek*:

Eine Leidenschaft für Licht und ein Eingehen auf Licht als einem Phänomen haben DeWain Valentine dazu gebracht, dessen flüchtige Aspekte einzufangen. Indem er ein visuelles Tagebuch der Unzahl von Veränderungen im Licht von Sonnenaufgang bis Sonnenuntergang schafft, filtert er Licht von Himmel und Meer durch eine Dichtheitszone in eine kontrollierte Umgebung. Valentine stellt fest, daß er immer noch mit transparentem farbigen Raum arbeitet, aber jetzt baut er ihn innerhalb einer gegebenen Fläche und bezieht dadurch Zugang zu Tageslicht in das Werk ein. Durch eine mehr direkte Benutzung von Licht fängt er die atmosphärischen Sensationen des Meeres und des Himmels ein. Diese sich ergebenden Umweltstücke sind eine logische Fortführung in einer zehnjährigen Involviertheit mit «Licht-Raum-Transparenz». [No. 26, 26. Juli 1975/3]

Open Diamond Diagonal, sepia, 1982, laminated glass
36 x 34 x 8″, 91 x 86 x 20 cm

Biographies

Robert Arneson

Born in Benicia, California, 1930
Resides in Benicia, California
Studied at the College of Marin, Kentfield, California; California College of Arts and Crafts, Oakland (Bachelor of Arts degree, 1954); and Mills College, Oakland, California (Master of Fine Arts degree, 1958)

Selected Solo Exhibitions
1960 Oakland Art Museum, Oakland, California
1962 M.H. de Young Memorial Museum, San Francisco, California
1963 Richmond Art Center, Richmond, California
1964 Allan Stone Gallery, New York, New York (also 1969)
1967 San Francisco Museum of Art, San Francisco, California (also 1974)
1000 Hansen Fuller Gallery, San Francisco, California (yearly through 1981)
1975 Allan Frumkin Gallery, New York, New York (also 1977, 79, 81, 83)
1976 Memorial Union Art Gallery, University of California, Davis, California
Allan Frumkin Gallery, Chicago, Illinois (also 1978)
1979 Hansen Fuller Goldeen Gallery, San Francisco, California (also 1980, 81)
1981 San Francisco Museum of Modern Art, San Francisco, California
1982 Fuller Goldeen Gallery, San Francisco, California (also 1984)
1984 Frumkin-Struve Gallery, Chicago, Illinois

Selected Group Exhibitions
1963 *California Sculpture*, Oakland Art Museum, Oakland, California
1965 *New Ceramic Forms*, Museum of Contemporary Crafts, New York, New York
1967 *Funk Art*, University Art Gallery, University of California, Berkeley, California
1968 *Dada, Surrealism and Their Heritage*, The Museum of Modern Art, New York, New York
1969 *Objects, USA*, National Collection of Fine Arts, Washington, D.C. (toured)
Human Concern—Personal Torment, Whitney Museum of American Art, New York, New York
1970 *Ceramics '70*, Everson Museum of Art, Syracuse,
New York
1971 *Clayworks: 20 Americans*, Museum of Contemporary Crafts, New York, New York
1972 *White on White*, Museum of Contemporary Art, Chicago, Illinois
A Decade of Ceramic Art, 1962-1972, San Francisco Museum of Modern Art, San Francisco, California
1973 *Painting and Sculpture by Young American Artists*, Cranbrook Academy of Art/Museum, Bloomfield Hills, Michigan
1974 *California Ceramic Sculpture, Part II*, Allan Frumkin Gallery, New York, New York
Clay, Whitney Museum of American Art, Downtown Branch, New York, New York
1977 *10th Anniversary Exhibition*, Museum of Contemporary Art, Chicago, Illinois
New Ceramic Sculpture, Allan Frumkin Gallery, New York, New York
1978 *Nine West Coast Clay Sculptors. 1978*, Everson Museum of Art, Syracuse, New York (toured)
1979 Whitney Museum of American Art, New York, New York
West Coast Ceramics, Stedelijk Museum, Amsterdam, The Netherlands
1980 *Sculpture in California, 1975-80*, San Diego Museum of Art, San Diego, California
20 American Artists, San Francisco Museum of Modern Art, San Francisco, California
1982 *100 Years of California Sculpture*, The Oakland Museum, Oakland, California
1983 *Ceramic Echoes*, William Rockhill Nelson Gallery and Atkins Museum of Fine Arts, Kansas City, Missouri
Art Itinera 83: Painterly Drawings, Castello Pasquini, Volterra, Italy
California Clay Works, San Francisco Museum of Modern Art, San Francisco, California
1984 *Drawings Since 1974*, Hirshhorn Museum and Sculpture Garden, Washington, D.C.
Return of the Narrative, Palm Springs Desert Museum, Palm Springs, California

Charles Arnoldi

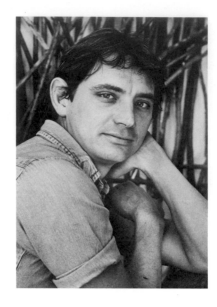

Born in Dayton, Ohio, 1946
Resides in Los Angeles and New York
Studied at Chouinard Art Institute, Los Angeles,
California (1968)

Awards
1969   Modern and Contemporary Art Council, Los Angeles
       County Museum of Art
1972   Wittkowsky Award, The Art Institute of Chicago
1974   Individual Artist Fellowship, National Endowment
       for the Arts
1975   John Simon Guggenheim Fellowship
1982   California Arts Council
       Individual Artist Fellowship, National Endowment
       for the Arts

Selected Solo Exhibitions
1971   Mizuno Gallery, Los Angeles, California
1972   Texas Gallery, Houston, Texas
       (also 1977, 79, 81, 83)
1974   Nicholas Wilder Gallery, Los Angeles, California
       (also 1975, 77, 78, 79)
1975   Robert Elkon Gallery, New York, New York
       (also 1978, 79)
1979   Dobrick Gallery, Chicago, Illinois
1980   James Corcoran Gallery, Los Angeles, California
       (also 1981, 82, 83)
1981   Hansen Fuller Goldeen Gallery, San Francisco,
       California

Selected Group Exhibitions
1969   *Fifteen Los Angeles Artists*, Pasadena Museum of
       Art, Pasadena, California
       The Power Survey of Contemporary Art, National
       Gallery of Victoria, Australia
1970   *Nine Artists*, Art Gallery, University of California,
       Irvine, California
       Permutations: Light and Color, Museum of
       Contemporary Art, Chicago, Illinois
1972   *Arnoldi/Cooper/McCollum/Wudl*, Art Gallery,
       California State University, Fullerton, California
       Working in California, Albright-Knox Art Gallery,
       Buffalo, New York
       Dokumenta 5, Kassel, West Germany
1973   *Ten Years of Modern and Contemporary Art*

Council Acquisitions, Los Angeles County Museum
of Art, Los Angeles, California
Market Street Program, San Francisco Museum of
Art, San Francisco, California
1974   *Fifteen Abstract Artists*, The Santa Barbara Museum
       of Art, Santa Barbara, California
1976   *Painting and Sculpture in California: The Modern
       Era*, San Francisco Museum of Modern Art,
       San Francisco, California (toured)
1978   *Painting and Sculpture Today*, Indianapolis Museum
       of Art, Indianapolis, Indiana
1979   *Aspects of Abstract*, Crocker Art Museum,
       Sacramento, California
1981   Whitney Museum of American Art, New York,
       New York
       Los Angeles Prints, 1883–1980, Los Angeles
       County Museum of Art, Los Angeles, California
       Polychrome, Hansen Fuller Goldeen Gallery,
       San Francisco, California
       Artists' Quilts, La Jolla Museum of Contemporary
       Art, La Jolla, California
1982   *L.A. Art: An Exhibition of Contemporary Paintings*,
       Nagoya City Museum, Nagoya, Japan
1983   *The 38th Corcoran Biennial Exhibition of American
       Painting: Second Western States Exhibition*,
       Corcoran Gallery of Art, Washington, D.C.
       A Century of Modern Sculpture, 1882–1982,
       The Museum of Fine Arts, Houston, Texas
       Charles Arnoldi and Laddie John Dill, Art Gallery,
       California State University, Fullerton, California

Bruce Beasley

Born in Los Angeles, California, 1939
Resides in Oakland, California
Studied at Dartmouth College, Hanover, New Hampshire
(1957–59), and the University of California, Berkeley
(Bachelor of Arts degree, 1962)

Awards
1960   Adele Morrison Memorial Medal, Oakland Art
        Museum Sculpture Annual
1961   Honorable Mention, San Francisco Art Institute
        Annual
1963   André Malraux Purchase Award, Biennale de Paris
1965   Frank Lloyd Wright Memorial Purchase Award,
        Marin Museum Association, San Rafael, California
1967   Purchase Prize, San Francisco Art Festival

Selected Solo Exhibitions
1961   Richmond Art Center, Richmond, California
1963   Everett Ellin Gallery, Los Angeles, California
1964   Kornblee Gallery, New York, New York
1965   Hansen Fuller Gallery, San Francisco, California
1966   David Stuart Gallery, Los Angeles, California
1971   André Emmerich Gallery, New York, New York
1972   M.H. de Young Memorial Museum, San Francisco,
        California
1973   The Santa Barbara Museum of Art, Santa Barbara,
        California
1974   San Diego Museum of Art, San Diego, California
1981   Hansen Fuller Goldeen Gallery, San Francisco,
        California

Selected Group Exhibitions
1960   *Painting and Sculpture Annual*, Richmond Art
        Center, Richmond, California
1961   *Art of Assemblage*, The Museum of Modern Art,
        New York, New York
1963   *Biennale de Paris*, Musée d'Art Moderne, Paris,
        France
1964   *Eleven American Sculptors*, University of California,
        Berkeley, California
        Albright-Knox Art Gallery, Buffalo, New York
1965   *Some Aspects of California Painting and Sculpture*,
        La Jolla Museum of Contemporary Art, La Jolla,
        California
1966   *Selected Acquisitions*, The Solomon R. Guggenheim

Museum, New York, New York
1967   *Plastics West Coast*, Hansen Fuller Gallery,
        San Francisco, California
1969   *Plastics and New Art*, Institute of Contemporary
        Art of the University of Pennsylvania, Philadelphia,
        Pennsylvania
        A Plastic Conference, The Jewish Museum,
        New York, New York (toured)
1970   Osaka Exposition, San Francisco Pavilion, Osaka,
        Japan
        Sculpture Here and Now, Stanford University
        Museum and Art Gallery, Stanford, California
        Pollution Show, The Oakland Museum, Oakland,
        California
        American Sculpture in Perspective, Sheldon
        Memorial Art Gallery, University of Nebraska,
        Lincoln, Nebraska
1973   *The Small Format*, Saint Mary's College,
        Moraga, California
        The Reflected Image, De Cordova Museum,
        Lincoln, Massachusetts
        Salon de la Jeune Sculpture, Musée d'Art Moderne,
        Paris, France
1974   *Public Sculpture, Urban Environment*, The Oakland
        Museum, Oakland, California
1979   *Spaces*, Civic Arts Gallery, Walnut Creek, California
1982   *Northern California Art of the Sixties*, deSaisset Art
        Gallery and Museum, University of Santa Clara,
        California
        100 Years of California Sculpture, The Oakland
        Museum, Oakland, California

Fletcher Benton

Born in Jackson, Ohio, 1931
Resides in San Francisco, California
Studied at Miami University, Oxford, Ohio (Bachelor of Fine
Arts degree, 1956)

Awards
1979   Award for Distinguished Service to the Arts,
        American Academy and Institute of Arts and Letters
1980   President's Scholar Award, California State
        University, San Jose
1982   Award of Honor for Outstanding Achievement in
        Sculpture, San Francisco Art Commission

Selected Solo Exhibitions
1964   California Palace of the Legion of Honor,
        San Francisco, California
1965   San Francisco Museum of Art, San Francisco,
        California (also 1970)
        Hansen Gallery, San Francisco, California
        (also 1966)
1967   Esther Robles Gallery, Los Angeles, California
        (also 1967, 72)
1968   Galeria Bonino Ltd., New York, New York
        (also 1969)
1969   Galerie Françoise Mayer, Brussels, Belgium
1970   San Francisco Museum of Art, San Francisco,
        California
        Albright-Knox Art Gallery, Buffalo, New York
        Galeria Bonino Ltd., Buenos Aires, Argentina
        Estudio Actual, Caracas, Venezuela
1971   Stanford University Museum and Art Gallery,
        Stanford, California
1972   La Jolla Museum of Contemporary Art, La Jolla,
        California
        Landry-Bonino Gallery Ltd., New York, New York
1973   Phoenix Museum of Art, Phoenix, Arizona
        University of California, Davis, California
        Galeria Bonino Ltd., Rio de Janiero, Brazil
1975   deSaisset Art Gallery and Museum, University of
        Santa Clara, Santa Clara, California
1978   Tortue Gallery, Los Angeles, California
        San Jose Museum of Art, San Jose, California
        (also 1982)
1979   The Art Club of Chicago, Chicago, Illinois
        Milwaukee Art Center, Milwaukee, Wisconsin

1980   Newport Harbor Art Museum, Newport Beach,
        California
        The Oakland Museum, Oakland, California
        John Berggruen Gallery, San Francisco, California
        Suermondt-Ludwig Museum, Aachen,
        West Germany
1981   Klingspor Museum, Offenbach, West Germany

Selected Group Exhibitions
1961   *Winter Invitational Exhibition*, California Palace of
        the Legion of Honor, San Francisco, California
        (also 1964)
1963   *Bay Area Artists*, The Santa Barbara Museum of
        Art, Santa Barbara, California
1964   *Twenty Bay Area Artists*, San Francisco Museum of
        Art, San Francisco, California
1965   *California Painting and Sculpture*, La Jolla Museum
        of Contemporary Art, La Jolla, California
        Kinetic Forces, San Francisco Museum of Art,
        San Francisco, California
1966   *Obelisk Without an Eye*, Walker Art Center,
        Minneapolis, Minnesota
        Kinetic Currents, San Francisco Museum of Art,
        San Francisco, California
        Whitney Museum of American Art, New York,
        New York (also 1968, 73)
1967   *American Sculpture of the Sixties*, Los Angeles
        County Museum of Art, Los Angeles,
        California (toured)
1968   *West Coast Now*, Portland Art Museum, Portland,
        Oregon (toured)
        28th Annual Exhibition, The Art Institute of
        Chicago, Chicago, Illinois
        Options, Walker Art Center, Minneapolis,
        Minnesota (toured)
1969   Albright-Knox Art Gallery, Buffalo, New York
        Impressions des USA, Galeria Françoise Mayer,
        Brussels, Belgium
        Galeria Bonino Ltd., Buenos Aires, Argentina
        (also 1972)
1970   *Expo '70*, International Museum of Fine Arts,
        Osaka, Japan
        Hayward Gallery, London, England
1971   The Oakland Museum, Oakland, California
1972   Stanford University Museum and Art Gallery,
        Stanford, California
1973   *Kinetic Exhibition*, University of California, Berkeley,
        California
1974   *Public Sculpture, Urban Environment*, The Oakland
        Museum, Oakland, California
        Inaugural Exhibition, Hirshhorn Museum and
        Sculpture Garden, Washington, D.C.
1975   Esther Robles Gallery, Los Angeles, California
1976   Elvehjem Museum of Art, University of Wisconsin,
        Madison, Wisconsin
        *Painting and Sculpture in California: The Modern
        Era*, San Francisco Museum of Modern Art,
        San Francisco, California (toured)
1977   *California Bay Area Update*, Huntsville Museum of
        Art, Huntsville, Alabama
1983   *The Planar Dimension: Geometric Abstraction by
        Bay Area Artists*, Civic Arts Gallery, Walnut Creek,
        California
        Bay Area Collects, San Francisco Museum of
        Modern Art, San Francisco, California

Guy Dill

Born in Duval County, Florida, 1946
Resides in Venice, California
Studied at Chouinard Art Institute, Los Angeles, California
(Bachelor of Fine Arts degree, 1970)

Awards
1972   Theodoron Award, The Solomon R. Guggenheim
        Museum
1974   First Prize, American Show, The Art Institute of
        Chicago
        Individual Artist Fellowship, National Endowment
        for the Arts
1981   Individual Artist Fellowship, National Endowment
        for the Arts

Selected Solo Exhibitions
1971   Ace Gallery, Los Angeles, California
        (also 1973, 77)
1972   Felicity Samuel Gallery, London, England
1974   Pace Gallery, New York, New York
1975   Morgon Thomas Gallery, Los Angeles, California
1976   Tortue Gallery, Los Angeles, California
1977   Dobrick Gallery, Chicago, Illinois
        ARCO Center for the Visual Arts, Los Angeles,
        California
1978   Rosamund Felsen Gallery, Los Angeles, California
        (also 1979)
1980   Janus Gallery, Venice, California (also 1981, 82)
        Ivory/Kimpton Gallery, San Francisco, California
        California State University, Bakersfield, California
1982   Flow Ace Gallery, Los Angeles, California
        (also 1983)
1984   Flow Ace Gallery, Paris, France

Selected Group Exhibitions
1971   24 Artists, Los Angeles County Museum of Art,
        Los Angeles, California
        Acquisitions, Pasadena Museum of Art, Pasadena,
        California
1972   Guy Dill/Laddie John Dill, Art Gallery, California
        State University, Fullerton, California
        Theodoron Show, The Solomon R. Guggenheim
        Museum, New York, New York
        Acquisition Show, Stedelijk Museum, Amsterdam,
        The Netherlands

Earth, Animal, Vegetable, Mineral, La Jolla
Museum of Contemporary Art, La Jolla, California
1973   Whitney Museum of American Art, New York,
        New York
        American Show, The Chicago Art Institute,
        Chicago, Illinois
1974   American Show, The Art Institute of Chicago,
        Chicago, Illinois
        Whitney Museum of American Art, New York,
        New York
1976   Sculpture Made in Place, Walker Art Center,
        Minneapolis, Minnesota
        Acquisitions, The Museum of Modern Art,
        New York, New York
1977   Current Direction in Southern California Art,
        Los Angeles Institute of Contemporary Art,
        Los Angeles, California
1979   Sculpture from the Permanent Collection,
        The Museum of Modern Art, New York, New York
1980   Across the Nation, Fine Art for Federal Buildings,
        1972-79, National Collection of Fine Arts,
        Smithsonian Institution, Washington, D.C.
        Furniture by Artists, Otis Art Institute of Parsons
        School of Design, Los Angeles, California
        In the Constructivist Spirit, Janus Gallery,
        Los Angeles, California
1981   Artists' Quilts, La Jolla Museum of Contemporary
        Art, La Jolla, California
        Anthony Caro, Guy Dill, Michael Heizer, Robert
        Rauschenberg, Flow Ace Gallery, Los Angeles,
        California
1984   Welton Becket Associates, Santa Monica, California

Jud Fine

Born in Los Angeles, California, 1944
Resides in Los Angeles, California
Studied at the University of California, Santa Barbara (Bachelor of Arts degree, 1966), and Cornell University, New York, New York (Master of Fine Arts degree, 1970)

Awards
1972   Modern and Contemporary Art Council,
        Los Angeles County Museum of Art
1974   The Laura Slobe Memorial Award, The Art Institute
        of Chicago
1978   Art in Public Places, National Endowment for
        the Arts
1982   Individual Artist Fellowship—Sculpture, National
        Endowment for the Arts

Selected Solo Exhibitions
1972   Mizuno Gallery, Los Angeles, California (also 1973)
        Ronald Feldman Fine Arts, New York, New York
        (also 1973, 75, 76, 78, 81)
1973   Dayton's Gallery 12, Minneapolis, Minnesota
        (also 1974)
1974   Lucrezia de Domizio, Pescara, Italy
1975   Galerie Alexandra Monett, Brussels, Belgium
1977   Margo Leavin Gallery, Los Angeles, California
        (also 1979, 81, 83)
        Marianne Deson Gallery, Chicago, Illinois
        Art Gallery, California State University, Fullerton
1978   Los Angeles Institute of Contemporary Art,
        Los Angeles, California
1979   Art Gallery, College of Creative Studies, Santa
        Barbara, California
1982   Anderson Gallery, Virginia Commonwealth
        University, Richmond, Virginia
        Dart Gallery, Chicago, Illinois
1983   Thomas Segal Gallery, Boston, Massachusetts

Selected Group Exhibitions
1971   *Drawing '71*, Art Museum, The University of New
        Mexico, Albuquerque, New Mexico
1972   *Dokumenta 5*, Kassel, West Germany
        Attitudes '72, Pasadena Museum of Art, Pasadena,
        California
        5 L.A. Artists, San Francisco Art Institute,
        San Francisco, California

        Art Council Acquisitions, Los Angeles County
        Museum of Art, Los Angeles, California
1973   *Biennale de Paris*, Musée d'Art Moderne, Paris,
        France
1974   *Seven Sculptors—New Involvement with Materials*,
        Institute of Contemporary Art, Boston,
        Massachusetts
        Edinburgh Summer Art Festival, Edinburgh,
        Scotland
1975   *Drawings—U.S.A.*, Stadtischen Museum,
        Leverkusen, West Germany
        Word/Number Image, Sarah Lawrence College,
        Bronxville, New York
1976   *Drawing/Disegno*, Cannaviello Studio d'Arte, Rome,
        Italy
        Painting and Sculpture Today '76, Indianapolis
        Museum of Art, Indianapolis, Indiana
1977   *View of a Decade*, Museum of Contemporary Art,
        Chicago, Illinois
        Words at Liberty, Museum of Contemporary Art,
        Chicago, Illinois
        *Watercolors and Related Media by Contemporary
        Californians*, Baxter Art Gallery, California Institute
        of Technology, Pasadena, California
1978   *Three Sculptors*, The Santa Barbara Museum of
        Art, Santa Barbara, California
1979   *California Hybrid*, Alex Rosenberg Gallery,
        New York, New York
        10 Sculptors/15 Works: Outdoors, California State
        College, San Bernardino, California
1980   *Sculpture in California, 1975–1980*, San Diego
        Museum of Art, San Deigo, California
1981   *Messages, Words and Images*, Freedman Gallery,
        Albright College, Reading, Pennsylvania (toured)
        Polychrome, Hansen Fuller Goldeen Gallery,
        San Francisco, California
        Downtown Los Angeles, Madison Art Center,
        Madison, Wisconsin (toured)
1982   *Security Pacific Collection*, Los Angeles Municipal
        Art Gallery, Los Angeles, California
        100 Years of California Sculpture, The Oakland
        Museum, Oakland, California
        Exchange Between Artists, 1931–1982, Musée
        d'Art Moderne, Paris, France (toured)
1983   *Young Talent Awards: 1963–1983*, Los Angeles
        County Museum of Art, Los Angeles, California
1984   *Japanese American Affinities*, Los Angeles
        Municipal Art Gallery, Los Angeles, California

Tom Holland

Born in Seattle, Washington, 1936
Resides in Berkeley, California
Studied at Willamette University, Salem, Oregon; University of California, Santa Barbara; and University of California, Berkeley

Awards
1959   Fulbright Award, Santiago, Chile
1975   Individual Artist Fellowship—Sculpture, National Endowment for the Arts
1979   John Simon Guggenheim Fellowship

Selected Solo Exhibitions
1960   Catholic University, Santiago, Chile
1962   Richmond Art Center, Richmond, California (also 1966, 76)
1963   Lanyon Gallery, Palo Alto, California (also 1964, 65)
1965   Nicholas Wilder Gallery, Los Angeles, California (also 1967, 68, 69, 72, 73, 76, 77)
Hansen Fuller Gallery, San Francisco, California (also 1968, 70, 72, 74, 76, 77)
1968   Arizona State University, Tempe, Arizona
1970   Neuendorf Gallery, Cologne and Hamburg, West Germany
Robert Elkon Gallery, New York, New York (also 1971)
1972   Multiples, Los Angeles, California
1973   Knoedler (Lawrence Rubin), New York, New York
Current Editions, Seattle, Washington
1975   Knoedler Contemporary Art, New York, New York
Dootson/Calderhead Gallery, Los Angeles, California
Greenberg Gallery, St. Louis, Missouri
1977   Watson/de Nagy Gallery, Houston, Texas
1978   Smith Anderson Gallery, Palo Alto, California
Charles Casat Gallery, La Jolla, California
Droll Kolbert Gallery, New York, New York
1983   Charles Cowles Gallery, New York, New York (also 1984)
Bank of America Galleries, San Francisco, California
James Corcoran Gallery, Los Angeles, California

Selected Group Exhibitions
1972   *California Prints*, The Museum of Modern Art, New York, New York
USA—West Coast, Hamburg, Hanover, and Cologne, West Germany
Works in Progress, San Francisco Museum of Art, San Francisco, California
1973   Whitney Museum of American Art, New York, New York (also 1978)
Small Format, Saint Mary's College, Moraga, California
New Work: Tom Holland, Don Kaufman, Sam Tchakalian, William T. Wiley, California State University, San Jose, Art Gallery, San Jose, California
1974   *Biennial of Painting and Sculpture*, Krannert Art Museum, Champaign, Illinois
1975   Virginia and Bagley Wright Collection, Denver Art Museum, Denver, Colorado
Corcoran Biennial, Washington, D.C.
Holland and Davis, Rowan Collection, Los Angeles Municipal Art Gallery, Los Angeles, California
1976   *Painting and Sculpture in California: The Modern Era*, San Francisco Museum of Modern Art, San Francisco, California (toured)
1977   *California Bay Area Update*, Huntsville Museum of Art, Huntsville, Alabama
Drawing Invitational, Fine Arts Gallery of San Diego, San Diego, California
Miniature, California State University, Los Angeles, California
Drawing Exhibition, Linda Farris Gallery, Seattle, Washington
New in the Seventies, University of Texas, Austin, Texas
1978   *Aspects of Abstract*, E.B. Crocker Art Gallery, Sacramento, California
1979   *Artists Born Between 1935-1945, 20 Painters*, Nancy Caldwell Gallery, New York, New York
1979   *Aspects of Abstract*, Crocker Art Museum, Sacramento, California
1981   *Works on Paper*, The Museum of Modern Art, New York, New York
1982   *Of No Particular Theme*, Baxter Art Gallery, California Institute of Technology, Pasadena, California
Northern California Art of the Sixties, deSaisset Art Gallery and Museum, University of Santa Clara, Santa Clara, California
1983   *On and Off the Wall: Shaped and Colored*, The Oakland Museum, Oakland, California
Huntsville Museum of Art, Huntsville, Alabama
1984   Greenberg Gallery, St. Louis, Missouri

Robert Hudson

Born in Salt Lake City, Utah, 1938
Resides in Cotati, California
Studied at the San Francisco Art Institute (Bachelor of Fine
Arts degree, 1962; Master of Fine Arts degree, 1963)

Awards
1961   Purchase Prize, San Francisco Art Festival
1964   San Jose State College
1965   Nealie Sullivan Award, San Francisco Art Institute
1972   Individual Artist Fellowship, National Endowment
        for the Arts
1976   John Simon Guggenheim Fellowship

Selected Solo Exhibitions
1961   Richmond Art Center, Richmond, California
1962   Bolles Gallery, San Francisco, California
1963   Allan Frumkin Gallery, New York, New York (also
        1965, 72, 76, 78, 81, 82, 84)
1967   Nicholas Wilder Gallery, Los Angeles, California
1969   Allan Frumkin Gallery, Chicago, Illinois
        (also 1971, 76)
1973   Hansen Fuller Gallery, San Francisco, California
        (also 1975, 77)
1977   Portland Center for the Visual Arts, Portland, Oregon
1978   University Memorial Center, University of Colorado,
        Boulder, Colorado
        Moore College of Art, Philadelphia, Pennsylvania
        (toured)
1979   Hansen Fuller Goldeen Gallery, San Francisco,
        California (also 1982)
1983   Morgan Gallery, Shawnee Mission, Kansas
        University of Wisconsin, Eau Claire, Wisconsin
1984   Fuller Goldeen Gallery, San Francisco, California

Selected Group Exhibitions
1959   *Richmond Ceramic Sculpture Annual Exhibition*,
        Richmond, California
        *Richmond Painting and Sculpture Annual
        Exhibition*, Richmond, California (also 1960, 61)
1962   *Bay Area Artists*, San Francisco Museum of Art,
        San Francisco, California
        79th Painting and Sculpture Annual Exhibition,
        San Francisco Museum of Art, San Francisco,
        California
        90-Year Retrospective of Bay Area Art,

San Francisco Museum of Art, San Francisco,
California
Some Points of View, Stanford University Museum
and Art Gallery, Stanford, California
1964   Lanyon Gallery, Palo Alto, California (also 1965)
        First Annual Sculpture Competition, San Jose City
        College, San Jose, California
        Allan Frumkin Gallery, Chicago, Illinois (also 1967)
        Bay Area Arts II, San Francisco Museum of Art,
        San Francisco, California
        Whitney Museum of American Art, New York,
        New York (also 1966, 67, 68, 69, 70)
1965   *The Drawing Society Regional Exhibition*, California
        Palace of the Legion of Honor, San Francisco,
        California
        Young America 1965, Whitney Museum of
        American Art, New York, New York
1967   The Chicago Art Institute, Chicago, Illinois
        Funk Art, University Art Museum, Berkeley,
        California
        American Sculpture of the Sixties, Los Angeles
        County Museum of Art, Los Angeles, California
1968   *West Coast Now*, Portland Art Museum, Portland,
        Oregon (toured)
        Looking Back, San Francisco Museum of Art,
        San Francisco, California
1969   *Fourteen Sculptors: The Industrial Edge*, Walker
        Art Center, Minneapolis, Minnesota (toured)
1970   *Centennial Exhibition*, San Francisco Museum of
        Art, San Francisco, California
1971   *Continuing Surrealism*, La Jolla Museum of
        Contemporary Art, La Jolla, California
        Good Drawing Show, Saint Mary's College Art
        Gallery, Moraga, California
1973   *Robert Hudson/Richard Shaw: Work in Porcelain*,
        San Francisco Museum of Art, San Francisco,
        California
1974   Whitney Museum of American Art, Downtown
        Branch, New York, New York
        A Drawing Show, Newport Harbor Art Museum,
        Newport Beach, California
1975   *34th Biennial*, Corcoran Gallery of Art,
        Washington, D.C.
        Hayward Gallery, London, England
1976   *Painting and Sculpture in California: The Modern
        Era*, San Francisco Museum of Modern Art,
        San Francisco, California (toured)
1977   *California Bay Area Update*, Huntsville Museum of
        Art, Huntsville, Alabama
1978   *Aesthetics of Graffiti*, San Francisco Museum of
        Modern Art, San Francisco, California
1979   *Drawing Invitational*, Central Washington
        University, Ellensburg, Washington
        Directions, Hirshhorn Museum and Sculpture
        Garden, Washington, D.C.
1981   *Polychrome*, Hansen Fuller Goldeen Gallery,
        San Francisco, California
1982   *First Annual Wild West Show*, Alberta College of
        Art Gallery, Calgary, Alberta, Canada
1983   *Sculpture: The Tradition in Steel*, Nassau County
        Museum of Fine Art, Roslyn, New York
1984   *Return of the Narrative*, Palm Springs Desert
        Museum, Palm Springs, California

Manuel Neri

Born in Sanger, California, 1930
Resides in Benicia, Caliornia
Studied at San Francisco City College (1949–50); University
of California, Berkeley (1951–52); California College of Arts
and Crafts, Oakland (1952–57); and California School of Fine
Arts, San Francisco (1957–59)

Awards
1953	First Award in Sculpture, Oakland Art Museum
1959	Nealie Sullivan Award, California School of Fine Arts, San Francisco
1963	82nd Annual Sculpture Award, San Francisco Art Institute
1965	National Art Foundation Award
1970	Sculpture Grant, University of California, Davis (also 1971, 72, 73, 74, 75)
1979	John Simon Guggenheim Fellowship
1980	Individual Artist Fellowship, National Endowment for the Arts
1982	Academy-Institute Award in Art, American Academy and Institute of Arts and Letters

Selected Solo Exhibitions
1957	Six Gallery, San Francisco, California
1960	Dilexi Gallery, San Francisco, California
1963	New Mission Gallery, San Francisco, California
1966	Quay Gallery, San Francisco, California (also 1968 71, 75)
1970	Saint Mary's College, Moraga, California
1971	San Francisco Museum of Art, San Francisco, California
1974	University Art Gallery, San Jose State University, San Jose, California
1976	Braunstein/Quay Gallery, New York, New York
1977	E.B. Crocker Art Gallery, Sacramento, California
1980	Whitman College, Walla Walla, Washington Richmond Art Center, Richmond, California
1981	Seattle Art Museum, Seattle, Washington Charles Cowles Gallery, New York, New York (also 1982) John Berggruen Gallery, San Francisco, California (also 1984)
1983	Gimpel-Hanover and André Emmerich Galerien, Zurich, Switzerland

Selected Group Exhibitions
1955	Six Gallery, San Francisco, California (also 1957)
1957	Richmond Art Center, Richmond, California
1959	Four-Man Show: Sam Francis, Wally Hendrick, Fred Martin, Manuel Neri, San Francisco Museum of Art, San Francisco, California
1961	Staempfli Gallery, New York, New York The Nude, California Palace of the Legion of Honor, San Francisco, California
1963	California Sculpture Today, Oakland Art Museum, Oakland, California
1964	Joan Brown/Manuel Neri, David Stuart Gallery, Los Angeles, California
1965	Bay Region: Prints and Drawings, San Francisco Museum of Art, San Francisco, California
1966	Abstract Expressionist Ceramics, University of California, Irvine, California
1967	Funk Art, University Art Museum, Berkeley, California Recorded Images/Dimensional Media, California State College, Fullerton, California
1968	West Coast Now, Portland Art Museum, Portland, Oregon
1970	Garden Show, Memorial Union Gallery, University of California, Davis, California Whitney Museum of American Art, New York, New York
1971	Good Drawing Show, Saint Mary's College Art Gallery, Moraga, California Quay Gallery, San Francisco, California (also 1972, 74)
1973	The Small Format, Saint Mary's College Art Gallery, Moraga, California
1974	A Third World Painting and Sculpture Exhibition, San Francisco Museum of Art, San Francisco, California Public Sculpture, Urban Environment, The Oakland Museum, Oakland, California
1976	Painting and Sculpture in California: The Modern Era, San Francisco Museum of Modern Art, San Francisco, California (toured) New Work: Bruce Connor and Manuel Neri, Braunstein/Quay Gallery, San Francisco, California
1977	California Bay Area Update, Huntsville Museum of Art, Huntsville, Alabama
1978	A Century of Ceramics in the United States, 1878–1978, Everson Museum of Art, Syracuse, New York
1979	Related Figurative Drawings, Hansen Fuller Goldeen Gallery, San Francisco, California
1980	Sculpture in California, 1975–80, San Diego Museum of Art, San Diego, California 20 American Artists, San Francisco Museum of Modern Art, San Francisco, California
1981	The Figure in Bronze: Small Scale, Middendorf/Lane Gallery, Washington, D.C.
1982	Benicia Sculptors, Benicia Art Studios, Benicia, California 100 Years of California Sculpture, The Oakland Museum, Oakland, California
1983	The United States of the Arts, Sarah Lawrence Gallery, Sarah Lawrence College, Bronxville, New York
1984	Drawings Since 1974, Hirshhorn Museum and Sculpture Garden, Washington, D.C.

Sam Richardson

Born in Oakland, California, 1934
Resides in Oakland, California
Studied at the California College of Arts and Crafts, Oakland
(Bachelor of Arts degree, 1956; Master of Fine Arts degree,
1960)

Selected Solo Exhibitions

1961   Hansen and Peterman Gallery, San Francisco,
        California
1966   Hansen Gallery/Tilman Place, San Francisco,
        California
1967   Humboldt State College, Arcata, California
1968   Hansen Fuller Gallery, San Francisco, California
        (also 1969, 71, 73, 75)
1969   Martha Jackson Gallery, New York, New York
        (also 1971, 72, 73, 75, 76)
1970   San Francisco Museum of Art, San Francisco,
        California
1972   Akron Art Institute, Akron, Ohio
1973   Mills College Art Gallery, Oakland, California
        Cranbrook Academy of Art/Museum, Bloomfield
        Hills, Michigan
        The Denver Art Museum, Denver, Colorado
1975   M.H. De Young Memorial Museum, San Francisco,
        California
1976   Dallas Museum of Fine Arts, Dallas, Texas
1977   Art Gallery, California State University, Fullerton,
        California
1978   The Oakland Museum, Oakland, California
1979   Hansen Fuller Goldeen Gallery, San Francisco,
        California (also 1980, 83)
1980   Janus Gallery, Los Angeles, California
1981   The Santa Barbara Museum of Art, Santa Barbara,
        California
1982   Klein Gallery, Chicago, Illinois

Selected Group Exhibitions

1961   *Third Winter Invitational*, California Palace of the
        Legion of Honor, San Francisco, California
1963   *Creative Casting*, Museum of Contemporary Crafts,
        New York, New York
1965   *Annual Exhibition*, Richmond Art Center, Richmond,
        California (also 1966, 67)
1967   *Painters Behind Painters*, California Palace of the
        Legion of Honor, San Francisco, California

Light and Movement, Esther Robles Gallery,
Los Angeles, California
Threshhold '67, Esther Robles Gallery, Los Angeles,
California
Bay Area South, Richmond Art Center, Richmond,
California
1968   *Plastic as Plastic*, Museum of Contemporary Crafts,
        New York, New York (circulated by the Smithsonian
        Institution)
        Whitney Museum of American Art, New York,
        New York
1969   *New Media—New Methods*, The Museum of
        Modern Art, New York, New York (toured)
        Contemporary American Sculpture: Selection 2,
        Whitney Museum of American Art, New York,
        New York
        Affect-Effect, La Jolla Museum of Contemporary
        Art, La Jolla, California
1970   *Pollution Show*, The Oakland Museum, Oakland,
        California
1971   *Spray*, The Santa Barbara Museum of Art,
        Santa Barbara, California
        White on White, Museum of Contemporary Art,
        Chicago, Illinois
1972   *Topography of Nature*, Institute of Contemporary
        Art, Philadelphia, Pennsylvania
        West Coast Sculpture Invitational, Stanford
        University Museum and Art Gallery, Stanford,
        California
1974   *Public Sculpture, Urban Environment*, The Oakland
        Museum, Oakland, California
1975   *Response to the Environment*, Rutgers University
        Art Gallery, New Brunswick, New Jersey
        California Landscape, The Oakland Museum,
        Oakland, California
1976   *Painting and Sculpture in California: The Modern
        Era*, San Francisco Museum of Modern Art,
        San Francisco, California (toured)
        A Sense of Scale, The Oakland Museum, Oakland,
        California
1978   *California 3x8 Twice*, Honolulu Academy of Arts,
        Honolulu, Hawaii
1979   Foster White Gallery, Seattle, Washington
1980   *Artists of the Pacific Coast States*, The Vice
        President's House, Washington, D.C.
1981   *California, the State of the Landscape:
        1872–1981*, Newport Harbor Art Museum,
        Newport Beach, California
        Then and Now: 1960–1980, Hansen Fuller
        Goldeen Gallery, San Francisco, California
1982   *100 Years of California Sculpture*, The Oakland
        Museum, Oakland, California
1983   *Chicago International Art Exposition, 1983*, Navy
        Pier, Chicago, Illinois
        The House that Art Built, Art Gallery, California
        State University, Fullerton, California

Michael Todd

Born in Omaha, Nebraska, 1935
Resides in Los Angeles, California
Studied at the University of Notre Dame, Notre Dame, Indiana
(Bachelor of Fine Arts degree, 1953), and the University of
California, Los Angeles (Master of Arts degree, 1959)

Awards
1957   Woodrow Wilson Fellowship (two years)
1961   Fulbright Fellowship, Paris (two years)
1974   Individual Artist Fellowship, National Endowment
        for the Arts

Selected Solo Exhibitions
1964   Hanover Gallery, London, England
        Pace Gallery, New York, New York
1965   Henri Gallery, Washington, D.C.
1968   Gertrude Kasle Gallery, Detroit, Michigan
        (also 1975)
1969   The Salk Institute, La Jolla, California
1970   University of California, Los Angeles, California
1971   Reese Palley Gallery, New York, New York
1972   University of Notre Dame, Notre Dame, Indiana
        California State University, Fullerton, California
        San Diego Museum of Art, San Diego, California
1974   Zabriskie Gallery, New York, New York (also 1976)
1975   Seder Creigh Gallery, Coronado, California
1976   Nicholas Wilder Gallery, Los Angeles, California
        Hammarskjold Plaza, New York, New York
1978   The Oakland Museum, Oakland, California
        Gallery Paule Anglim, San Francisco, California
        (also 1980, 82)
1979   ARCO Center for the Visual Arts, Los Angeles,
        California
        Diane Brown Gallery, Washington, D.C. (also 1981)
        Tortue Gallery, Santa Monica, California (also
        1980, 82)
1981   Charles Cowles Gallery, New York, New York
        (also 1983)
1983   Klein Gallery, Chicago, Illinois

Selected Group Exhibitions
1962   American Cultural Center, Paris, France
1965   Whitney Museum of American Art, New York,
        New York (also 1967, 68)
1966   *Primary Structures*, The Jewish Museum,
        New York, New York
1967   *American Sculpture of the Sixties*, Los Angeles
        County Museum of Art, Los Angeles, California
1968   Corcoran Gallery of Art, Washington, D.C.
1974   *Public Sculpture, Urban Environment*, The Oakland
        Museum, Oakland, California
1976   *Painting and Sculpture in California: The Modern
        Era*, San Francisco Museum of Modern Art,
        San Francisco, California (toured)
1978   *Photographs by Sculptors*, Los Angeles County
        Museum of Art, Los Angeles, California
1980   *Sculpture in California, 1975–80*, San Diego
        Museum of Art, San Diego, California
        Crocker Art Museum, Sacramento, California
1982   *20 American Artists: Sculpture 1982*, San
        Francisco Museum of Modern Art, San Francisco,
        California
        100 Years of California Sculpture, The Oakland
        Museum, Oakland, California
        Exchange Between Artists, 1931–1982, Musée
        d'Art Moderne, Paris, France (toured)
1983   *Urban Sculpture: Architectural Concerns*, Security
        Pacific Bank, Los Angeles, California
        Matthews Hamilton Gallery, Philadelphia,
        Pennsylvania

DeWain Valentine

Born in Fort Collins, Colorado, 1936
Resides in Venice, California
Studied at the University of Colorado, Boulder (Bachelor of
Fine Arts degree, 1958; Master of Fine Arts degree, 1960),
and Yale Norfolk Art School, Norfolk, Connecticut (Yale
University Fellowship, 1958)

Awards
1980   John Simon Guggenheim Fellowship
1981   Individual Artist Fellowship, National Endowment
        for the Arts

Selected Solo Exhibitions
1958   University of Colorado Fine Arts Gallery, Boulder,
        Colorado (also 1960)
1964   The Gallery, Denver, Colorado
1968   Douglas Gallery, Vancouver, British Columbia,
        Canada
        University of California, Santa Barbara, California
1969   Henry Art Gallery, University of Washington,
        Seattle, Washington
        Fine Arts Gallery, University of British Columbia,
        Vancouver, British Columbia, Canada
        Galerie Bischofberger, Zurich, Switzerland
1970   Pasadena Museum of Art, Pasadena, California
1973   Galerie Denise René, New York, New York
1974   San Jose Museum of Art, San Jose, California
1975   La Jolla Museum of Contemporary Art, La Jolla,
        California
1977   The Santa Barbara Museum of Art, Santa Barbara,
        California
1979   Los Angeles County Museum of Art, Los Angeles,
        California
        University of California, Irvine, California
1980   Malinda Wyatt Gallery, Venice, California
        (also 1982)
1981   Projects Studio One, Institute for Art and Urban
        Resources, New York, New York
1982   Laumeier International Sculpture Park, St. Louis,
        Missouri
1983   Madison Art Center, Madison, Wisconsin
1984   Center for the Fine Arts, Miami, Florida

Selected Group Exhibitions
1958   *Joslyn Biennial Exhibition*, Joslyn Art Museum,
        Omaha, Nebraska (also 1960)

1959   Dallas Museum of Fine Arts, Dallas, Texas
1960   University of Colorado Fine Arts Gallery, Boulder,
        Colorado
1962   Amarillo Art Center Association, Amarillo, Texas
1965   *Eight Colorado Artists*, University of Colorado Fine
        Arts Gallery, Boulder, Colorado
        Plastic Relief Painting, University of Colorado Fine
        Arts Gallery, Boulder, Colorado
1966   Whitney Museum of American Art, New York,
        New York (also 1968, 70)
1967   *American Sculpture of the Sixties*, Los Angeles
        County Museum of Art, Los Angeles, California
1968   *Plastics West Coast*, Hansen Fuller Gallery,
        San Francisco, California
        West Coast Now, Portland Art Museum, Portland,
        Oregon (toured)
        Plastic as Plastic, Museum of Contemporary Crafts,
        New York, New York
1969   *Fourteen Sculptors: The Industrial Edge*, Walker Art
        Center, Minneapolis, Minnesota (toured)
        Plastic Presence, The Jewish Museum, New York,
        New York (toured)
1970   *Permutations: Light and Color*, Museum of Contem-
        porary Art, Chicago, Illinois
1971   *First International Biennial of Small Sculpture*,
        Budapest, Hungary
        Society of Contemporary Art Drawing Exhibit, The
        Art Institute of Chicago, Chicago, Illinois
        Bell, Cooper, Alexander, McCracken, and Valentine,
        Ace Gallery, Los Angeles, California
1973   *American Art, 1948–1973*, Seattle Art Museum,
        Seattle, Washington
1974   Margo Leavin Gallery, Los Angeles, California
        (also 1975, 76, 77)
        Galerie Denise René, New York, New York
        (also 1975)
1975   Libra Gallery, Claremont College, Claremont,
        California (also 1976)
1976   Artworks, Milwaukee, Wisconsin
1977   *Private Images*, Los Angeles County Museum of
        Art, Los Angeles, California
        100+, Los Angeles Institute of Contemporary Art,
        Los Angeles, California
1978   *Drawings for Outdoor Sculpture*, John Weber
        Gallery, New York, New York (toured)
        Change, Inc., West Exhibition, Los Angeles County
        Museum of Art, Los Angeles, California
        The Museum of Drawers, by Herbert Distel,
        Los Angeles Institute of Contemporary Art,
        Los Angeles, California
1979   *California Perceptions: Light and Space*, Art Gallery,
        California State University, Fullerton, California
1980   *Structural Imagery*, University of California, Irvine,
        California
        Sculpture in California, 1975–80, San Diego
        Museum of Art, San Diego, California
1981   Lonny Gans, Venice, California
        California Innovations, Art Gallery, California State
        University, Fullerton, California (toured)
1982   *100 Years of California Sculpture*, The Oakland
        Museum, Oakland, California
        Exchange Between Artists: 1931–82, Musée d'Art
        Moderne, Paris, France (toured)
1983   *Urban Sculpture, Architectural Concerns*, Security
        Pacific National Bank, Los Angeles, California

Bibliographies

Robert Arneson

Adrian, Dennis. "Robert Arneson's Feats in Clay." *Art in America*, vol. 62, no. 3, September-October 1974, pp. 80-83.

Albright, Thomas. "The Cream of California Ceramics." *San Francisco Chronicle*, 10 April 1982.

Armstrong, Lois. "Los Angeles: Roy De Forest and Robert Arneson." *Artnews*, vol. 68, no. 7, October 1969, pp. 74-76.

Arneson, Robert. *My Head in Ceramics*. Self-published, 1972.

Ball, Fred. "A Decade of Ceramic Art: 1962-1972." *Ceramics Monthly*, vol. 21, no. 1, January 1973, pp. 18-20.

_____. "Arneson." *Craft Horizons*, vol. 34, no. 1, February 1974, pp. 28, 30, 63, 64.

Brown, Christopher. "Bob Arneson—From Comic Books to Self-Portraits." *Artweek*, vol. 7, no. 35, 16 October 1976, p. 13.

Caldwell, John. "Contemporary Artists in Summit Exhibit." *The New York Times*, 28 March 1982.

Coffelt, Beth. "Arneson's Whistling is Blowing Everybody's Mind at the Whitney." *San Francisco Sunday Examiner & Chronicle*, 17 July 1977.

_____. "Arneson and Sculpture, Beyond City Limits." *Newsweek*, 22 March 1982, p. 53.

Einbeck, Jean. "Letters: Arneson's Ceramics." *Craft Horizons*, vol. 25, no. 1, January-February 1965, p. 6.

Ellenzweig, Allen. "Arts Reviews: Robert Arneson." *Arts*, vol. 49, no. 7, April 1975, p. 14.

_____. "Arts Reviews: Robert Arneson." *Arts*, vol. 52, no. 1, September 1977, p. 75.

Frankenstein, Alfred. "Mind Blower of Century." *San Francisco Chronicle*, 5 October 1972.

_____. "The Ceramic Sculpture of Robert Arneson: Transforming Craft into Art." *Artnews*, vol. 75, no. 1, January 1976, pp. 48-50.

French, Palmer D. "Reviews: Robert Arneson." *Artforum*, vol. VII, no. 8, April 1969, pp. 75, 76.

Glueck, Grace. "Art: Robert Arneson." *The New York Times*, 13 May 1983.

Hughes, Robert. "Molding the Human Clay." *Time*, 18 January 1982, p. 66.

Judd, Donald. "In the Galleries: Robert Arneson." *Arts*, vol. 39, no. 4, January 1965, p. 69.

Kramer, Hilton. "Ceramic Sculpture and the Taste of California." *The New York Times*, 20 December 1981.

Last, Martin. "Reviews: Robert Arneson." *Artnews*, vol. 68, no. 8, December 1969, p. 8.

McCann, Cecile N. "Arneson, Richardson." *Artweek*, vol. 1, no. 21, 23 May 1970, p. 1.

_____. "Membrane Paintings, Arneson's Feast." *Artweek*, vol. 2, no. 36, 23 October 1971, pp. 1, 8.

_____. "Arneson and Trowbridge—Hot and Cool." *Artweek*, vol. 4, no. 35, 20 October 1973, p. 3.

_____. "About Arneson, Art and Ceramics." *Artweek*, vol. 5, no. 36, 26 October 1974, pp. 1, 6, 7.

McFadden, Sarah. "Reviews: Robert Arneson." *Art in America*, vol. 66, no. 4, July-August 1977, p. 100.

McGuignan, Cathleen. "Newsmakers." *Newsweek*, 22 March 1982.

Meisel, Alan R. "Letter from San Francisco: Robert Arneson." *Craft Horizons*, vol. 24, no. 5, September-October 1964, p. 53.

_____. "Letter from San Francisco: Robert Arneson." *Craft Horizons*, vol. 27, no. 5, September-October 1967, pp. 41, 42.

_____. "Funky Figurines." *Time*, 26 April 1968, p. 76.

_____. "Letter from San Francisco: Robert Arneson." *Craft Horizons*, vol. 32, no. 4, August 1972, p. 49.

Morch, Al. "Westerners with Feats of Clay." *San Francisco Examiner*, 9 April 1982.

The Museum of Modern Art. *Dada, Surrealism and Their Heritage*. New York: The Museum of Modern Art, 1968.

The National Museum of Modern Art. *Contemporary Ceramic Art: Canada, USA, Mexico and Japan*. Kyoto: The National Museum of Modern Art, 1971; Tokyo: The National Museum of Modern Art, 1972.

Oakland Art Museum. *Ceramics and Sculpture by Robert Arneson*. Oakland: Oakland Art Museum, 1960.

Plagens, Peter. *Sunshine Muse*. New York: Praeger Publishers, 1974.

Selz, Peter. *Funk*. Berkeley: University Art Museum, 1967.

Stephan, R.F. "Arneson's Landscape." *Artweek*, vol. 7, no. 4, 24 January 1976, pp. 5, 6.

Stevens, Mark. "Brave Feats of Clay." *Newsweek*, 11 January 1982, pp. 67, 68.

Tarshis, Jerome. "Robert Arneson, How to be a Non-Artist." *Coast*, January 1977, pp. 48-50.

Temko, Allan. "A Shocker from the Ever Controversial Robert Arneson." *San Francisco Chronicle*, 28 May 1982.

Wilson, William. "S.F. Exhibit: Clay and Now Moscone." *Los Angeles Times*, 25 April 1982.

Wolff, Theodore F. "When Clay Came into its Own as Art." *Christian Science Monitor*, 14 January 1982.

Zack, David. "The Ceramics of Robert Arneson." *Craft Horizons*, vol. 30, no. 1, January-February 1970, pp. 36-41.

Charles Arnoldi

Albright-Knox Art Gallery. *Working in California*. Buffalo: Albright-Knox Art Gallery, 1972.

Art Gallery, California State University, Fullerton. *Arnoldi/Cooper/McCollum/Wudl*. Fullerton: Art Gallery, California State University, Fullerton, 1972.

_____. *Charles Arnoldi and Laddie John Dill*. Fullerton: Art Gallery, California State University, Fullerton, 1983.

The Art Museum, California State University, Long Beach. *Selections from the Frederick Weisman Company Collection of California Art*. Long Beach: California State University, Long Beach, 1979.

Atkins, Robert. "Art: Modern Painted Sculpture." *Architectural Digest*, vol. 40, August 1983, p. 112.

Baker, Elizabeth C. "Los Angeles, 1971." *Artnews*, vol. 70, September 1971, pp. 28, 33, 34.

Ballatore, Sandy. "Charles Arnoldi's Mazes." *Artweek*, vol. 5, 2 March 1974, p. 5.

Baum, Hank, editor. *The Los Angeles Art Review*. Chicago: The Krantz Company, Publishers, 1981.

Canavier, Elena. "Contemporary Art Council's Acquisitions." *Artweek*, vol. 4, 13 January 1973, p. 1.

Contemporary Arts Museum. *America: The Landscape*. Houston: Contemporary Arts Museum, 1981.

Corcoran Gallery of Art. *The 38th Corcoran Biennial Exhibition of American Painting: Second Western States Exhibition*. Washington, D.C.: Corcoran Gallery of Art, 1983.

Dokumenta 5. Kassel, West Germany, 1972.

Frank, Peter. "New York Reviews." *Artnews*, vol. 74, Summer 1975, p. 136.

Glueck, Grace. "Two Biennials: One Looking East and the Other Looking West." *The New York Times*, 27 March 1983.

Hansen Fuller Goldeen Gallery. *Casting: Survey of Cast Metal Sculpture*. San Francisco: Hansen Fuller Goldeen Gallery, 1982.

Hopkins, Henry T. *50 California Artists*. San Francisco: Chronicle Books, 1981.

Indianapolis Museum of Art. *Painting and Sculpture Today*. Indianapolis: Indianapolis Museum of Art, 1978.

Kalil, Susie. "American Landscape—Contemporary Interpretations." *Artweek*, vol. 12, 25 April 1981, pp. 9, 10.

_____. "Art: Charles Arnoldi." *The Houston Post*, 6 February 1983.

Krantz, Les, editor. *The Chicago Art Review*. Chicago: The Krantz Company, Publishers, 1981.

La Jolla Museum of Contemporary Art. *Artists' Quilts*. La Jolla: La Jolla Museum of Contemporary Art, 1981.

Livingstone, Jane. "Four Los Angeles Artists." *Art in America*, vol. 58, September-October 1970, p. 131.

Los Angeles County Museum of Art. *Los Angeles Prints, 1883–1980*. Los Angeles: Los Angeles County Museum of Art, 1981.

Los Angeles Municipal Art Gallery. *L.A. Art: An Exhibition of Contemporary Painting*. Los Angeles: Los Angeles Municipal Art Gallery, 1982.

McDonald, Robert H. "Contemporary Abstraction—South." *Artweek*, vol. 5, 23 February 1974, pp. 1, 16.

Museum of Contemporary Art. *Permutations: Light and Color*. Chicago: Museum of Contemporary Art, 1970.

Museum of Fine Arts. *Graham Gund Collection*. Boston: Museum of Fine Arts, 1982.

The Museum of Fine Arts, Houston. *A Century of Modern Sculpture, 1882–1982*. Houston: The Museum of Fine Arts, 1983.

Pace Gallery. *A Decade of California Color*. New York: Pace Gallery, 1970.

Pasadena Museum of Art. *Fifteen Los Angeles Artists*. Pasadena: Pasadena Museum of Art, 1969.

Plagens, Peter. "The Decline and Rise of Younger Los Angeles Art." *Artforum*, vol. X, May 1972, p. 80.

San Francisco Museum of Modern Art. *Painting and Sculpture in California: The Modern Era*. San Francisco: San Francisco Museum of Modern Art, 1976.

The Santa Barbara Museum of Art. *Fifteen Abstract Artists*. Santa Barbara: The Santa Barbara Museum of Art, 1974.

Whitney Museum of American Art. *The Whitney Biennial Exhibition of Painting and Sculpture*. New York: Whitney Museum of American Art, 1981.

Wilson, William. "A Cocktail Party of the Second Kind." *Los Angeles Times*, 1 March 1981.

Bruce Beasley

American Sculpture. Lincoln: University of Nebraska Press, 1970.

Artforum. "California Sculptors." Vol. II, no. 2, August 1963.

Artforum. "Plastics West Coast." Vol. VI, no. 7, March 1968.

Artnews. "Bruce Beasley in Sacramento." 1970.

Bush, J. *A Decade of Sculpture*. Cranbury: Art Alliance Press, 1974.

Faulkner-Ziegfield. *Art Today: 1969*. New York: Holt Rinehart Winston, 1969.

Illinois University. *Contemporary American Painting and Sculpture*. Urbana: University of Illinois Press, 1969.

Lucie-Smith, E. *Late Modern, The Visual Arts Since 1945*. New York: Praeger Publishers, 1969.

Newman, Thelma. *Plastics as an Art Form*. Radnor: Chilton Book Company, 1969.

Seitz, William. *The Art of Assemblage*. New York: The Museum of Modern Art, 1961.

Thalacker, D. *The Place of Art in the World of Architecture*. New York: Chelsea House Publishers, 1980.

Time. "The Crystal Clear Scene." 9 February 1968.

Time-Life Books. *Nature-Science Annual*. 1970.

Fletcher Benton

Albright, Thomas. "Three Masterful Artists." *San Francisco Chronicle*, 15 January 1970.

_____. "Benton at The Oakland Museum." *Artweek*, 17 January 1970.

_____. "Fletcher Benton at the San Francisco Museum of Art." *Artweek*, 17 January 1970.

_____. "Benton's Kinetic Sculpture." *San Francisco Chronicle*, 12 June 1970.

_____. "Fletcher Benton's Subtle Sculptures." *San Francisco Chronicle*, 10 March 1980.

John Berggruen Gallery. *Fletcher Benton: Recent Sculpture*. San Francisco: John Berggruen Gallery, 1981.

Butterfield, Jan. "An Interview with Fletcher Benton." *Art International*, November-December 1980.

Cortright, Barbara. "Fletcher Benton Sculpture." *Artweek*, 27 April 1974.

Curtis, Stephanie. "Conceptual Art Changes." *Palo Alto Times*, 19 October 1972.

Dickson, Joanne. "San Jose Museum Showcases Artwork of Faculty Members." *Palo Alto Times*, January 1978.

Davis, Douglas. *Art and the Future*. New York: Praeger Publishers, 1973.

Frankenstein, Alfred. "Art's Most Moving Moments." *San Francisco Examiner-Chronicle*, 27 March 1966.

_____. "Kinetic Forces." *San Francisco Chronicle*, 12 January 1965.

_____. "Impressive Sculpture Show." *San Francisco Chronicle*, 25 November 1970.

Hagberg, Marilyn. "Benton's Moving Paintings." *Artweek*, 29 April 1972.

Hopkins, Henry T. *50 West Coast Artists*. San Francisco: Chronicle Books, 1981.

Jenson, Dean. "Fletcher Benton: Folded Circle-Triangle." *Milwaukee Sentinel*, 23 November 1979.

Los Angeles County Museum of Art. *American Sculpture of the Sixties*. Los Angeles: Los Angeles County Museum of Art, 1967.

McCann, Cecile N. "Fletcher Benton Color Flow. *Artweek*, 23 October 1971.

Morch, Al. "Bronzing the Alphabet." *San Francisco Examiner*, 24 March 1980.

The Oakland Museum. *Public Sculpture, Urban Environment*. Oakland: The Oakland Museum, 1973.

_____. *100 Years of California Sculpture*. Oakland: The Oakland Museum, 1982.

Plagens, Peter. *Sunshine Muse*. New York: Praeger Publishers, 1974.

Rickey, George. "Kinesis Continued." *Art in America*, December-January 1965–66.

Seldis, Henry J. "U.S. Sculpture Exhibit Looks Beyond the '60s." *Los Angeles Times*, 7 May 1967.

Stiles Knute. "Fletcher Benton at John Berggruen." *Art in America*, Summer 1980.

Tall, William. "Exploring the Mystery of Kinetic Art." *Detroit Free Press*, 5 April 1970.

Temko, Allan. "Public Sculpture Out in the Open." *San Francisco Chronicle*, 11 March 1981.

Walls, Jim. "Experimental Artist Explores New Domain." *San Francisco Chronicle*, 20 January 1960.

Wallace, Dean. "Polychrome Sculpture Says 'Please Touch.'" *San Francisco Chronicle,* 24 August 1964.

Weimers, Leigh. "A Rather Involved Slice of Real Life." *San Jose News*, 26 September 1980.

Wilson, William. "Air of Pageantry in Banner Art." *Los Angeles Times*, 26 July 1965.

_____. "Benton's Sculpture Shines." *Los Angeles Times*, 6 May 1966.

Guy Dill

Armstrong, Richard. *Sculpture in California*. San Diego: San Diego Museum of Art, 1980, p. 31.

Art Gallery, California State University, Fullerton. *Guy Dill and Laddie John Dill*. Fullerton: Art Gallery, California State University, Fullerton, 1983.

Askey, Ruth. *A View Through*. Long Beach: The Art Galleries, California State University, Long Beach, 1975, pp. 19–22.

_____. "Guy Dill's Dado Line." *Artweek*, 1 July 1975.

Ballatore, Sandy. "In the Constructivist Spirit—1980 at the Janus Gallery." *Images & Issues*, vol. I, no. 3, Winter 1980/81, pp. 94, 95.

Baur, John I.E. *1973 Biennial Exhibit*. New York: Whitney Museum of American Art, 1973, p. 21.

_____. *General Exhibition Catalogue/Permanent Collection*. Long Beach: Long Beach Museum of Art, 1973, p. 21.

Collins, Dan. "Formalizing the Familiar." *Artweek*, 21 March 1981, p. 3.

Glicksman, Hal. *Furnishings by Artists*. Los Angeles: Otis Art Institute of Parsons School of Design, 1980, p. 22.

_____. "Guy Dill." *Artweek*, vol. XI, no. 22, 7 June 1980, p. 6.

Hopkins, Henry T. *50 West Coast Artists*. San Francisco: Chronicle Books, 1981, pp. 94, 95.

Hopps, Walter. *Six L.A. Artists*. Washington, D.C.: Federal Reserve Board, 1980, pp. 9–11.

Kramer, Hilton. "Guy Dill." *The New York Times*, 19 January 1974.

_____. "Guy Dill." *The New York Times*, 17 January 1976.

Larson, Phillip. "Guy Dill." *Arts*, April 1976, p. 9.

_____. *Dill, Gennover, Madsen*. Minneapolis: Walker Art Center, April 1976, pp. 1, 2, 7.

Lobdell, Nancy. *A Museum Without Walls*. Long Beach: California State University,Long Beach, 1980, pp. 27, 28.

Mead, Katherine Harper. "Head Way." *Gallery Notes*. Santa Barbara: The Santa Barbara Museum of Art, September 1976.

Muchnic, Suzanne. "Guy Dill's New Direction." *Artweek*, vol. IV, no. 23, 17 June 1976, p. 16.

Neuberg, George, and Balomey, Robert. *Forgotten Dimension—A Survey of Small Sculpture in California Now*. Fresno: Fresno Arts Center, 1982, p. 21.

Smith, Barbara. "Guy Dill Sculptures." *Artweek*, 13 January 1973, p. 3.

Smith, Michael. *Jack Brogan Projects*. Pasadena: Baxter Art Gallery, 1980, p. 6.

Strauss, Ludy. *Artists' Quilts*. La Jolla: La Jolla Museum of Contemporary Art, 1981, pp. 8, 20.

Thalacker, Donald. *The Place of Art in the World of Architecture*. London: Chelsea House, 1980, pp. 8, 20.

Waldman, Diane. *Theodoron Catalogue*. New York: The Solomon R. Guggenheim Museum, 1972.

Wilson, William. Review. *Los Angeles Times*, 26 May 1976.

_____. "A Brace of Space Shapers." *Los Angeles Times*, 17 March 1981.

Jud Fine

Art in America, Summer 1979.

Artforum, October 1972.

Artnews, November 1973.

Artnews, October 1978.

Arts, May 1972.

Arts, December 1973.

Arts, September 1974

Arts, June 1975.

Artweek, October 1977.

Artweek, June 2, 1979.

Boston Globe. 10 March 1974.

Case, William D. Review. *Arts*, vol. 46, no. 7, October 1973, p. 72.

Fine, Jud. *Walk*. Self-published, 1976.

_____. "Polynesian/Polyhedron." *LAICA Journal*, Winter 1981, pp. 44, 45.

Frackman, Noel. "Jud Fine." *Arts*, vol. 49, no. 7, March 1975, p. 6.

_____. Review. "Jud Fine." *Arts*, vol. 52, no. 10, June 1978, p. 36.

Goya, March-April 1974.

Hugo, Joan. "Jud Fine's Visual Paradigms." *Artweek*, vol. 12, no. 40, 28 November 1981, p. 1.

Kelly, James J. *Living Materials: A Sculptor's Handbook*. New York: Holt Rinehart Winston, 1972.

Los Angeles Herald Examiner, 22 October 1978.

Los Angeles Times, 10 October 1977.

Los Angeles Times, 23 October 1978.

Los Angeles Times, 17 October 1981.

McCann, Cecile N. "Cross-Culture Vanguard Art." *Artweek*, vol. 4, no. 33, 6 October 1973, p. 4.

Moore, Alan. "Jud Fine, Ronald Feldman Fine Arts." *Artforum*, vol. XII, no. 8, April 1975, p. 79.

Muchnic, Suzanne. "A Museum on a Campus Mall." *Los Angeles Times*, 30 April 1979.

Naylor, C., and Orridge, G.P., editors. *Contemporary Artists*. London: St. James Press, 1978.

The New York Times, 7 July 1974.

The New York Times, 11 January 1975.

The New York Times, 17 April 1976.

Plagens, Peter. "Jud Fine, Riko Mizuno Gallery." *Artforum*, vol. XII, no. 3, November 1973, pp. 85, 86.

Santa Barbara, Spring 1978.

Straight Turkey, Spring 1974.

Tracks: A Journal of Artists' Writings, vol. 2, no. 2, Spring 1976.

The Village Voice, 4 June 1979.

Wilson, William. "Muddied on Philosophy's Turf." *Los Angeles Times*, 20 September 1976.

Wortz, Melinda. "Measurements of Time and Structures for Experience." *Artweek*, vol. 11, no. 36, 1 November 1980, p. 5.

Tom Holland

Albright, Thomas. "The Nation: San Francisco: Star Streaks: Exhibition at San Francisco Art Institute." *Artnews*, April 1979, p. 101.

_____. "San Francisco: Different and Indifferent Drummers." *Artnews*, vol. 81, no. 1, January 1982, p. 89.

_____. "San Francisco Kinetic Painting: Exhibition at Hansen Fuller Gallery." *Artnews*, February 1976, pp. 77, 78.

_____. "Bay Area Art." *Horizon*, July 1980, p. 30.

Andre, Michael. "Tom Holland: Exhibition at Knoedler Gallery." *Artnews*, December 1973, p. 90.

Ashberry, John. "Pleasures of Paperwork." *Newsweek*, 16 March 1981, pp.93, 94.

Bell, Jane. "Tom Holland: Exhibition at Droll Kolbert Gallery." *Artnews, January 1979, p. 157.*

Bradley, Laural. "Tom Holland: Exhibition at Blum/Helman, New York." *Arts*, vol. 54, no. 5, January 1980, p. 34.

Breckenridge, Betty. "San Francisco: 12th Annual Oil and Sculpture, Richmond Art Center." *Artforum*, February 1963, p. 45.

Cohen, Ronnie. "New Editions: Tom Holland -Pace Editions." *Artnews*, vol. 81, no. 4, April 1982, p. 102.

Gollin, Jane. "Tom Holland: Exhibition at Lawrence Rubin Gallery." *Artnews*, December 1972, p. 12.

Henry, Gerrit. "New York Letter: Cote at Reese Palley." *Art International*, February 1971, p. 81.

King, Mary. "St. Louis—Tom Holland: Exhibition at Greenberg Gallery." *Arts*, November 1974, p. 27.

Kramer, Hilton. "Show of New Works Sets Example at Modern." *The New York Times*, 13 February 1981.

Leider, Philip. "San Francisco: The Construction as an Object of Illusion." *Artforum*, October 1962, p. 40.

Magloff, Joanna C. "San Francisco: Tom Holland, Exhibition at Lanyon Gallery." *Artforum*, May 1963, p. 12.

Martin, Fred. "Tom Holland, the Byron Burford Paintings, Richmond Art Center." *Artforum*, August 1962, p. 35.

Pincus-Witten, Robert. "New York: Alan Cote at Reese Palley." *Artforum*, March 1971, p. 62.

_____. "New York: Exhibition at Robert Elkon Gallery." *Artforum*, December 1970, p. 83.

Plagens, Peter. "Los Angeles: Exhibition at Nicholas Wilder Gallery." *Artforum*, December 1969, p. 75.

Polley, Elizabeth M. "2D-3D at Richmond Art Center." *Artforum*, June 1966, pp. 49, 50.

_____. "San Francisco: Tom Holland, Exhibition at Lanyon Gallery." *Artforum*, May 1964, p. 46.

Ratcliff, Carter. "New York: Exhibition at Robert Elkon Gallery." *Art International*, Summer 1970, p. 144.

Richardson, Brenda. "Bay Area Survey: Exhibition at Hansen Fuller Gallery." *Arts*, November 1970, p. 54.

Smith, Griffin. "Reviews and Previews—Miami: Exhibition at Corcoran Gallery." *Artnews*, January 1975, p. 82.

TARSHIS, Jerome. "San Francisco: Exhibition at Hansen Fuller Gallery." *Artforum*, December 1970, p. 84.

Tucker, Marcia. *The Structure of Color*. New York: Whitney Museum of Amrican Art, 1971.

Whittet, G. "London: Exhibition at Felicity Samuel Gallery." *Art and Artists*, June 1973, p. 42.

Robert Hudson

Adrian, Dennis. "Sculpture and Print Annual, Whitney Museum." *Artforum*, vol. 5, no. 7, March 1967, PP. 54, 56.

Albright, Thomas. "Mythmakers." *The Art Gallery*, February 1975, pp. 12–17, 44, 45.

Bloomfield, Arthur. "Artist Takes Imagination on a Joy Ride." *San Francisco Examiner*, 25 March 1977.

Bourdon, David. *The Village Voice*, 21 October 1965, p. 11.

Brown, Christopher. "Robert Hudson." *Art International*, vol. 24, August-September 1981, pp. 119, 120.

California Palace of the Legion of Honor. *The Drawing Society—Regional Exhibition*. San Francisco: California Palace of the Legion of Honor, February 1965.

Coplans, John. "Sculpture in California." *Artforum*, vol. 2, no. 2, August 1963, pp. 5, 31.

_____. "Circle of Styles on the West Coast." *Art in America*, vol. 52, no. 3, June 1964, pp. 28, 30.

_____. "West Coast Notes." *Art International*, vol. IX, no. 1, February 1965, pp. 46, 47.

Constable, Rosalind. "Is It Painting or Is It Sculpture?" *Life International*, vol. 39, no. 12, 20 December 1965, p. 132.

Danieli, Fidel A. "American Sculpture of the Sixties at the Los Angeles County Museum." *Studio International*, vol. 173, no. 890, June 1967, p. 321.

_____. "Robert Hudson: Space and Camouflage." *Artforum*, vol. VI, no. 3, November 1967, pp. 32, 34, 35.

Dills, Keith. "Robert Hudson's New Work." *Artweek*, 6 April 1977, pp. 1, 16.

Frank, Peter. "Robert Hudson." *Artnews*, November 1976, pp. 149, 150.

Friedman, Martin. "Vestiges of Pop and Funk: Hudson and Randell." *Fourteen Sculptors: The Industrial Edge*. Minneapolis: Walker Art Center, May 1969, p. 39.

Allan Frumkin Gallery. *Robert Hudson: Visions of Eyes and Hands*. New York: Allan Frumkin Gallery, 1976.

Kozloff, Max. "West Coast Art: Vital Pathology." *The Nation*, vol. 199, no. 4, 24 August 1964, p. 79.

Leider, Philip. "Some New Art in the Bay Area." *Artforum*, July 1963, p. 7.

Linville, Kasha. "Robert Hudson, Frumkin Gallery." *Artforum*, vol. IX, no. 10, June 1971, p. 86.

Lippard, Lucy R. "As Painting is to Sculpture: A Changing Ratio." *American Sculpture of the Sixties*. Los Angeles: Los Angeles County Museum of Art, 1967, p. 33.

McCann, Cecile N. "Hudson—Images of Tension." *Artweek*, vol. 1, no. 14, 4 April 1970, p. 1.

_____. "Robert Hudson Paintings." *Artweek*, 15 December 1973, pp. 1, 16.

McChenney, Mary Fuller. "Porcelain by Richard Shaw and Robert Hudson." *Craft Horizons*, October 1973, pp. 34–37.

Monte, James. "Making It with Funk." *Artforum*, vol. V, no. 10, June 1967, pp. 56, 57.

Moore College of Art. *Robert Hudson*. Philadelphia: Moore College of Art Gallery, 1977.

The Oakland Museum. *100 Years of California Sculpture*. Oakland: The Oakland Museum, 1982.

Palm Springs Desert Museum. *Return of the Narrative*. Palm Springs: Palm Springs Desert Museum, 1984.

Pincus-Witten, R. "New York: Robert Hudson." *Artforum*, December 1965, p. 132.

Platt, Susan. "Hudson's World." *Artweek*, vol. 13, no. 44, 25 December 1982, p. 3.

Polley, Elizabeth M. "Young Artists." *Artforum*, March 1963, p. 12.

Rhodes, Rod. "The 1st Western States Biennial: A Difficult Birth." *Artweek*, 7 April 1979.

San Francisco Museum of Modern Art. *Painting and Sculpture in California: The Modern Era*. San Francisco: San Francisco Museum of Modern Art, 1976.

San Francisco Museum of Modern Art. *Robert Hudson and Richard Shaw: Works in Porcelain*. San Francisco: San Francisco Museum of Art, 1973.

Selz, Peter. *Funk*. Berkeley: University Art Museum, 1967.

Shapiro, Lindsay Stamm. "New York Sculpture." *Craft Horizons*, December 1976, p. 53.

Tuten, Frederic. "American Sculpture of the Sixties." *Arts*, vol. 41, no. 7, May 1967, pp. 42, 43.

Wilson, William. "Six Robert Hudson Sculptures Displayed." *Los Angeles Times*, 8 December 1967.

Manuel Neri

Albright, Thomas. "Rooted in the Tradition of the Human Figure—A Sense of Magical Equilibrium." *San Francisco Chronicle*, 13 November 1971, p. 38.

_____. "Forceful Masterpieces from Manuel Neri." *San Francisco Chronicle*, 17 May 1979, p. 47.

_____. "The Growth of Manuel Neri." *San Francisco Chronicle*, 11 March 1980, p. 58.

_____. "Manuel Neri's Survivors: Sculpture for the Age of Anxiety." *Artnews*, vol. 80, no. 1, January 1981, pp. 54–59.

Anderson, Wayne. *American Sculpture in Process: 1930–1970*. Boston: New York Graphic Society, 1975.

Blum, Walter. "A Showcase for Contemporary Art." *San Francisco Examiner*, 10 August 1980, pp. 16–20.

Bolomey, Roger. *Forgotten Dimension—A Survey of Small Sculpture in California Now*. Fresno: Fresno Arts Center, 1982.

Boynton, James, editor. *San Francisco 9*. Houston: Houston Contemporary Arts Museum, 1962.

Butterfield, Jan. "Ancient Auras—Expressionist Angst: Sculpture by Manuel Neri." *Images & Issues*, Spring 1981, pp. 38–43.

Castellon, Rolando. *A Third World Painting and Sculpture Exhibition*. San Francisco: San Francisco Museum of Art, 1974.

Clark, Garth, and Hughto, Margie. *A Century of Ceramics in the United States, 1878–1978*. New York: E.P. Dutton in association with the Everson Museum of Art, 1979.

Coplans, John, editor. *Abstract Expressionist Ceramics*. Irvine: University of California, Irvine, 1966.

Charles Cowles Gallery. *Manuel Neri*. New York: Charles Cowles Gallery, 1981.

Dunham, Judith. "Manuel Neri: Life with the Figure." *Artweek*, 13 November 1976, pp. 1, 7.

Figoten, Sheldon. "Building and Painting the Figure." *Artweek*, 20 June 1981, pp. 5, 6.

Hansen Fuller Goldeen Gallery. *Casting: A Survey of Cast Metal Sculpture in the '80s*. San Francisco: Hansen Fuller Goldeen Gallery, 1982.

Hopkins, Henry T. *50 West Coast Artists*. San Francisco: Chronicle Books, 1981.

Kramer, Hilton. "Art: First Solo Show for Manuel Neri." *The New York Times*, 27 February 1981.

LaPlante, John D., editor. *Some Points of View—1962*. Stanford: Stanford University Art Gallery, 1962.

Lewis, Jo Ann. "Peopled Paradox." *The Washington Post*, 3 February 1983.

McDonald, Robert. "Manuel Neri." *Artweek*, 9 June 1979, pp. 1, 8.

Richard L. Nelson Gallery. *Sculptors at UC Davis: Past and Present*. Davis: University of California, Davis, 1982.

Neuberg, George. *Manuel Neri, Sculptor*. Oakland: The Oakland Museum, 1976.

Nordland, Gerald. *Arts of San Francisco: Manuel Neri*. San Francisco: San Francisco Museum of Art, 1971.

The Oakland Museum. *100 Years of California Sculpture*. Oakland: The Oakland Museum, 1982.

Plagens, Peter. *Sunshine Muse*. New York: Praeger Publishers, 1974

Rannells, Susan, and Richardson, Brenda. *Free*. Berkeley: University Art Museum, 1970.

Saint Mary's College Art Gallery. *The Small Format*. Moraga: Saint Mary's College Art Gallery, 1973.

_____. *The Good Drawing Show*. Moraga: Saint Mary's College Art Gallery, 1976.

Seattle Art Museum. *Manuel Neri Sculpture and Drawings*. Seattle: Seattle Art Museum, 1981.

Selz, Peter. *Funk Art*. Berkeley: University Art Museum, 1967.

Shere, Charles. "Show by Sculptor-Painter Neri One of Magnificence." *Oakland Tribune*, 3 December 1981.

Stiles, Knute. "San Francisco: Manuel Neri at Paule Anglim." *Art in America*, October 1979.

Sam Richardson

Art Gallery, California State University, Fullerton. *Coordinate Line—Motion Broken by Boulder*. Fullerton: California State University, Fullerton, 1977.

Art International, December 1969.

Art International, 29 January 1971.

Art International, 20 April 1975.

Art International, March/April 1976.

Artnews, November 1972.

Arts, April 1975.

Butterfield, Jan. *Sam Richardson*. New York: Martha Jackson Gallery, 1976.

_____. *To Ponder Rather than to Know*. Chicago: Klein Gallery, 1982.

Craft Horizons, December/January 1969.

Derfner, Phyllis. "New York Letter." *Art International*, vol. XIX, no. 4, 20 April 1975, p. 58.

Foley, Suzanne. *Sam Richardson*. San Francisco: San Francisco Museum of Art, 1970.

French, Palmer D. Review. *Artforum*, vol. VII, no. 5, January 1969, p. 67.

Garver, Thomas H. *Light-Line*. San Francisco: The Fine Arts Museums of San Francisco, 1975.

Hopkins, Henry T. *50 West Coast Artists*. San Francisco: Chronicle Books, 1981.

Livingston, Jane. Review/Los Angeles. *Artforum*, vol. VI, no. 9, May 1968, p. 67.

Murdock, Robert. *Sight-Line/Snow Drift*. Dallas: Dallas Museum of Fine Art, 1976.

Neubert, George W. *Bentwood/Landlines*. Oakland: The Oakland Museum, 1978.

Pollock, Duncan. "San Richardson at The Denver Art Museum." *Art in America*, vol. 62, no. 1, January-February 1974, p. 105.

Polley, E.M. Review/San Francisco. *Artforum*, vol. IV, no. 10, June 1966, p. 50.

Selvig, Forrest Hall. "Whitney Annual: Sculpture 1968, "Old Stars and New Talent." *Arts*, vol. 43, no. 3, December-January 1969, pp. 25–27.

Smidt, Sam. *New Ground*. New York: Martha Jackson Gallery, 1973.

Spurlock, William. *Sam Richardson—Landscape Constructs*. Santa Barbara: The Santa Barbara Museum of Art, 1981.

Thompson, Orrel E. *Sam Richardson*. Akron: Akron Art Institute, 1972.

Visual Dialog, September 1975.

Visual Dialog, December 1975.

Michael Todd

Albright, Thomas. Review. *Artnews*, vol. 78, no. 1, January 1979, pp. 107, 108.

Artner, Alan G. Review. *Chicago Tribune*, 28 October 1983.

Art in America, February 1964, p. 98.

Art in Ameica, May 1976.

Art in America, January 1979.

Art in America, October 1980.

Art in America, May 1981.

Art in America, April 1982.

Artforum, May 1974, p. 15.

Artforum, May 1976, p. 16.

Artforum, September 1978.

Artforum, January 1979.

Artforum, October 1980.

Artnews, vol. 70, no. 9, January 1972, p. 62.

Artnews, October 1974, p. 115.

Artnews, January 1979.

Arts, May 1967, p. 42.

Arts, February 1972.

Arts, March 1972.

Arts, May 1976.

Arts, June 1976.

Arts, April 1979.

Arts, October 1980.

Artweek, 6 January 1979.

Artweek, 1 November 1980.

Battcock, Gregory. *Minimal Art—A Critical Anthology.* New York: E.P. Dutton, 1968.

Cebulski, F. "Function and Art." *Artweek*, 3 April 1982.

Cummings, Paul. *Dictionary of Contemporary Artists.* New York: St. Martin's Press, 1982, p. 559.

Fitz Gibbon, John. *Michael Todd: Sculpture 1983.* Dominguez Hills: California State University, Dominguez Hills, 1983.

Garver, Thomas H. Review. *Artforum*, March 1970, p. 84.

Goley, Mary Anne, and Hopps, Walter. Introduction to *6 L.A. Sculptors*. Washington, D.C.: The Federal Reserve, 1980.

Harrison, J. Review. *Arts*, May 1964, p. 41.

Hugo, Joan. "Lightness of Form and Spirit." *Artweek*, 9 January 1982, p. 5.

Kessler, Charles. "Painterly Sculpture." *Arts*, June 1975, pp. 86, 87.

Mashek, J. "Sorting Out the Whitney Annual." *Artforum*, February 1971, pp. 71, 72.

Miller, Tressa Ruslander. Introduction to *Urban Sculpture: Architectural Concerns*. Los Angeles: Security Pacific National Bank, 1983.

Perlmutter, Elizabeth. Review. *Artnews*, vol. 75, no. 4, April 1976, p. 68.

Rubin, D.S. Review. *Arts*, June 1979, p. 25.

Rykwert, J. "Fetish Objects at the Hanover Gallery." *Domus*, March 1964, p. 48.

Stevens, E. Review. *Arts*, March 1966, p. 48.

Stiles, K. Review. *Art in America*, February 1983, p. 141.

Zimmerer-McKelvie, Kathy. "Michael Todd: Sculpture and Painting." *Images & Issues*, March-April 1983, pp. 25–27.

DeWain Valentine

Baker, Elizabeth C. "Los Angeles, 1971." *Artnews*, vol. 70, no. 5, September 1971, pp. 27–39.

Bordeaux, Jean-Luc. "DeWain Valentine, Light Explored." *Art in America*, vol. 67, no. 8, December 1979, pp. 102–06.

_____. "Los Angeles: A New Center for Contemporary Art." *Connaissance des Arts*, no. 22, November 1981, U.S. edition, pp. 98–105.

_____. "Un Musée Américain en pleine croissance." *Connaissance des Arts*, no. 286, December 1975, p. 75.

Danieli, F.A. "DeWain Valentine." *Art International*, vol. XII, no. 9, November 1969, pp. 36–39.

_____. "Two Showings of Younger Los Angeles Artists." *Artforum*, vol. V, no. 2, October 1966, pp. 24–26.

Frank, J. "The Gallery (Denver) Group." *Artforum*, vol. III no. 1, September 1964, p. 50.

Frank, Peter. "DeWain Valentine." *Artnews*, vol. 72, no. 3, March 1973, p. 76.

Friedman, Martin. "14 Sculptors: The Industrial Edge." *Art International*, vol. 14, no. 2, February 1970, pp. 36–38.

Hastings, Nory. "DeWain Valentine." *Western Plastics,* November 1974, p. 1.

Hazlitt, Gordon J. "Venice, Unique Among the World's Bohemias." *Artnews*, vol. 79, no. 1, January 1980, pp. 94–98.

Hemmerdinger, William. "California Innovations." *Palm Springs Life*, vol. XXIV, no. 4, pp. 78, 79.

Hoffman, Fred. "DeWain Valentine, New Work." *Artforum*, vol. XVIII, no. 5, January 1980, pp. 77–78.

Hopkins, Henry T. *50 West Coast Artists*. San Francisco: Chronicle Books, 1981, pp. 118, 119.

Hugo, Joan. "The Behavior of Materials." *Artweek*, vol. 10, no. 33, 18 October 1979, p. 7.

Hunter, Sam. *American Art of the 20th Century*. New York: Abrams, 1972, p. 399.

Kosloff, Max. "Whitney Annual: Sculpture, Whitney Museum." *Artforum*, vol. III, no. 6, February 1969, pp. 6, 64.

Lindsley, Carol. "Plastics Into Art." *Art in America*, vol. 56, no. 3, May/June 1968, p. 115.

Livingston, Jane. "Plastics, L.A." *Artforum*, vol. 6, no. 9, May 1968, pp. 65–66.

Lockwood, Charles. "Wheels and Deals Keep California Venice Spinning." *Smithsonian*, vol. 10, no. 12, March 1980, pp. 112–19.

Mellow, James B. "New York Letter." *Art International*, vol. III, no. 8, October 1968, p. 61.

Montgomery, Cara. "Los Angeles Report." *Arts*, vol. 47, no. 7, May/June 1973, p. 53.

Opiger, Curt. "New Images, New Materials." *Artforum*, vol. IV, no. 4, December 1965, pp. 14–16.

Passoni, Franco. *Art and Plastics*. Milano: Industria Pubblicazioni Audiovisivi, 1975, p. 140.

Peck, Stacy. "Home Magazine Q&A." *Los Angeles Times*, 27 January 1980.

Plagens, Peter. "Five Artists Ace Gallery." *Artforum*, vol. X, no. 2, October 1971, pp. 86, 87.

_____. *Sunshine Muse*. New York: Praeger Publishers, 1974, pp. 120, 122–124, 168.

Preisman, Fran. "DeWain Valentine, Seizing Light." *Artweek*, 26 July 1975, p. 3.

Restany, Pierre. "USA, 76, The Year of Recycling." *Domus*, no. 565, December 1976, pp. 52–54.

Smith, Roberta Pancoast. "DeWain Valentine." *Arts*, vol.47, no. 5, p. 75.

Taylor, John Lloyd. "DeWain Valentine." *Art International*, vol. 17, no. 7, pp. 21–24, 48, 76.

Von Meier, Kurt. "An Interview with DeWain Valentine." *Artforum*, vol. VII, no. 9, pp. 36–39.

_____. "Los Angeles." *Art International*, vol. X, no. 10, December 1966, p. 54.

_____. *Time*, vol. 89, no. 19, 12 May 1967, p. 82.

Wechsler, Judith. "Why Scale." *Artnews*, vol. 66, no. 4, Summer 1967, p. 35.

All portraits are by Mimi Jacobs, except page 83 by Thomas P. Vinetz.

All color photography is by Thomas P. Vinetz, except pages 87, 95, and 127.

Additional photography is by M. Lee Fatherree, pages 48, 104, 113, 114, and 122; Wayne McCall, page 121; Joe Schopplein, page 120; Frank J. Thomas, page 89; and Thomas P. Vinetz, page 57.